Sutton 66-5808
Modern American criticism

Date Due

FEB 14 '67			
AUG 15 '67			
APR 30 '68			
		JUN 09	
		JUL X X 2015	

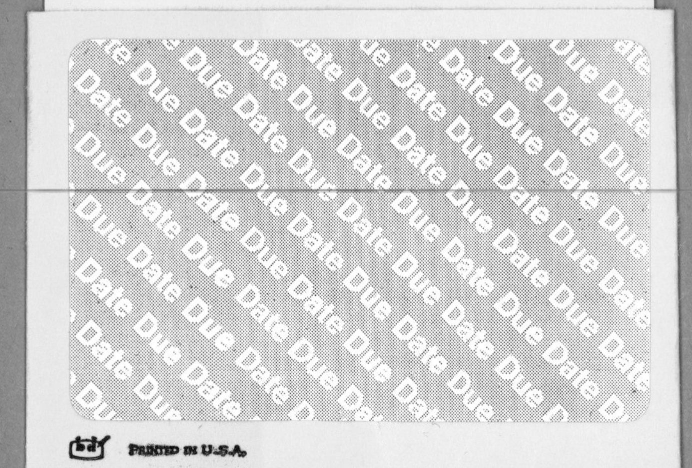

PRINTED IN U.S.A.

RICHARD SCHLATTER, GENERAL EDITOR

Humanistic Scholarship in America

THE PRINCETON STUDIES

THE COUNCIL OF THE HUMANITIES
WHITNEY J. OATES, CHAIRMAN
PRINCETON UNIVERSITY

The Books and

ART AND ARCHAEOLOGY

James S. Ackerman Rhys Carpenter
Wen Fong

CLASSICS

Eric A. Havelock

HISTORY

Felix Gilbert John Higham
Leonard Krieger

LINGUISTICS

William Haas Roman Jakobson
Rulon Wells

LITERATURE

David Daiches Howard E. Hugo

MODERN AMERICAN CRITICISM

Walter Sutton

Their Authors

MUSICOLOGY

Frank Ll. Harrison   Mantle Hood
Claude V. Palisca

THE ORIGINS OF AMERICAN HUMANISTIC SCHOLARS

Robert H. Knapp

PHILOSOPHY 1930-1960

Roderick M. Chisholm   Herbert Feigl
William Frankena   John Passmore
Hilary Putnam   Manley Thompson

RELIGION

Paul Ramsey, ed.
James Luther Adams   Philip H. Ashby
Robert M. Grant   James H. Nichols
Harry M. Orlinsky   John E. Smith
Claude Welch

RELIGION, A HUMANISTIC FIELD

Clyde A. Holbrook

The aim of these volumes is to present a critical account of American humanistic scholarship in recent decades. They have been commissioned by the Council of the Humanities, Whitney J. Oates, Chairman, of Princeton University and were made possible by a grant from the Ford Foundation.

—Richard Schlatter, General Editor.

MODERN AMERICAN CRITICISM

WALTER SUTTON

PRENTICE-HALL, INC. ENGLEWOOD CLIFFS NEW JERSEY

 Manufactured in the United States of America. Library of Congress Catalog Card Number: 63-8462.

58625-C

PRENTICE-HALL INTERNATIONAL, INC.
London · Sydney · Tokyo
PRENTICE-HALL OF CANADA, LTD.
PRENTICE-HALL OF INDIA (PRIVATE), LTD.

Second printing........June, 1965

FOREWORD

What is the purpose of humanistic scholarship? What, in fact, does the humanist scholar do?

The job of the humanist scholar is to organize our huge inheritance of culture, to make the past available to the present, to make the whole of civilization available to men who necessarily live in one small corner for one little stretch of time, and finally to judge, as a critic, the actions of the present by the experience of the past.

The humanist's task is to clear away the obstacles to our understanding of the past, to make our whole cultural heritage—primitive, pre-Columbian, African, Asian, aboriginal, Near Eastern, classical, medieval, European, American, contemporary, and all the rest—accessible to us. He must sift the whole of man's culture again and again, reassessing, reinterpreting, rediscovering, translating into a modern idiom, making available the materials and the blueprints with which his contemporaries can build their own culture, bringing to the center of the stage that which a past generation has judged irrelevant but which is now again usable, sending into storage that which has become, for the moment, too familiar and too habitual to stir our imagination, preserving it for a posterity to which it will once more seem fresh.

The humanist does all this by the exercise of exact scholarship. He must have the erudition of the historian, the critical abilities of the philosopher, the objectivity of the scientist, and the imagination of all three. The scholar who studies the history of science, for example, must combine a knowledge of languages, history, and philosophy with the knowledge of a scientist. And so on with the scholars who study music, art, religion, literature, and all the rest.

The job is, obviously, impossible for any man; and the humanist scholar, knowing he can never attain his true goal, is always tempted to run after wooden idols whose cults are less exacting and which proffer an easy bliss.

Sometimes the humanist is tempted to bypass the rigorous training of the scholar and to wrap himself in the cloak of the sophist. Then he lapses into a painful wooliness and becomes the "literary" sort of humanist whose only accomplishment is a style which achieves the appearance of sublimity at the cost of an actual inanity. His opposite number is the hardheaded humanist who reacts against empty loftiness by becoming a pedant: he devotes himself to antiquarian detail no less trivial than the banalities of some social science or the mere collecting spirit which is sometimes found in the natural sciences. "Physical science can be at least as trivial as any other form of inquiry: but this is less obvious to the outsider because the triviality is concealed in the decent obscurity of a learned language."

Given the magnitude of his task and the impossibility of total perfection, the humanist scholar must, of course, specialize and his works will often be esoteric. But the belief persists that somehow specialization must be converted to generalization if the humanist scholar is to complete his job. Humanist scholars have not solved the problems of excessive specialization and must share the blame for that catastrophe of communication which besets modern learning.

Humanist scholars have been accused of being overly genteel, contemptuous of popular culture, snobbish and anti-democratic after the fashion of their aristocratic Renaissance progenitors, backward looking, hostile to the present, fearful of the future, ignorantly petulant about science, technology, and the Industrial Revolution—"natural Luddites." "It is a sad thought indeed that our civilization has not produced a *New Vision,*" a modern technologist complains, "which could guide us into the new 'Golden Age' which has now become physically possible, but only physically. . . . Who is responsible for this tragi-comedy of Man frustrated by success? . . . Who has left Mankind without a vision? The predictable part of the future may be a job for electronic predictors but the part of it which is not predictable, which is largely a matter of free human choice, is not the business of the machines, nor of scientists . . . but it ought to be, as it was in the great epochs of the past, the prerogative of the inspired humanists." (Dennis Gabor, "Inventing the Future," *Encounter,* May 1960, p. 15.)

Scholars in the humanities may modestly reject the suggestion that they can ever be the inspired prophets of a new age. But their scholarship is essential to enable us to distinguish the inspired prophets from the fanatical Pied Pipers.

The Ford Humanities Project under the direction of the Council of the Humanities of Princeton University is looking at American humanistic scholarship of recent decades, describing it, and attempting to sift the imaginative, the original, and the admirable from the pedantic, the conventional, and the superficial.

We have commissioned about a dozen volumes by recognized scholars in each field. These volumes will give us an account of American humanistic scholarship enabling us to see just what that scholarship has contributed to the culture of America and the world.

Professor Sutton's essay is one of three which will examine recent literary scholarship and criticism in America. The authors in the Ford Humanities Project were asked to act both as objective historians and as critics and the General Editor, who is a historian, has emphasized the criticism since the besetting sin, I think, of "projects" and "surveys" is objective dullness. Walter Sutton has given us solid history; but his own critical principles shine forth clearly and powerfully. He tells us what American criticism has been and what has been wrong with it. I am grateful to him for both telling the story and giving us matter for that sharply critical arguing without which humanistic scholarship dies.

RICHARD SCHLATTER
General Editor

PREFACE

In this survey of modern American literary criticism I have considered five representative groups in a roughly chronological order: the New Humanists, psychological and myth critics, liberal and radical critics, New Critics, and neo-Aristotelians. The treatment of individual critics in relation to these larger groups supplies a focus for the consideration of the problems of terminology and standards of judgment that have peculiarly complicated American criticism of the past twenty or thirty years. The result is a combined historical and critical discussion that will, I hope, do justice to both the positive contributions and the limitations of our leading critical traditions.

There are some critics who are not easily identifiable with the groups considered, and I regret that their work is slighted. But the distinctive positions of the major groups provide a context necessary for the understanding of modern criticism. Although my primary interest has been in the theory and the theoretical implications of the writings of the critics discussed, from a point of view defined in the last chapter, I have made use of many examples of practical criticism of literature that should be familiar to students and nonspecialist readers.

I have noted the impact of modern science upon literary critics (who have responded negatively as well as positively), but I am not here concerned with the question of the extent to which criticism may be regarded as a science. Too much has been made of the differences between our ways of knowing—and the academic disciplines that represent them. Arbitrary distinctions between the sciences and the humanities and, within the humanities, between historical and critical studies have tended to obscure the fact that all intellectual disciplines depend upon systematic inquiry subject to the tests of consistency and verification by experience—as the older and broader usage of the word *science* reminds us. After a period of extreme specialization in most fields, the time is ripe, in literary criticism at least, for more integrative studies relating the forms of literature to their increasingly complex social environment.

This or any discussion of modern criticism must make frequent references to the romantic tradition. But the full spectrum of romantic ideas is not to be found in contemporary criticism, in which the revelation doctrines and the organicism deriving from Coleridge have been fostered to the exclusion of attention to the theories of the language and the function of literature of figures like Wordsworth, Shelley, and Whitman. This imbalance is in need of correction by critics humanistically interested in all resources of the past.

I wish to thank Richard Schlatter of the Ford Humanities Project and the Literature Committee of the Princeton Council of the Humanities for providing the opportunity for this most congenial study. I am particularly indebted to C. L. Barber for his reading of chapters in rough draft form, and for his generous suggestions, and to Carlos Baker for a thoughtful reading of the completed manuscript. My greatest assistance in final revision has come from my closest reader, Vivian R. Sutton.

The transformation of manuscript to printed book has been facilitated by the editorial skill and helpfulness of Claude Conyers.

PREFACE

Brief passages in the following pages have appeared, in another form, in articles in the *Journal of Aesthetics and Art Criticism*, *The Minnesota Review*, the *Rivista di Estetica*, and *Symposium;* and I am grateful to their editors for permission to reprint this material.

W. S.

Syracuse University

CONTENTS

1

INTRODUCTION

In 1910, in his lecture "The New Criticism," Joel Elias Spingarn proclaimed, "We have done with all the old Rules." Rejecting all earlier methods in favor of the expressionism of Croce, he continued, "We have done with the *genres* or literary kinds. . . . We have done with the moral judgment of literature. . . . We have done with technique as separate from art. . . . We have done with the race, the time, the environment of a poet's work as an element in criticism. . . . When criticism first propounded as its real concern the oft-repeated question: 'What has the poet tried to express and how has he expressed it?' Criticism prescribed for itself the only possible method."

In attacking moral, sociological, and classical genre criticism, Spingarn was dismissing, prematurely, traditions that were to exert a continuing influence on criticism through the practice of the New Humanists, the liberal and radical critics of the 1930's, and the neo-Aristotelians. The strongest feature of his argument, and the most useful for his time, was its defense of literature against those who would regard it simply as documentary support for ethical or historical principles —or those who would substitute for criticism what Ezra Pound called the china egg of Germanic scholarship.

The critical movement Spingarn prophesied failed to materialize (he has no direct connection with the later New Criticism). His iconoclasm, however, was in keeping with the intransigent spirit of the war decade, a time of cleavage between traditional and modernist tendencies in the arts and between old and new social usages. Although the break was not absolute, the period was one of ferment and change and intellectual excitement, as developments in science and technology, as well as politics, were transforming the world. While the investigations of Freud and the new psychologists were introducing unsettling concepts of human nature, the old certainties of time and space were dissolving in the universe envisioned by the new physics, which no longer permitted even the solace of a simple materialism. At the same time, advances in technology speeded the building of the machine world by modern man as Promethean engineer. Reacting to this constantly changing environment, the arts produced a succession of intense and short-lived revolutionary programs—Futurism, Imagism, Vorticism, Dadaism, Surrealism. Each had its day and declined, but all contributed in one way or another to the formulation of aesthetic and critical theories. Although the exact origins of modern literary criticism within the present century cannot easily be isolated, certain events can be related to its growth.

On the eve of World War I, the international Imagist movement led by T. E. Hulme and Ezra Pound announced specifications for a new poetry distinguished by objectivity, economy of language, and freedom of form. The Imagist tenets published in 1913 insisted on a hardness and precision to counter the diffuseness and verbosity of much Victorian poetry; they rejected the confines of conventional rhyme and meter, substituting the free "sequence of the musical phrase" for the mechanical rhythm of the metronome.

Pound was reacting also against the impressionistic criticism of Pater and his contemporaries—which he dismissed as senseless "yatter"—and focusing attention upon the work itself, and its technique. He was supported by T. S. Eliot, who began his career as a critic during the war years and whose collection *The Sacred Wood: Essays on Poetry and Criticism* appeared in 1920. Objecting to both impressionism and moralism, Eliot stimulated, by precept and example, a technical criticism concerned with the structural principles of literature—"classical" in its traditionalism and its emphasis on impersonality.

The postwar decade saw further developments. Besides the criticism of Pound and Eliot, there was a continuation of the liberal and radical tradition of the prewar era of protest and reform, and the New Humanism, inaugurated by Irving Babbitt and Paul Elmer More early in the century, was enjoying its greatest prestige. The growth of the physical and social sciences, especially psychology, was also affecting criticism. By 1924, when I. A. Richards' *Principles of Literary Criticism* combined the study of psychology and literary theory, the main lines of modern criticism were established.

Many of the "modernists" were anything but hostile to the past. (As a Vorticist Pound objected to the Futurists' compulsion to destroy "past glories.") Although they rebelled against the nineteenth century, blasting its bourgeois Victorianism, it was in order to fix their eyes upon a more remote idealized past—prescientific, preindustrial, sometimes pre-Christian—before the unity of vision of Greek or medieval Christian ideals had been lost in the "dissociation of sensibility" which accompanied the rise of modern science. Unlike the liberal social critics and psychological critics, who were hospitable to science and looked to it for inspiration, many of the modernist followers of Hulme, Pound, and Eliot fostered a romantic antagonism.

Yet, like all critics, they were inevitably affected by the

rise of modern science. As the sciences increasingly overshadowed humanistic studies, the proven efficiency of their procedures heightened the sensitivity of literary critics to problems of language and method and to the question of their contribution to human knowledge. A concern for scientific method and discipline can be seen in the psychological criticism of the 1920's, the sociological criticism of the Thirties, and the New Criticism of the 1940's and 1950's.

Even earlier, among aesthetic and technical critics like Pound and Eliot, there was evidence of a desire to make critical procedures more precise and objective and to associate literary and scientific processes. T. S. Eliot's well-known essay, "Tradition and the Individual Talent" (1919), makes use of chemical terms to describe the poetic process. The "impersonal theory" is explained by analogy with a catalytic reaction that occurs when a "bit of filiated platinum is introduced into a chamber containing oxygen and sulphur dioxide." The resultant "sulfurous acid," containing no trace of platinum, is the literary work; the "mind of the poet is the shred of platinum." Obviously, this is not a "scientific" explanation of what happens in the mind of the writer but a figure of speech designed to support an argument for an "objective" and "distanced" poetry. Still, the device confers upon the statement, which is an important contribution to modern theory, the aura if not the substance of scientific sanction.

As early as 1913, Ezra Pound had explicitly likened literature to science and asserted its cognitive function. In "The Serious Artist" he argues, "The arts, literature, poesy, are a science, just as chemistry is a science. Their subject is man, mankind and the individual." Like the sciences, the arts produce knowledge: "I have said that the arts give us our best data for determining what sort of creature man is. As our treatment of man must be determined by our knowledge or conception of what man is, the arts provide data for ethics." These data, Pound insists, are sound and even more reliable than those provided by the social scientist because the serious artist is more precise and "scientific" than the "social theorician."

Pound's awareness of psychoanalysis is revealed in his famous definition of the image, published in the same year as "The Serious Artist" and the tenets of Imagism. After describing the *image* as "that which presents an intellectual and emotional complex in an instant of time," he continues, "I use the term 'complex' rather in the technical sense employed by the newer psychologists, such as Hart, though we might not agree absolutely in our application." Bernard Hart, the British psychologist who helped to introduce Freud's ideas into England, had published an essay, "The Conception of the Subconscious" (1910), in which he defined *complexes,* in the context of Freudian theory, as systems of "unconscious ideas . . . agglomerated into groups with accompanying affects." He also observed—and his comment may well have attracted Pound's attention—that "a single idea or image in consciousness may be conditioned (constellated) by a multiplicity of unconscious complexes."

Since psychology is the science which has long been most intimately associated with literature, it is not surprising that Pound should have made use of its ideas and terms. In doing so, he anticipated, characteristically, the fuller application of psychology to literary criticism and theory in the postwar years.

⸎ 2 ⸎

EARLY PSYCHOLOGICAL CRITICISM

1—I. A. Richards' eclectic Principles of Literary Criticism; *2—F. C. Prescott's* The Poetic Mind; *3—Freudian biographies—V. W. Brooks and J. W. Krutch; 4—Ludwig Lewisohn's* Expression in America

Freud's early works, *The Interpretation of Dreams* and *Three Contributions to a Theory of Sex,* were introduced to America through translations published during the prewar decade. While his ideas stimulated experimentation in such literary techniques as dream symbolism and stream-of-consciousness narration, popular Freudianism dramatized the libido and reinforced the social revolt against Victorian or "Puritan" mores. As a result, the psychoanalytical theory of Freud was the most important of the psychological influences upon the criticism of the 1920's.

Literary critics were interested in psychology as a discipline that might provide them with better terms and standards. While they were drawn mostly to the theory of Freud, and later of Jung, other schools of modern psychology also affected their work. Among these, behaviorism enjoyed its greatest prestige during the 1920's. At the same time, Gestalt psychology was contributing to the beginnings of the contextualist theory later developed by the New Criticism. But literary critics have usually not been adherents of a single psychological system. They have been more often eclectics than orthodox Freudians or Jungians. Among such uncommitted critics the most prominent was I. A. Richards.

I

The groundwork of I. A. Richards' critical position was laid in a series of books that began to appear during the 1920's. Of these the most important is *Principles of Literary Criticism* (1925 [1924]), probably the most influential work of literary theory to appear during the decade. Richards' wide range of interests includes psychology, literary theory and criticism, and linguistics. In *Principles* Richards expresses a desire to relate criticism to a "systematic exposition of psychology." Typical of his early position (sometimes called "positivist"), the book attempts to bring the methods of the laboratory to literary study and to place criticism upon an experimental basis.

The exact composition of Richards' eclectic psychology is difficult to determine. His emphasis on the unified nature of the literary experience is in keeping with Gestalt psychology, but he is heavily indebted to behaviorism for his explanation of literary experience in physiological terms and for his idea of the function of literature as the organization and control of impulses. In other respects, especially its concern for values, his theory is at odds with behavioral psychology.

Richards makes a point of the need for an improved critical language. While he recognizes that his own terminology may seem uncouth to some readers, he justifies it on the grounds that he is more interested in words capable of practical definition than in those possessing "emotive power." (Richards has since reversed this position completely and now considers the ideal critical language to be the complex and emotive language of poetry.) In a chapter entitled "The Language of Criticism" he disapproves of terms that attribute effects to the aesthetic object and obscure the fact that the poem or literary work is a subjective experience of the reader. He dislikes the use in art criticism of such words as *construction, form, balance, composition, unity,* and *expression,* and in literary criticism of *rhythm, stress, plot,* and *character.*

In describing the poem as an experience of the reader, Richards maintains that literary or aesthetic experience is not unique, and that it differs from other common experiences only in degree and not in kind. By taking this position (which follows John Dewey's earlier discussions of the relation of art to experience) Richards rules out the possibility of an aesthetic idealism or art-for-art's-sake attitude and insists upon communicability as a necessary function of literature. An account of value and of communication are for him the "two pillars upon which a theory of criticism must rest."

It is his intention to ground these in psychology. He finds the key to a "Psychological Theory of Value" (the title of his seventh chapter) in the individual and social problem of organizing impulses and attitudes in a manner least wasteful of human possibilities. Art is valuable because it is able to organize opposing attitudes efficiently. (Subsequently Richards cites Coleridge's discussion of the poetic imagination's "reconciliation of opposite or discordant qualities.") Richards makes use of Arnold's phrase to describe the artist as a "critic of life" who gives order to attitudes that exist in confusion in most minds. Among various techniques employed by the poet to secure an equilibrium, Richards singles out *irony,* making it a standard of poetic value and providing later critics with one of their most widely used criteria.

The similarity of experienced responses to a given stimulus is the basis for the communicative quality of literature, a necessary quality if literature is to be granted any social use or function beyond the organizing of an individual's attitudes. In a not very fully developed chapter entitled "Art, Play and Civilisation," Richards treats the question of literature's social contribution. Although most concerned with the negative social effects of bad art, he touches on the idea that the shared experience of art may contribute to a more coherent social order. (A decade later, in *Coleridge on Imagination* [1935], he adds that poetry as myth provides a "necessary channel for the reconstitution of order" in the modern world.)

Principles of Literary Criticism deals with several important problems of critical theory. One of these is Richards' well-known emotive-referential distinction between the language of poetry and that of science: "A statement may be used for the *reference,* true or false, which it causes. This is the *scientific* use of language. But it may also be used for the sake of the effects in emotion and attitude produced by the reference it occasions. This is the *emotive* use of language." Or, again, in his discussion of the question of belief: "The sense in which we believe a scientific proposition is not the sense in which we believe emotive utterances." Scientific belief is the "readiness to act as though the reference symbolized by the proposition which is believed were true." Emotive beliefs, however, are "provisional acceptances . . . made for the sake of the 'imaginative experience' which they make possible." Richards concludes that "the difference between these emotive beliefs and scientific beliefs is not one of degree but of kind."

These distinctions, typical of a romantic as well as a positivist point of view, have been extremely influential and, as emphases, very useful. However, the language of literature may also express propositional truths and even compel scientific belief as Richards defines it. To deny this possibility is to seal off the poetic experience from the realm of common experience in which propositional truths and literal beliefs exist.

Another problem raised is that of the standards for determining the form of a poem when the poem is identified with the experience of the reader. Is the poem to be considered the experience of any one reader or the aggregate of the experiences of an indefinite number of more-or-less competent readers? Recognizing the dangers of an uncontrolled relativism, Richards proposes as a standard "the relevant experience of the poet when contemplating the completed composition." By extension, a poem can be judged not only by its author, but by "anyone whose experience approximates in this degree to the standard experience [of the writer]." The difficulty with this solution is that the experience of the writer cannot easily be determined, and the critic is left with a standard of dubious value.

Despite his concern for precise terminology and a desire to base his theory on psychology, Richards follows no one accepted body of theory, and his citations of poets and critics, particularly the romantics, are far more copious than his references to psychologists. Jung and Freud are mentioned in passing but are not listed in his index, which includes a total of twenty-three page references to Wordsworth and Coleridge. Richards considers the transcendental theory of the romantics the most important resource for an understanding of the nature of poetry and the function of criticism. In his concluding chapters he comments that the "Revelation Doctrines [of Coleridge], when we come to know what they are really about, come nearer, we shall see, to supplying an explanation of the value of the arts than any of the other traditional accounts." In contrast, he cavalierly dismisses the theory of both Freud and Jung: "The Vienna School would merely have us away with antiquated lumber; the Zürich School would hand us a new outfit of superstitions."

Despite the "positivism" attributed to Richards at this time, the conclusion of *Principles of Literary Criticism* quite clearly points toward the view of poetry as myth which later emerges in *Coleridge on Imagination.* In this volume Richards echoes Coleridge in describing poetry as the myth-making faculty "which most brings 'the whole soul of man into activity.' " Even in the earlier *Principles* the distinction between the two uses of language and two kinds of belief parallels the romantic distinction between the language of the understanding and that of the higher reason and between the "two truths" identified with these faculties. Thus, although ostensibly developing a critical theory "scientific" in its language and methods, Richards is actually using the resources of science to refurbish and translate into twentieth century terms nineteenth century romantic ideas.

2

An earlier work of literary theory influenced by modern psychology is *The Poetic Mind* (1922) by Frederick C. Prescott, who had been interested in the relation of literature and psychoanalysis for more than a decade and whose article, "Poetry and Dreams," had appeared in the *Journal of Abnormal Psychology* in 1912.

In *The Poetic Mind,* the account of the nature and function of poetry owes much to Freud. The poem is likened to a dream which provides in disguised form the fulfillment of repressed wishes. The imaginative shaping of the literary work by the writer involves the processes of condensation and displacement Freud attributed to the dreaming mind. In the literary work, as in the dream, there is an unconscious or latent meaning as well as a manifest meaning. On its deeper level the mind is merged with the general or universal mind of the race and expresses itself through symbols that constitute an archaic universal language. Through the symbolically veiled expression of repressed desires, a release or catharsis is achieved by the writer. Since this release is also experienced by the reader, literature serves a social function, and Aristotle's theory of catharsis can be understood in psychoanalytic terms.

Although deeply interested in psychoanlysis, Prescott is not orthodox, and his work reveals several omissions and modifications of Freud's ideas. Prescott avoids the concept of infantile sexuality or sexuality in general. He likens the mind of the poet to that of a child, but his conception of the child is much closer to Wordsworth's than to Freud's. Like Richards, Prescott is most sympathetic to the literature of the romantics although he is less interested in the critical theory of Coleridge than in the poetic statements of Wordsworth and Shelley, whom he frequently cites.

In keeping with his idealization of human nature, most apparent in his treatment of the child, Prescott glosses over certain features of Freud's theory. Although he explains the writing of poetry as wish fulfillment, he insists that the desires satisfied represent our higher nature rather than our animal instincts: "To be valuable, to be what we ordinarily include under the term, poetry must be the product of high desire . . . ," and the greatest poetry is inspired by our most nearly universal desires. Prescott does not suggest a relationship between aspiration and biological impulse, to Freud the basis of all artistic expression. He does not use the term *libido,* although his familiarity with the Freudian concept is apparent in his discussion of the relation of poetic to physiological rhythm. While comparing a literary work to a dream and interpreting its symbolism, Prescott ignores sexual meanings. He discusses the use of a *house* as a symbol for the body in Shakespeare, Hawthorne, and Poe, even citing Freud's *Interpretation of Dreams,* but does not mention that the house not only might be, but according to Freud inevitably would be, a specifically sexual symbol.

Prescott goes beyond Freud in claiming for the poet the role of a seer. For him, as for the romantic, the poet, the prophet, and the priest are one. Just as the fantasy play of the child is a preparation for maturity, the artful play of the poet contributes to the development of mankind. Echoes of Whitman's democratic bard and of Shelley's poet as the "unacknowledged legislator" of mankind can be heard in Prescott's conclusion that poetry "provides a symbolical, fictional, and concealed plan of action" for the race.

Principles of Literary Criticism and *The Poetic Mind* are alike in combining an interest in psychology with an affinity for romanticism. Richards psychologizes the romantic theory of Coleridge while Prescott romanticizes the psychoanalytic theory of Freud. Prescott is more consistent in his use of psychological terminology and in his adherence to one body of theory. His deviations may result from his social conditioning. His work was begun in an era in which stringent taboos against the discussion of sex were still in force and completed during a period in which violent reactions against such taboos were being expressed by a younger generation. Prescott did not participate directly in its rebellion, but by helping to spread a knowledge of Freud's ideas, however modified, he contributed to the displacement of an older system of thought and manners that had not encouraged either a scientific theory of literature or its frank and honest criticism.

3

Early literary studies inspired by psychoanalysis were focused more upon the author than his work, and Freudian literary biographies enjoyed something of a vogue during the 1920's. Among these, two of the best known and most controversial at the time of their publication dealt with nineteenth century figures, Mark Twain and Edgar Allan Poe.

In *The Ordeal of Mark Twain* (1920; revised, 1933), Van Wyck Brooks presents the thesis that Twain suffered from a "miscarriage in his creative life, a balked personality, an arrested development of which he was himself almost wholly unaware, but which for him destroyed the meaning of life." The source of his difficulty was a conflict between his will and his creative "unconscious self," which could find fulfillment only through the life of the artist. This creative impulse was opposed and defeated by Twain's compulsion to bend his will to his mother's desire that he be "good" and "successful"—a compulsion originating in a crucial experience: the exaction of a promise from the impressionable boy at the deathbed of his father. The mother's repressive mores and materialistic values were reinforced by the emerging business society with which Twain consciously identified himself after a brief period in which his creative nature found scope in the craft of a river pilot. His marriage to Olivia Langdon (a substitute mother) and his life as an editor and publisher further encouraged his conformist tendencies and neutralized his impulse toward art.

In Brooks's opinion, Twain's career as a humorist and entertainer was a disastrous compromise because the humorist must identify himself with the popular audience upon whose favor his success depends. To do so Twain suppressed many of his true opinions and pandered to the Philistinism of a middle-class audience by ridiculing beauty and the life of the intellect. His life-long delight in violent profanity and obscenities, a reaction to his repressive environment, was a "waste of a priceless psychic material" that could have been utilized by the artist in a society more willing to recognize the needs of the body and the passions.

Twain's creative impulse might have found expression through satire, toward which his talents inclined, had it not been for certain obstacles. One was that he could not be a serious satirist and also be a "success." Another was that he lacked standards by which the deficiencies of his society could be judged. But most important, in Brooks's opinion, was Twain's fear of flying in the face of public opinion.

Brooks relates his analysis to Twain's writing in only a limited way, sometimes by the association of themes with the author's attitudes but more often by an identification of the author with his characters. To support his thesis he frequently establishes a direct relationship between author and character. In *Captain Stormfield's Visit to Heaven,* the angelic character of Edward J. Billings of Tennessee had been in life a poet scoffed at by his fellow villagers—in a milieu similar to Twain's—but in heaven he gains his reward as his talents are recognized by such peers as Shakespeare and Homer. Brooks's application of a wish-fulfillment formula to this story is too pat, too simple. While the element of wish is present, there is lacking the kind of disguise, involving condensation and displacement, typical of the dream work and the work of art in Freud's view. In a similar fashion, Brooks identifies Twain's interest in twins and dual characters with the author's own conflicts, equating the twinned characters of *Pudd'nhead Wilson, The Gilded Age,* and *The Prince and the Pauper* with the two sides of his nature, the unconscious "artist" self and the conformist, socially conditioned personality.

More convincing is the recognition of the regressive nature of Twain's identification with child characters and the antebellum past, a preoccupation interpreted as the result of frustration: "When people in middle age occupy themselves with their childhood it is because some central instinct in them has been blocked by internal or external obstacles: their consciousness flows backward until it reaches a period in their memory when life still seemed to them open and fluid with possibilities." One of Twain's favorite fancies was that "life should begin with old age and progress backwards," and his nostalgia found its freest and fullest expression in his stories of boy life along the Mississippi in the years before the war.

Although Brooks cites Freud in discussing Twain's humor and alludes to him briefly on other occasions, as in his reference to the dream as the expression of a suppressed wish, there is no serious or intensive application of Freud's ideas. Despite the use of such words as *repression, regression,* and *unconscious self,* Brooks does not employ Freud's basic terminology. Although Twain's relationship to his mother is

stressed, there is no recognition of an Oedipal situation. And, finally, although Brooks mentions Twain's recurrent dreams as evidence of his conflict, these are subjected to only superficial interpretation and not in Freudian terms.

Brooks is most concerned with an analysis of American society in which the figure of Twain as frustrated artist occupies the role of a victim hero. In developing this theme, he amply documents his discussion of a nineteenth century business society hostile to artistic creativity; thus his psychological speculations are used as supporting devices for social criticism. His "ordealist" theory, which has been much debated, is a development of the larger theme of the alienated American artist which originated in the romantic period. The question of whether Twain was thwarted or aided by his society in finding appropriate expression continued to be debated. Bernard DeVoto wrote *Mark Twain's America* (1932) as a refutation of Brooks's thesis.

In *Edgar Allan Poe: A Study in Genius* (1926), Joseph Wood Krutch also isolates an early conflict as the key to his subject's life and writing. But this conflict, crippling though it was to Poe personally, was the enabling act that unlocked his peculiar genius and compelled its expression: "The forces that wrecked his life were those that wrote his works." (Krutch recognizes the Freudian principle of sublimation which Brooks ignored.)

Like Twain's, Poe's difficulties originated in childhood experience. Not only did his father desert him while he was still an infant, but his mother died when he was not quite three. His removal to the home of the Allans provided him with a mother surrogate but with no substitute for his father except as an object of resentment and hate. Recognizing the

failure of a normal sexual development in the young Poe, Krutch speculates that it was perhaps the memory of his mother that "stood between him and any normal fruition of love." Poe's marriage to his child wife, Virginia, whom he called "Sis," and his life with her and her mother provided the appearance but not the reality of a normal adjustment: "In Mrs. Clemm he both loved and used the mother whose Shadow haunted him; in Virginia he had bodily before his eyes that consumptive angel who figures in all his dreams. They were ghostly shadows whose unreality seemed to make unnecessary the physical union which he could not offer."

Another conflict, involving Poe's sense of social identity, came to its climax during his brief stay at the University of Virginia. Trained to think of himself as a Southern gentleman but having no real social position (John Allan never adopted him nor made him his heir), Poe sought relief from insecurity in drinking and gambling with the cockfighting rioters at Jefferson's training school for the republic's natural aristocracy.

For Poe the dream of literary fame provided a compensation for lack of status and sexual maladjustment. Both problems are reflected in his writing, in the sterile isolation of his heroes and his death-ridden heroines. In his heroines—Lygeia, Ulalume, Lenore—Krutch sees the "phantom projection of the hero's need, born of no parents except his conflict of desires and encountered nowhere except in one of these phantasies to which the needs give rise." Krutch speculates upon possible references of these characters, whether to Virginia, his mother, or any of a number of other women with whom Poe became involved: "To this question no final answer can be given. Psychiatrists may quarrel over the question of whether or not an inhibition such as his must

actually arise from a previous experience and a consequent fixation or whether it may have some organic cause. But one thing is fairly certain. Poe could not love in the normal fashion and the reason lay, or at least seemed to him to lay [*sic*], in the death of some woman upon whom his desire had irrevocably fixed itself. If we knew who lay behind the doors of that tomb in the ghoul-haunted woodland of Weir, we should know the answer to the greatest riddle of Poe's life." In view of his earlier reference to the "consumptive angel" who figured in all Poe's dreams, it is strange that Krutch should leave this question hanging. According to the Freudian theory he had been following, all of these figures are images of the mother from whose embrace Poe never freed himself.

Neurotic compensation is also apparent in Poe's tales of ratiocination, the prototypes of the modern detective story. In his constant struggle against maladjustment and insecurity, the systematized events of these stories provided an escape from disorder and emotion: "Poe invented the detective story," according to Krutch, "in order that he might not go mad." The forces of disorder were to prevail in Poe's life, however, and they manifested themselves in his work. With the psychic disintegration that followed his loss of Virginia, Poe finally surrendered any pretense of rationality. *Eureka,* the prose poem that he regarded as his masterpiece, represents a megalomaniacal wish fulfillment achieved through an identification with the Cosmos.

In conclusion, Krutch acknowledges the importance of Poe's influence upon French symbolist poetry, particularly through Baudelaire. As for American literature, he feels that Poe's influence has been "almost exclusively . . . upon form rather than upon matter or tone."

Displaying more psychological insight than Brooks, Krutch makes a greater use of Freudian concepts in interpreting Poe's writing, as well as his life. Poe's work lends itself to this kind of treatment, which has been most exhaustively developed by Marie Bonaparte in *The Life and Works of Edgar Allan Poe* (1949). Read on a plain-sense level, the Gothic elements of his tales and poems are often childish and shoddy. But if the reader credits his statement that the horror of his tales was not of Germany but of the soul and if the soul is identified with the psyche, another dimension of meaning opens, and one may well feel that Poe's real power lies in a realm that can best be charted by depth psychology.

It is surprising that Krutch did not go further in his interpretation of the perversion and alienation patterns in Poe's work. If he had, he could not have concluded that Poe's influence in America lay primarily in matters of form rather than content (inseparable though these are except for purposes of emphasis). Poe has often been treated as an anomaly among the romantics; some critics have even suggested that he is not only atypical but un-American. But he is very much of his time and place, a fact as evident in his work as in that of Hawthorne, whom he resembles in his somber treatment of themes of isolation and withdrawal and his use of Gothic conventions. His "blackness" (the lack of any redeeming vision) and his sense of alienation and unreality have made him a representative figure, and his influence is reflected in theme and tone as well as in technique. Poe's work cannot be considered atypical if one recognizes the persistence of the Gothic mode in American literature.

4

Ludwig Lewisohn's *Expression in America* (1932), reissued in 1939 as *The Story of American Literature,* represents the culmination of the early critical use of Freudianism, combining the preoccupation of the Twenties with the individual psyche and the necessary interest of the Thirties in the social environment. Lewisohn's treatment of the romantics reveals this psychological and sociological interest. Like Krutch, he views Poe's work as "genetically a defense-neurosis" or compensatory fantasy. Like Parrington, he thinks of the nineteenth century writers of romances as "escapists" whose work had little to do with "the quality of American life."

He is less sympathetic than Parrington, however, to Emerson and Thoreau, whom he describes as "chilled under-sexed valetudinarians." Although he recognizes Emerson's theory of expression as a "liberating doctrine" and Thoreau's style as having a classic solidity, Lewisohn believes that the work of both suffered from the limitations of the "Puritan" temperament. It is quite obvious that Lewisohn, in his wholehearted support of the revolt against Victorian mores, considers lusty sexuality a necessary precondition of good writing.

He is even more unfavorable in his estimate of Herman Melville's work, which was just beginning to receive renewed attention after a long period of neglect. It is Lewisohn's opinion that Melville never attained the ability to project a successful work, that after his brief career as a novelist he lapsed into silence with the demon in his soul still unexorcised. This failure Lewisohn explains as the result of an intense mother fixation (the condition that Krutch had diagnosed as the cause of Poe's achievement). Left fatherless at thirteen, Melville repressed his Oedipal hatred and substituted a defensive idealization, which later broke down—a pattern that can be seen in his novel *Pierre.* Because of his unresolved conflict, Melville never achieved "creative discipline or serenity" and cannot be considered "even a minor master." The real voice that comes through Melville's work is that of a "big bearded violently excited man trying to shout down the whimpering, lonely child in his soul."

This sweeping dismissal confuses biographical and literary circumstances. Like most artists, Melville suffered conflicts which he projected in his writing. What is important is the way in which these are utilized and controlled as formal elements of a work of art, and this is a question ignored by Lewisohn. If he had recognized and considered it, he could not so easily have denied Melville's achievement. Although Melville's talents often resisted close discipline and some of his narratives are sprawling and ill-proportioned when measured by the standards of the "well-made" novel, works as closely crafted and consistent in tone as *The Confidence-Man, Bartleby the Scrivener,* and *Billy Budd* testify to his formal mastery and control.

In a preface Lewisohn asserts his intention of using the method of Freud, saying that "the portrayer of any aspect of human life or civilization who does not do so today will soon be like some mariner of old, who, refusing to acknowledge the invention of mathematical instruments because their precision was not yet perfect, still stubbornly sailed his vessel by the stars." At the same time he expresses his belief in the writer as a prophet and in literature as the source of truth. With the rise of science and the consequent loss of a supernatural authority, the reader necessarily became a seeker, "one to whom literature was no longer an eloquent diversion or an illustration of the foreknown and fixed, but moral research, a road to salvation, the bread of life." Although he is not explicit, Lewisohn suggests that the absolutes that have been lost to modern man may be restored through the poet in the role of Whitman's "divine literatus."

Lewisohn believes, however, that it is necessary to substitute Freud's scientific view of human nature and of literature for the optimistic supernaturalism of the romantic. He is accordingly more sympathetic to the literary naturalists than to the romantics or the genteel realists. He considers Stephen Crane and Frank Norris "Sowers and Pathfinders" who struggled to liberate literature from the moral imperatives and inhibitions of Victorian gentility. Rejecting Brooks's view, Lewisohn sees Twain as a folk artist who spoke in the voice of his people and created an "epical" account (the comparison is with Homer) of expansionist America. Howells and James were escapists whose work suffers the blight of gentility. Howells was, like his age, "acutely and negatively sex-conscious." In discussing his ambivalence, Lewisohn cites Freud's *Totem and Taboo.* As for Henry James, flight from self was the motive of his life and frustration the theme of his fiction.

At this point Lewisohn's reader may well ask, "So what?" Neurotic tendencies in Howells and James have been discussed and acknowledged. What is lacking here, as in the judgment of Melville, is a critical analysis of the work to support the generalizations made. James, for example, had his inhibitions, but as an artist he did not avoid the implications of whatever human experience he considered. His treatment of love was not that of D. H. Lawrence, but it is difficult to think of any of his contemporaries who explored the subject as thoroughly as he.

Expression in America was not really freed, Lewisohn thinks, until the emergence of the twentieth century naturalists. The delayed appearance of *Sister Carrie* after its suppression in 1900 was a milestone not only because Dreiser created in it the folk legend of industrial America but also because he represented the struggle of the individual, in spite of overwhelming forces, to satisfy his desires. A want of art in Dreiser, a crudeness of language, is offset by a brooding pity for the human waif in a meaningless world and by the honest and direct treatment of sex as a basic reality, the primal creative force, whether in its carnal or mystical manifestations. In effect, Dreiser is valued as a poet of the *libido,* although Lewisohn does not use the term.

And yet—to use one of Dreiser's favorite phrases—and yet, nature is not enough for Lewisohn. Committed though he professes to be to the "organon or method of knowledge associated with the venerated name of Sigmund Freud," Freud's "scientific" view of human life is not enough. His demonstration of the sexual basis of all experience was necessary for the rejection of older conventional values supported by a now-deposed authority, but other values must arise to take their place, and the obvious source of these is art. Lewisohn shares Freud's idea that art is expression and that its motive is self-catharsis and communication. But to Lewisohn art is more because it can provide the ends or values ignored by the naturalistic sciences. For these, we must look beyond nature in our lives and beyond naturalism in literature.

Lewisohn finds the prospects discouraging. Because the field of prose fiction is dominated by naturalism, the only hope for constructive values seems to lie in the poets, and here he is somewhat graveled for matter (as Parrington less justly said of Hawthorne). He can say little for the newer poetry of Pound, Eliot, Williams, and Cummings, believing rather that the future lies with E. A. Robinson, William Ellery Leonard, and Vachel Lindsay.

Such eccentricity of judgment is common in Lewisohn's work. His simplified Freudian ideas are often relevant to the lives of American writers, but he fails to use them as tools of literary criticism. *Expression in America* is essentially a study of culture rather than of literature. In combining an interest in psychoanalysis and the romantic tradition, it is typical of early psychological criticism. Many critics, unable to accept the full implications of Freud's thought, attempted the difficult task of reconciling it with revelation theories and similar romantic ideas. In later years, critics thus inclined identified themselves with Jungian myth criticism, while Freudian criticism developed along lines more consistent with psychoanalytical principles.

⧼ 3 ⧽

THE NEW HUMANISM

1—Irving Babbitt; 2—Paul Elmer More; 3—Gorham B. Munson and Stuart Sherman; 4—The battle of the symposia; 5—George Santayana

Many intellectuals sensitive to the confusion and disorder of the early twentieth century looked to the past for sustaining values. In the midst of the rebellion against "Puritanism," they defended the principles of decorum and restraint against what seemed to them the excesses of modern scientific, literary, and social thought.

In criticism the staunchest defenders of an older order were the New Humanists, led by Irving Babbitt and Paul Elmer More. Establishing their position in the first decade of the century and gaining support from followers in the universities, the Humanists remained a power to be reckoned with for nearly a generation. From their ivied bastions they fired salvos against avant-garde and liberal critics in a latter-day version of the battle of the Ancients and the Moderns. Most active in the 1920's, this pamphlet warfare culminated in the appearance of rival Humanist and anti-Humanist symposia in 1930. Although the New Humanism disintegrated as a movement during the Thirties, when the depression encouraged the growth of socially conscious liberal and radical criticism, it remained a recognizable though indirect influence upon individual critics.

The New Humanists sought their standards in the pre-nineteenth century past. Insistent upon the dualism of man and nature and of the moral and the animal nature within man, they were militantly opposed to both romanticism and literary naturalism. Against the "beautiful necessity" of the romantics and the pessimistic determinism of the naturalists, they argued for the freedom of the will and the possibility of moral choice. Against the romantics' expansiveness and celebration of impulse, they preached the gospel of the middle way and the need of the discipline of conscience operating through the "inner check." While they did not deny the creative power of the imagination, they disapproved of its apotheosis, feeling that romantic intuition needed the corrective of reason and judgment. They also distrusted the revolutionary spirit and the ideology of popular democracy, which seemed to them the indulgence of a sentimental humanitarianism. Identifying themselves with the classes rather than the masses, the Humanists promoted the idea of a cultural and social elite as the source of needed intellectual and moral leadership.

I

Irving Babbitt was the chief prophet and lawmaker of the New Humanism. Schooled in the classics of the West and the East, Babbitt began his long academic career in the mid-Nineties as an instructor of French at Harvard. Of the series of books that established his reputation, four are most useful as a definition of his position: *Literature and the American College* (1908), *The New Laokoön* (1910), *Rousseau and Romanticism* (1919), and *Democracy and Leadership* (1924). Although *Rousseau and Romanticism* is probably the best known of these, most of Babbitt's later ideas are anticipated in *Literature and the American College,* which begins with a quotation from Emerson's "Ode to Channing":

> *There are two laws discrete*
> *Not reconciled—*
> *Law for man, and law for thing. . . .*

That Babbitt should have chosen lines from America's chief romantic as the motto for his Humanist dualism may seem ironic. But the Humanist shares other ideas and attitudes of the transcendentalist. Babbitt also endorses Emerson when he asserts that Humanism is interested in "the perfecting of the individual rather than in schemes for the elevation of mankind as a whole."

From the beginning Babbitt makes clear his aristocratic and antidemocratic views. He divorces *humanism* from any association with *utopianism* or *humanitarianism* by citing a late Latin authority, Gellius, to the effect that "*Humanitas* . . . is incorrectly used to denote a 'promiscuous benevolence, what the Greeks call philanthropy,' whereas the word really implies doctrine and discipline and is applicable not to men in general but only to a select few,—it is, in short, aristocratic and not democratic in its implication." Babbitt believes that a person who is so misguided as to have "sympathy for mankind in the lump, faith in its future progress, and desire to serve the great cause of this progress, should be called, not a humanist, but a humanitarian." It is not surprising that he considers the proper function of the American college to be the training of an elite for the leadership of the less disciplined masses. After appealing to the English ideal of the gentleman and scholar, he declares that "in one sense the purpose of the college is not to encourage the democratic spirit, but on the contrary to check the drift toward a pure democracy." What is desirable is "an aristocratic and selective democracy."

The need for order is intensified by a confusion of values resulting from the rise of naturalism. Babbitt distinguishes two phases within the naturalistic movement: one is the "positivist and utilitarian movement" fathered by Bacon; the other is the romantic stemming from Rousseau. These twin humanitarianisms, one scientific and one sentimental, are both dependent on the gospel of progress and blind to evil and to human imperfection and limitation. By promoting a belief in progress and substituting the "cult of humanity" for "our real religion," naturalism has succeeded in placing the Golden Age in the future instead of the past.

In education the rise of naturalism undermined the traditional academic disciplines. The humanities are in need of defense against the inroads of the sciences, just as in an earlier age they were in need of defense against theology. The study of literature has been weakened by a growing emphasis on modern literature, which even before the development of romanticism permitted too much scope for personal emotions. The only antidote for the sentimental and subjective in modern literature is a firm grounding in what Babbitt describes as the "rational study" of the classics, which would also provide a common stock of values for the cultured elite.

Both the college and the graduate school have suffered from the progressive and scientific traditions. The college should stand "not for the advancement, but for the assimilation of learning and for the perpetuation of culture." As for the graduate school, Babbitt sees the chief threat to humane scholarship in the rising prestige of Germanic philology. The new scholars, servile rather than creative in spirit, he identifies with the scientists in their dedication to "law for thing" rather than "law for man." (The Humanist here echoes not only Emerson's "Ode" but the theme of his "American Scholar" as well.) The pedantry of the philological tradition not only "dehumanizes" literary study; it also drives away good men who cannot stomach the existing requirements for the Ph.D. degree.

In *Rousseau and Romanticism,* Babbitt again links Bacon and Rousseau as corruptors of civilization, with Rousseau as head devil. Against them he places Aristotle, whose *Poetics* affords "the best theory of classicism," one that recognizes man as the creature of two laws and advocates the "law of measure." The classical emphasis on restraint and proportion is a corrective to the romantic indulgence of temperament and the idea of art as self-expression. Babbitt approves the classical standards of *general nature, imitation, probability,* and *decorum* while recognizing the necessity of flexibility in the understanding of these terms. Reacting against the narrowness of neoclassical standards, here as in *The New Laokoön,* Babbitt insists that "true classicism does not rest on the observance of rules or the imitation of models but on an immediate insight into the universal." (In promoting these classical criteria Babbitt anticipates the later neo-Aristotelians.)

In his concluding chapter, "The Present Outlook," Babbitt acknowledges that Humanism is not enough: "Though religion can get along without humanism, humanism cannot get along without religion." He finds in the "middle way" of Buddhism a harmony of the meditative and religious life and the ethical and humanistic life—a harmony that Aristotle fails to provide. Babbitt turns, significantly and characteristically, not to a religion of revelation but to one in which the ideal of right conduct exists apart from any concept of God or divinity.

The central and enduring values needed to redeem the modern world can be established only by leaders exercising what Babbitt calls "the highest use of the imagination." He distinguishes between the "Arcadian" imagination, representing individual impulses, and the "ethical imagination," expressing with a "high seriousness" a common or universal self.

In the light of this distinction, with its echoes of Arnold, Babbitt examines the work of the leading romantics. The quality of imagination displayed by both Keats and Shelley does not rise above the Arcadian or pastoral level. Babbitt regards Wordsworth with mixed feelings: he is rather attracted by his high moralizing and didacticism but distrusts his sentimentalization of common life and his regressive cult of the child. He treats Coleridge with more sympathy, but condescendingly. The romantic he most respects is Goethe, who in mid-career had the wisdom to turn from an emotional striving toward the unlimited to an acceptance of boundaries. Babbitt regrets that the humanistic Goethe has had fewer followers than the romantic.

For the most part, Babbitt's literary criticism is incidental to his moralistic social criticism and his Humanist version of history. Such highly loaded terms as *the two laws, the ethical imagination, humanitarianism,* and *the philosophy of flux* are used not so much to interpret literature as to pass moral judgment. Even if a distinction could be made between two types of imagination—one "ethical," the other "Arcadian" or "pastoral"—what grounds are there for calling one "higher" than the other?

The Humanist is hostile to contemporary literature, which reflects a world view that he does not wish to or cannot accept and which employs artistic conventions that he refuses to understand. Babbitt can dismiss Joyce's *Ulysses,* the carefully wrought product of years of conscious artistry, by saying that it "marks a more advanced state of psychic disintegration than anything that has come down to us from classical antiquity." He lumps Theodore Dreiser with Sherwood Anderson, H. L. Mencken, Sinclair Lewis, John Dos Passos, and Carl Sandburg, as end products of a long descent from *religious* to *humanistic* to *naturalistic realism*—a realism he describes as "romanticism on all fours." The only possible escape from the life of sensation in which this group is absorbed must come from a renewal of the "inner life," of which, for America, Jonathan Edwards is the exemplar. Babbitt admits that Edwards' theology is no longer acceptable and that a secular substitute must be found; the quest for this is the vocation of the Humanist leader.

The invocation of Edwards is a key to the cultural genealogy of the Humanist. In his idealism and his religious aspiration, Emerson was also the heir of Edwards; and the Humanist, like the transcendentalist, is seeking in what he regards as the modern wasteland (Emerson's "sty" of nature) for something to replace the divine and supernatural light of which the Puritan was confident. For both the answer seems to lie in an "ethical," "higher" imagination. It is not only in the recognition of two laws and of the need for supranaturalistic values, but also in the idealizing tendency, the revulsion from the gross life of the senses, that the New Humanist is at one with the romantic transcendentalist.

2

A Thoreau to Babbitt's Emerson, Paul Elmer More has sometimes been called "the hermit of Princeton." Author of a number of historical works on Christianity and the classics, More is best known for the *Shelburne Essays,* issued in eleven volumes comprising two series (1904-10; 1913-21) and consisting largely of reviews and articles which had appeared in *The Nation* and other periodicals. In the bulk of his output, More is the foremost Humanist critic, and his discussions of American and chiefly English literature (the ratio of essays on these is about one to three) reveal a point of view very close to Babbitt's.

Inspired by Thoreau, More retired, early in his career, to a small house in New Hampshire for two years of meditation and writing. The title of the *Shelburne Essays*—like *Walden,* named after a place of withdrawal—represented for the author the contemplative spirit in which his writings were conceived.

The essays begin with "A Hermit's Notes on Thoreau," in which More sees Thoreau as a kindred spirit who turned from civilization to the solitude of nature. His Humanism is apparent in his praise of Thoreau's moral rigor and roots in New England Puritanism. More ignores the pantheistic feeling for nature that Thoreau courted in periods of meditation, believing that he found nature not so much a stimulant to "pantheistic reverie" as a "discipline of the will." For the Humanist, Thoreau's chapter on "Higher Laws" is more compelling than those on "Solitude" or "Spring."

Other American writers treated sympathetically in the

earlier essays are Hawthorne, Poe, Emerson, and Whitman. Hawthorne, the inheritor of the Puritan idea of depravity, also communicates the Hindu sense of loneliness and illusion. More links his and Poe's treatment of moral isolation to the Puritan feeling of alienation from nature, evident in its hysterical extreme in the witchcraft demonstrations of the seventeenth century. Like Babbitt, More praises Emerson for his dualism, but he considers transcendentalism a "fatally easy philosophy" in its denial of sin and suffering. A poet preacher of sometimes amorphous sermons, Whitman does not rise to the height of Emerson but is nevertheless richer in temperament; Americans should accept him as "one of the most original and characteristic of their poets." (More does not comment upon Whitman's proclamation that the body is no greater than the soul, nor the soul than the body.)

More condemns the English romantics for their surrender to flux. Wordsworth, however, he praises for his contemplative love of nature. Most of nineteenth century English literature (More hardly touches the twentieth) is seen as a progressive decline from the romantics through the Victorians, who were demoralized by the "philosophy of change" which Darwinism introduced. In the midst of disintegration Arnold stands out as a lonely and heroic figure in his quest for enduring values and his attempt to see life steadily and whole.

Among earlier writers, Milton is preeminent for his qualities of aspiration, high seriousness, and discipline. The true theme of *Paradise Lost* is not sin or the problem of the relationship of man to God in theological terms but rather the desire of man for "Paradise itself," the "longing of the human heart for a garden of innocence, a paradise of idyllic delights." The theme is universal, expressed not only in the classics but in the Celtic dream of Avalon and the Wordsworthian idea of the heaven "which is our home." It presents a vision of purity set off against the evil and corruption of the world: "As Adam in his morning hymn gave thanks for the glories of the outstretched and still uncontaminated earth, so almost are we ready to render praise to the poet's creative genius for this sweet refuge of retirement he has builded for the heart of our fancy." (The withdrawal theme defined by More anticipates the myth critic's rebirth archetype, although More apparently is not aware either of its psychological or mythic implications—or of its romanticism.)

In the absence of a fully developed theory, clues to More's critical principles are discoverable in the essay "Criticism" in the seventh volume of the *Shelburne Essays* (1910) and in the "Definitions of Dualism" presented in the next volume, entitled *The Drift of Romanticism* (1913). More accepts Arnold's idea of literature as a "criticism of life," but he considers inadequate his definition of criticism as the effort "to know the best that is known and thought in the world." With all his earnestness, Arnold lacked a positive principle to integrate his moral and his aesthetic sense. Arnold's "sweetness and light" is "little more than the modern term for the deist's nature and reason." Although More is obviously indebted to Arnold's humanism, he is eager to distinguish his own position from that of the English Victorian.

Like Arnold, More looks to the past as a source of standards for literary and social criticism, which he does not regard as separate functions. Arnold, he feels, tended to regard the past as a dead storehouse; it is rather a repository of events which interact with those of the present and which the critic is able to interpret creatively. Adapting from an essay of Wilde's the idea of literature as the collective memory of mankind's emotions and experiences, More suggests, with almost Jamesian indirection, that "this larger memory, in its transmuting and unifying power, may not unmeaningfully be regarded as the purpose of activity, and literature may not too presumptuously be cherished as the final end of existence." In this "theory" of memory, criticism can play an important role. Since the critic's function of valuing is a form of creating, "the critical spirit is akin to that force of design or final cause in the Aristotelian sense, which we are beginning once more to divine as the guiding principle, itself unchanged, at work within the evolutionary changes of nature; and in so far as it becomes aware of this high office it introduces into our intellectual life an element outside of alteration and growth and decay, a principle to which time is the minister and not master."

Here More again anticipates some of the functions of the later myth criticism as he tentatively formulates not a method but a mystique of criticism. His reader, however, is left unenlightened as to how the general and familiar tenets of academic Humanism are to be applied to practical criticism.

Characteristic features of More's Humanism can be seen in his "Definitions of Dualism." Tradition is the experience of society, which can be transferred to the individual through education. "Art is the experience of the individual in tradition. Serious art is thus almost necessarily concerned with the past and with ambitions of the future." Although this idea foreshadows the argument of Eliot's "Tradition and the Individual Talent," More's preoccupation with the past amounts almost to a fixation. The need of "checking the enthusiasm of the living by the authority of the dead" belies his earlier profession of a vital interaction between past and present and helps to explain his hostility to contemporary art. Among the dead, despite his veneration of Milton, his closest ties and deepest responses are with the English and American romantics. Although critical of the limitations of poets like Keats and Wordsworth, he is temperamentally closer to them than to Dryden or Pope, whom he considers classics of English prose.

More's distrust of reason is another link with the romantics: "Rationalism is the attempt to erect reason into an independent power within the soul taking the place of the inner check. The union of science and rationalism, that is to say, the reassumption of nature and the soul under the same law, gives the false philosophy of naturalism." The idea of a scientific philosophy is cavalierly rejected: "Scientific monism is a kind of sterile hybrid from the union of naturalism and idealism. It need be named and no more." For More as for the romantics it is the imagination, or the "faculty which sensualizes the data of experience," that produces art or poetry.

But in his moral and social attitudes More like Babbitt rigidly opposes the romantic idea of human goodness. He appeals to the authority of St. Augustine, feeling that the rigor of Augustinian orthodoxy is needed to correct modern Pelagianism in an age when a "so-called Christian sociology" is being substituted for the older faith. More's religious conservatism and deep distrust of human nature are consistent with his social attitudes, which are most explicitly set forth in *Aristocracy and Justice* (1915), the ninth volume of the *Shelburne Essays.* He stresses the need of a ruling class or elite, but he exceeds Babbitt in identifying his elite with the propertied class and the interests of the republic with those of property. Against the background of the bloody Colorado mine strikes, in which women and children were shot down, More asserts that "to the civilized man the rights of property are more important than the right to life." Since civilization rests on property and must recognize the inequality of man, "in view of the interests involved, it is better that legal robbery should exist along with the maintenance of law, than that legal robbery should be suppressed at the expense of law." In a society in which the unequal distribution of property proves, to the Humanist as to the Puritan, the inherent inequality of men, the Humanist must resist the false idea of equality before the law.

This denial of the basic premises of democracy cuts More off from the author of *Walden, Civil Disobedience,* and *A Plea for Captain John Brown,* with whom he had sought to identify himself. In *Walden* Thoreau sees property as an evil and a deterrent to the development of a humane culture. In all his writing but most emphatically in the civil disobedience essay, Thoreau asserts unequivocally the right of the individual regardless of status or support to consideration before the law. In contrast with the vital expansive spirit of the earlier American, the posture of the Humanist is mean and self-regarding. More's denial of these human values is the utterance of a humanism wanting in humanity.

3

The term *humanism* is fortunately too broad to be confined within these narrow limits. Many critics considered themselves humanists who were antipathetic to the outlook of Babbitt and More. And even among their followers there was some latitude of opinion.

In *Destinations* (1928), Gorham B. Munson considers

Babbitt's Humanism a sound basis for literary criticism, "counter-impressionistic and counter-relativistic in its assumptions and aims." He praises More as "probably the best living American critic," with the "greatest maturity of judgment now displayed in the American literary scene." Munson differs from them, however, in his interest in contemporary literature. He appreciates the efforts of the experimental poets even though he does not approve of their attitudes. He recognizes the use of wit, eloquence, and mockery by Wallace Stevens, exotic though his verse may seem, as one means, though not the Humanist's, of establishing order. The unconventional poetry of Marianne Moore is admirable in its "style" and "design," though it falls short of major work because it does not "see totalities" or treat experience "as a whole." William Carlos Williams is "a United States poet," distinguished by force of diction, freshness of observation, and roots in the sensual life.

Munson feels the need of what he calls a new symbolism in American literature if it is to develop beyond the pessimistic naturalism of Dreiser and Sherwood Anderson. Less inclined than Babbitt and More to look to the past for values, he is also more sensitive critically and does not depend so mechanically on terms like *dualism, higher will, ethical imagination,* and *inner check.* His discussions of modern literature, and especially modern verse, show a greater responsiveness to poetic language and awareness of its dynamics.

The reputation of Stuart Pratt Sherman, a defector from the ranks of Humanism, has suffered from the dispraise of former associates. A native of the Midwest, he came under the influence of Irving Babbitt at Harvard. His early books, *Matthew Arnold: How to Know Him* (1917) and *On Con-*

temporary Literature (1917), reflect his tutelage. But during the postwar period, when he left an academic post to become literary editor of the New York *Herald Tribune,* he turned more and more to the tradition of democratic liberalism.

His apostasy (or liberation) can be seen in several later books. In *Americans* (1922) he follows the Humanists in praising Milton, not, however, for his dualism and his ethical imagination so much as for his doctrine of individualism. Among the Americans to whom the book is chiefly devoted, Emerson is preeminent because of his resistance to authority, a characteristic which the elder Humanists had understandably neglected. Hawthorne is praised not as an heir to Calvinism but rather as a "subtle critic and satirist of Puritanism from a transcendentalist point of view" and Whitman is esteemed for his humanitarianism and democratic faith. The mystery at the heart of this faith is not human iniquity but the "co-existence of personal freedom with social authority," epitomized in the verse motto of *Leaves of Grass:* "One's-self I sing, a simple separate person, / Yet utter the word Democratic, the word En-Masse."

Sherman's strongest repudiation of Humanism occurs in a satiric "Imaginary Conversation with Mr. P. E. More." Beginning with the statement that "if W. D. Howells was the dean of our fiction, Mr. More is the bishop of our criticism," he ironically flays More and his associates for their acceptance of the idea of depravity and their aristocratic contempt for the *mobile vulgus.* In discussing the eighteenth century, More "can forgive Pope his virulent personal satire but not his deistic optimism"; he prefers Swift to Pope because of his view of man as a species of vermin. Of the antidemocratic bias of the Humanist, Sherman says that More and his fellow conservatives "have never felt one generous throb of the faith, regenerative and sustaining and uniting, which Jefferson poured broadcast upon the spirit of the American people—faith in the sense and virtue of the community and in the sense and virtue of the majority of its components." This faith Sherman recognizes as the true religion of democracy, "consisting of a little bundle of general principles" which make the average man respect himself and his neighbors and keep him from "lapsing into Yahooism."

In a genial aside in *Critical Woodcuts* (1926), Sherman comments on the change in his views and his increasing sympathy with the work of his contemporaries: "Rigorous teachers seized my youth and taught me some phrases about the desirability of seeing things steadily and seeing them whole. But experience has taught me that it is exceedingly difficult to see steadily and whole any object which is alive and moving rapidly."

4

A bitter conflict began during the war decade between the New Humanists and numerous younger critics who objected to their social and literary principles. In the Twenties this became a running battle that culminated in the publication, in 1930, of rival symposia setting forth, in no very systematic fashion, Humanist and anti-Humanist arguments. Though these were often repetitious, particularly on the Humanist side, they reveal some of the critical attitudes of members of the opposing camps.

The first to appear was *Humanism and America*, edited by Norman Foerster, who had already applied Humanist doctrines to criticism in several volumes including *Nature in American Literature* (1923), *American Criticism* (1928),

Reinterpretation of American Literature (1928), and *Towards Standards* (1930). His practice adds little to the basic position already established by Babbitt and More. His theory, set forth in *American Criticism,* will be discussed in a later chapter.

The symposium represents twelve contributors besides Foerster, Babbitt, and More. Foerster's preface summarizes the Humanist position and echoes its standard terminology (*vital restraint, law of measure, discipline, centrality, modernism, humanitarianism*). Babbitt's "Humanism: An Essay at Definition" is noteworthy chiefly for its religious emphasis, its author feeling that there is need for cooperation between the Humanist and the authentic Christian in opposing the "behaviourists and other naturalistic psychologists who are to be regarded at present as among the chief enemies of human nature": "For my own part I range myself unhesitatingly on the side of the supernaturalists."

Paul Elmer More's essay, "The Humility of Common Sense," reprinted from *The Demon of the Absolute* (1928), shows a deep hostility to the new theoretical science of Whitehead and the "Einsteinian relativists." Whitehead's *Science and the Modern World* is criticized for legislating mechanism (and matter) out of existence, leaving only *events* and thus eliminating, for More, any distinction between body and soul and depriving mankind of "what is distinctively human." "Science as an accumulation and classification and utilization of observed facts may go on from victory to victory; but science as a name for such hypothetical theories of time and space, matter and motion and life, as those broached by the Darwinians of the nineteenth century, or the Einsteinian relativists of the twentieth, is not a progress of insight but a lapse from one naive assumption to another in a vicious circle of self-contradicting monisms." We must throw over the idol of unity, the demon of the rationalistic absolute which has sprung from the "union of science and metaphysics."

Acting from some inner emotional necessity, More denies the truths of modern science because they conflict with his theory of existence. In his excursion into the field of scientific theory, he is guided by his brother, a professor of physics at the University of Cincinnati. Louis T. More's essay, entitled "The Pretensions of Science," appears at the beginning of the symposium, perhaps to provide scientific support for the antiscientism of the Humanists. Professor More objects to theoretical scientists as men "who are not content to work in their limited field, but are really metaphysicians who have created a fictitious world of the imagination made out of aethers, electrons, and mathematical symbols, and have confused it in their own and other minds with the sensible world of brute fact." This latter world is the sphere of true science, which is concerned not with all knowledge, but with *objective* knowledge.

A clue to the viewpoint of most of the contributors is revealed by the titles of some of the essays: G. R. Elliott's "The Pride of Modernity"; F. J. Mather, Jr.'s "The Plight of the Artist"; A. R. Thompson's "The Dilemma of Modern Tragedy"; and H. H. Clark's "Pandora's Box in American Fiction."

In "Religion Without Humanism," T. S. Eliot, a former student of Babbitt, finds humanism not so much a sustaining philosophy as a leavening agent in "the full realization and balance of the disciplined intellectual and emotional life of man." After commenting upon the mutual need of humanism and religion and science, Eliot concludes, "It is the spirit of humanism which has operated to reconcile the mystic and ecclesiastic in one church; having done this in the past, humanism should not set itself up now as another sect, but strive to continue and enlarge its task, labouring to reconcile and unite all the parts into a whole."

Although *Humanism and America* contains more polemic than criticism, there are a few essays in which doctrine is brought to bear upon literature. Robert Shafer's "An American Tragedy" treats Dreiser, a favorite target, as a slave to temperament, "the chaotic flow of 'natural' impulses" that denies our humanity and ends in despair. *This* is our "American tragedy." However, Shafer recognizes that Dreiser, in struggling to express the truth as he sees it from a deterministic point of view, has lived a "rationally purposive life"—that in reducing his truth to consistency and giving it coherent form, he has refuted his own philosophy.

The Critique of Humanism, hastily prepared as a counterblast, is introduced by its editor, C. Hartley Grattan, as an "experiment in pamphleteering in the modern manner." Thirteen contributors attack the Humanist position with arguments in which three themes recur: the hostility of the Humanists to science and modern culture, the inadequacy of their philosophical and moral theory, and their insensitivity to aesthetic considerations.

In "The New Humanism and the Scientific Attitude," Grattan regrets the appropriation of the word *humanism* by a doctrinaire group interested in deriving values from "past formulations" rather than experimentally from a study of contemporary society and its needs. He asserts the continuity of man and nature, believing that values, which are conditioned by culture, should be scientifically based. The Humanist view of literature as a repository of moral values Grattan considers a failure to recognize art as an independent mode of experience.

Edmund Wilson takes the Humanists to task for their limited, moralistic criticism of literature and for their failure to recognize the moral ordering of experience in Joyce's "stream of consciousness" technique. Wilson's "Notes on Babbitt and More" also questions Babbitt's scholarship in his essay in *Humanism and America,* in which, according to Wilson, Babbitt misrepresents a Greek text in order to turn Sophocles into a Harvard Humanist.

In "The Fallacy of Humanism," Allen Tate points to the inconsistency of Babbitt's attitude toward reason, which combines the expression of a faith in reason with the desire to go *beyond reason* through the intuitive "ethical imagination." The attempt to base values in the culture of the past is a futile process involving an "infinite regression to authoritative judgment."

The discipline that the Humanist talks about so much is, for R. P. Blackmur (in "The Discipline of Humanism") a repressive moralism ignorant of the nature of art: "This adverse criticism never refers to the kind of discipline in which the artist is interested—the discipline of his subject matter—but chiefly examines that discipline which involves a view of life or the apprehension of the higher will; discipline, that is, in which the artist need not be directly concerned at all. Humanism has refrained, and no doubt this is an admirable instance of vital restraint, from all that a novelist or poet would mean by literary criticism. There was nothing to compel it to refrain, so that it must have been an act of choice; either Humanism is not interested in the content of literature and the problems surrounding it, or it has had no experience therein." The Humanists have, in effect, substituted censorship for criticism.

The *dualism* upon which the Humanists pride themselves is "merely a kind of double life in the mind" which "divides life into the material and the spiritual, the lower and the higher wills, and asserts that the spiritual, the higher will, is the meaning of the material. The Humanists, lacking either the dogma of Christianity or the body of Greek civilization to infuse the spiritual with the nourishment of earth, tend to divorce their higher will from experience altogether, and to employ it, so divorced, as a standard by which to judge others' experience. It is no wonder then, that what the humanists call their insight, their imagination, their discipline, should seem to us their arrogance, their blindness, and their censorious ignorance."

The bitterness that comes through these lines is shared by other contributors, especially those concerned for social and political as well as literary problems.

In "Humanizing Society," Malcolm Cowley asserts that a preoccupation with morality has prevented the Humanists from understanding the true humanizing function of art, while their antipathy to contemporary literature has blinded them to the way in which writers help to humanize and make comprehensible the world in which modern man must live. The Humanists wilfully ignore the social realities pressing upon the artist—realities that the anti-Humanist critic finds especially importunate in the early years of the depression: "What . . . has Humanism to do with the scene outside my window: with the jobless men who saunter in the dusk, or the dying village, or the paper mill abandoned across the river—this mill whose owners have gone South where labor is cheap?"

Many contributors note the limitation resulting from the Humanists' hostility to contemporary life and literature. In "Poetry, Morality, and Criticism," Yvor Winters defends the work of the experimental poets and novelists against Humanist attacks. Although Winters later modified his own views, he here justifies such leading experimental poets as William Carlos Williams and Marianne Moore: their poetry, like all genuine poetry, is a kind of moral discipline that the Humanists are unable to understand, a discipline in the confrontation of reality, rather than an escape from it to a stereotyped traditionalism.

The concluding essay, Lewis Mumford's "Toward an Organic Humanism," suggests an alternative to the official Humanist view. The New Humanism of which Babbitt and More are the leaders is a partial philosophy, as is that of the New Mechanism, promulgated by Dewey and Beard. (The one group has made a fetish of morality, the other of the machine.) Just as the former is too narrowly preoccupied with conventional moral judgments based on standards derived from the past, the latter is too limited in its quantitative treatment of objective phenomena and its avoidance of questions of value. Mumford points out that science, contrary to the opinion of the Humanists, inculcates in its followers discipline and humility, a subordination of pride and selfish interest to the realities of experience.

The Humanist dualism of soul and body, man and nature, is false because it denies the interrelationship of the individual and his environment. Human life and development depend upon an organic relationship between man and his world, a world within which the human personality is central, since all the data of the external universe demand the existence of a living observer, whose presence is necessary for the development of history, itself a human creation: "Our thought itself, our concepts, our grammatic structure, are the products of the multitude of human beings that came before us; and the existence of human society is a much surer fact of experience than the existence of Betelgeuse, or, for that matter, the whole physical universe—all of which is derivative and inferential, since it assumes the existence of human instruments like language, mathematics, measurements." What is needed for further advancement is a new synthesis through an "organic humanism"—an open synthesis that recognizes the relative and incomplete state of knowledge and that has room for new truths, thus differing from "the synthesis which satisfied St. Thomas Aquinas and Dante, for that was unable to absorb the discoveries as to the nature of the physical world which followed so soon after its formulation."

The main problem, for Mumford, is to keep the organism and its environment in a state of tension within which growth and renewal will be continuous. "An organic attitude towards life can truly be called humanism; for it will reconcile by its superior comprehension the one-sided philosophies which men have formulated out of a raw and imperfect experience."

Mumford's naturalistic humanism is a far cry from the doctrine preached by Babbitt and More. In its acceptance of scientific techniques and its belief in growth and renewal, it offers more hope for the future of humanity than the New Humanists would allow.

5

One of the most distinguished opponents of the New Humanism was the philosopher George Santayana, a master of satiric irony. In a rapier-slim volume entitled *The Genteel Tradition at Bay* (1931), he characterizes the New Humanists as genteel heirs to a spiritually bankrupt Puritan tradition and their morality as narrow and parochial rather than universal. Of the Humanists' distinction between man's lower and higher nature, and their identification of naturalism with the lower, Santayana quietly asks, "Why is naturalism supposed to be favourable to the lower sides of human nature? Are not the higher sides just as natural?" Morality, far from being above the level of nature, is necessarily grounded there.

As for the controls of reason and the inner check prescribed by the Humanists, Santayana observes, "True reason restrains only to liberate; it checks only in order that all currents, mingling in that moment's pause, may take a united course." The New Humanism by its very nature leads one to expect an apocalyptic revelation, or at least some supernatural sanction for its inner check. But one receives only prudent admonitions encouraging a "cautious allegiance to the genteel tradition." Santayana concludes that the Humanists are perverted in their denial of nature and a relativistic morality: "When . . . a tender conscience extends its maxims beyond their natural basis, it not only ceases to be rational in its deliverances, and becomes fanatical, but it casts the livid colours of its own insanity upon nature at large. . . . No true appreciation of anything is possible without a sense of its *naturalness,* of the innocent necessity by which it has assumed its special and perhaps extraordinary form. In a word, the principle of morality is naturalistic. Call it humanism or not, only a morality frankly relative to man's nature is worthy of man, being at once vital and rational, martial and generous; whereas absolutism smells of fustiness as well as of faggots."

It was not so much the attacks of their enemies as the times that defeated the Humanists. The depression decade, following the numbing shock of the 1929 crash, saw their decline from a position of importance to one of obscurity if not insignificance. Babbitt died in 1933 and More in 1937, but the dissolution of the critical group cannot be attributed to their passing. It is rather that the Humanists had so little to say to the 1930's. In the midst of economic disaster and social suffering, their genteel moralizing seemed trivial and irrelevant, while their aristocratic pretensions were more offensive than they had been during the gilded Twenties.

☙ 4 ❧

LIBERAL AND MARXIST CRITICISM

1—The pattern of liberal and Marxist criticism; 2—Radical journals: The Masses—*Floyd Dell and Max Eastman; 3—*The Modern Quarterly—*V. F. Calverton; 4—*The New Masses—*Philip Rahv and Granville Hicks; 5—The* Partisan Review *and the shift to formalist criticism; 6—Critics of Marxist theory; 7—Independent revolutionary critics—Newton Arvin, Kenneth Burke, Edmund Wilson; 8—The Thirties bracketed—V. L. Parrington and F. O. Matthiessen*

1

Criticism concerned with the economic, social, and political implications of literature has a long history in America beginning with the growth of cultural nationalism in the early nineteenth century. Whitman and Howells, and Emerson to a lesser degree, were the transmitters of this tradition, which was reinforced by new liberal and radical political movements in the early years of the twentieth century. The struggles of labor during the period of industrial expansion, the growth of monopolies, and the corruption of government on all levels stimulated many vigorous if uncoordinated voices of protest and programs of reform. In the field of journalism and popular literature this was the time of the "muckraking" movement, christened by Theodore Roosevelt in 1906. It included Ida Tarbell, Lincoln Steffens, and writers associated with *Arena, McClure's,* and other magazines and newspapers. *The Jungle* (1906), Upton Sinclair's novel of protest against conditions in the Chicago meat-packing industry, was written to appear serially in the Socialist *Appeal to Reason.*

For many writers and critics the solution to existing evils seemed to lie in the aims of the Socialist Party of the United States, which was organized in 1900 and grew rapidly under the leadership of Eugene Debs. Weakened during the war years by dissension over policy, it was seriously crippled by the Socialist-Communist split in 1919. In the decade that followed, both the Red scare and prosperity helped reduce the party to comparative insignificance.

During the period of its early growth, however, socialism was a force in both creative writing and criticism. Before the war, "New Realists" like John Macy, Randolph Bourne, and Van Wyck Brooks were staunch adherents. Macy, who is best known for his *Spirit of American Literature* (1913), also wrote *Socialism in America* (1916), in the preface of which he described himself as a "member of the Socialist party and of the Industrial Workers of the World." He went on to say, "I have no official position in either. I express only my own opinions or the opinions of others which happen to appeal to me." Such independence and eclecticism, typical of many of the early radicals, is in sharp contrast to the orthodoxy of later Marxist critics.

Van Wyck Brooks, in *America's Coming of Age* (1915), saw in our national life and literature, with the conspicuous exception of Whitman's poetry, a falling away from the democratic ideal of the good life. He urged a rejection of the barren tradition of Puritanism—the source of our genteel conventions and our materialism—and the formulation of new social ideals. He took for granted that on the economic plane "this change implies socialism; on every other plane it implies something which a majority of Americans in our day certainly do not possess—an object in living." However, like many other "radicals" of the time, Brooks was less interested in accomplishing a socialist revolution than in renovating the native liberal-democratic tradition and adopting its values as standards for social and literary criticism.

His radicalism was indeed a passing phase, and his criticism, in retrospect, seems dated. His biographies of Mark Twain and Henry James, published in the 1920's, supported only negatively his earlier appeals for a rediscovery of the American spirit and evidenced more debunking than crusading zeal. At the beginning of the 1930's, when a new radical criticism was developing, he was turning from serious criticism to the genial reconstruction of the earlier American literary scene that was to attract a popular audience to *The Flowering of New England* (1936) and its companion volumes. His earlier work, nevertheless, stands as a contribution to liberal literary criticism.

The United Communist Party was organized in 1920, becoming the Workers Party in 1921, and finally, in 1928, the Communist Party of the U.S.A. Although weakened by attacks from without and by internal dissension during the 1920's, it grew in strength and influence during the depression years, when proletarian literature and criticism flourished, with an increasing stress on conformity. The attitudes and standards of writers and critics were examined for their adherence to a "Party line" which was itself subject to discomfiting fluctuations. To be sure, not all Communist sympathizers submitted to Party discipline gracefully (in fact, some of the better radical critics remained independent), but most critics—even those who did not wish any association with the movement—were sensitive to the demands of pressing social problems and felt compelled to come to terms at least with the standards of criticism proclaimed by official spokesmen. In the later Thirties the movement was seriously weakened by the Moscow purge trials and the Spanish Civil War, and the Soviet-Nazi nonaggression treaty of 1939 was the final disabling blow. Leftist literary criticism never recovered from this period of intense disillusionment. The outlook of the critics of the Thirties came to be viewed as a facile Utopianism, and Marxism was succeeded by a "New Liberalism," representing a retreat from an exposed position on the left to a newer vantage point, never too clearly defined, but closer to the "vital center" of the political scene.

2

Although not all critics who attempted to explain literature in terms of its social, economic, and political environment identified themselves politically with socialism or communism, the revolutionary criticism published in several periodicals had an immense influence.*

The most colorful and important of the early radical magazines was *The Masses,* begun in Greenwich Village in 1911 and succeeded by *The Liberator* (1918-24). The two were edited from 1912 to 1923 by Max Eastman and Floyd Dell; and associates and regular contributors included John Reed, Louis Untermeyer, Lincoln Steffens, Mary Heaton Vorse,

* Readers interested in these and other modern literary periodicals have an indispensable guide and aid in *The Little Magazine: A History and Bibliography* (1947), by Frederick J. Hoffman, Charles Allen, and Carolyn F. Ulrich.

Michael Gold, Joseph Freeman, and Upton Sinclair. *The Masses* attacked bourgeois economic, social, and political institutions with a verve and abandon that involved it in libel suits, loss of mailing privileges, suspension, and eventual suppression by the government at the end of 1917. *The Liberator* continued in the same tradition for several years until its Communist ties gradually tightened and it became absorbed by the *Workers' Monthly* in 1924.

Both *The Masses* and the early *Liberator* printed better social and political essays than creative writing or criticism. The Paterson and Colorado strikes were effectively reported, as was the Bolshevik revolution, covered by John Reed, who wrote for *The Liberator* dispatches later incorporated in *Ten Days that Shook the World* (1919). Generous in their enthusiasms and sympathies, the editors vigorously supported the feminist movement and Margaret Sanger's birth-control crusade. Much of the verse published in the magazines was, in contrast, sentimental and traditional, revealing no awareness of the problems or objectives of Pound, Williams, or other serious experimental poets of the time.

Floyd Dell, who wrote most of the reviews and critical articles, was sympathetic to literature that supported socialist ideals. His judgments were often inconsistent because of strong subjective responses which tended to get in the way of effective discussion of form or technique. His assessment of Dreiser, made when *The Genius* appeared in 1915, is typical: he acknowledges the power of Dreiser's vision of social struggle and injustice but regrets his confusion and cynicism. Less typical is an article on Walt Whitman that appeared in *The Liberator* (1919) in a time of postwar disillusionment. Unlike most proletarian critics, Dell emphasizes Whitman's sense of self-contradiction as well as his democratic vision. In a self-revealing analysis, Dell asserts that Whitman's temperament was typically American in its mixture of self-doubt and Utopian faith. The application to the postwar period is explicit: Whitman set the keynote of the later struggle toward the realization of social ideals. The struggle will be supported, even in the face of almost hopeless odds, by Americans, who share this paradoxical heritage.

Dell's *Intellectual Vagabondage* (1926), which originally appeared in *The Liberator* as a series of articles entitled *Literature and the Machine Age,* also shows the postwar mood of the revolutionary critic. A rather simple personalized history of literature, chiefly English, from the eighteenth century to the twentieth, it explains developments in terms of social causes. In it, Dell identifies himself with the questing intellectuals in a period of confusion in values. For his generation, coming of age in the first decade of the century, the image of a new Utopia, of which H. G. Wells was the prophet, was foreshadowed in the plays of Ibsen and Shaw. Shaw's skepticism, however, introduced a sobering question: "Can you create a new civilization upon the ruins of the old? Can you even get along in such a new civilization if someone else creates it for you?"

The question is one Dell considers with serious doubts. His last chapter, "Intellectual Shell-Shock," expresses disillusion with the results of the Russian experiment and suggests that it must remain for a younger generation, growing up under different conditions, to reconstruct the "shattered social, political and economic ideals . . . we have left them." Perhaps the younger generation will be able to formulate values appropriate to a machine civilization from which Dell and his contemporaries, heirs to a romantic individualism, feel increasingly alienated.

Partly because of his personal conflicts and his resistance to conformity and doctrinaire limitations, Dell's critical standards were disorganized. He was responsive to protest, magnanimous and tolerant of inconsistency, and humanitarian in a way that both the Humanist and the orthodox Marxist would condemn. In these respects he was typical of his generation, and his criticism represents not only the ideas but the emotions of a period in which liberals and anarchists and socialists and communists and feminists and reformers of many kinds banded together, in a very ragged front, to wage war against the established order.

As Dell's editorial colleague, Max Eastman directed most of his attention to social and political topics, but he also wrote literary criticism and theory. Two of his books—*The Enjoyment of Poetry* (1913) and *The Literary Mind: Its Place in an Age of Science* (1931)—are well known, the former enjoying a continuing popularity. Eastman is less concerned than his revolutionary associates with the problem of the relation of literature to political ideology because of a distinction which he makes between poetic and practical activities: science is the province of knowledge and truth while poetry, or imaginative literature, is concerned with the unique personal feelings and qualities of experience left out of scientific generalizations. In *The Literary Mind* poetry is described as an art "totally distinct from the art of general knowledge." Since poetry has surrendered to science the search for truth, it does not matter whether the "truths" of literature, which contribute to the reader's enjoyment and heightened consciousness of life, are scientifically verifiable.

With the passing of the Twenties, Eastman, like Dell, became increasingly disillusioned. His *Artists in Uniform*

(1934) is a protest against the straitjacketing of writers by official Communism in both Russia and the United States, and *The End of Socialism* (1937) treats the rise of Stalin and the purge trials of 1936 as the death of revolutionary socialist ideals.

3

The Modern Quarterly, A Journal of Radical Opinion (later *The Modern Monthly*) was founded in Baltimore in 1923 by the youthful V. F. Calverton and edited by him, with the assistance of Samuel D. Schmalhausen and—briefly, during the mid-Thirties—of Max Eastman and Edmund Wilson. It ceased publication in 1938, although a special memorial issue was brought out after Calverton's death in 1940. A lively journal in which Marxian and Freudian viewpoints predominated, *The Modern Quarterly* included, among many well-known contributors, John Dewey, Max Eastman, Sidney Hook, Waldo Frank, Floyd Dell, Herbert Read, Ernest Sutherland Bates, Diego Rivera, and Sherwood Anderson.

While the *Quarterly* covered a wide range of topics, one of its most important features was a symposium, "The Revolution of the Word," in the fall of 1929, the issue being whether literature, or art, is to be considered as the expression of an individual sensibility or as communication. The immediate cause of the controversy was the campaign for the "Revolution of the Word" being conducted in Eugene Jolas's *transition,* where installments of Joyce's *Work in Progress,* later *Finnegans Wake,* were appearing. Inspired by Joyce and by the surrealists, Jolas was proclaiming a new synthesis of poetic language which would tap the resources of the unconscious mind through the language of the dream and thus enrich the sensibility of modern man, a prisoner of a machine society and its rationalism. In his symposium essay, "Necessity for the New Word," Jolas distinguishes himself from the surrealists by insisting that the conscious mind is not to be ignored but rather complemented and reinforced by the subconscious: there must be "a fusion of a physical and supernatural reality." "With the new word and its arrangements we hope to burst the metallic age. We hope to destroy the world with an apocalyptic vision. We hope to create a new and more magical universe with words that approximate the synthetist reality we dream of."

Because of its professed revolutionary nature and its preoccupation with the private dream life rather than social reality, Jolas's program was a challenge to the radical social critic. In his reply V. F. Calverton agrees that a new age requires a new and revolutionary literature, but he questions the appropriateness of the kind of revolution proposed by the *transition* critics: they are moving in the direction of less rather than greater communicability and thus encouraging an "anarchy in the arts that is destructive of all esthetic progress."

By combining an emphasis on the dislocation of language and the coining of neologisms with the proposition that "the writer expresses, he does not communicate," the revolutionists assume a nihilist position. For Calverton, words are primarily "social forms, not individual ones," and any attempt to frustrate their communicability is both an offense against the community and a perversion of language. He concludes by saying, "We are, then, for all kinds of experimentation in modern writing, but experimentation which remains communicative in whatever form it takes." The *revolution-in-the-wordists* are not revolutionary but reactionary. "To be revolutionary one must experiment with better means of communication rather than with more muddled methods of expression, for the aim of our age, with its new science and new logic, is to clarify rather than confuse."

The ideological position of the proletarian critic places him in a dilemma. Although he should logically be on the side of an experimentation and revolution in the arts paralleling the revolution in social forms, he must resist the modernist tendency to distort or reshape conventions so radically as to place a barrier between the artist and a large popular audience. He is inclined to disapprove of difficult free verse arrangements like those of Cummings or Pound and to favor traditional rhymed verse or Whitmanesque long-line verse. While such a stand may encourage poetry of greater comprehensibility, it also encourages tameness and dullness.

Victor Francis Calverton (born George Goetz), a native of Baltimore and a graduate of Johns Hopkins, became a convert to socialism at the age of eighteen. Although attracted to Communism in the Twenties, he never became a member of the Party; in fact, he broke his association with orthodox Communists in 1931 because of the Party's totalitarianism. As editor of the *Modern Quarterly* he accepted contributions from Trotskyites and other dissenters.

In *The Newer Spirit* (1925) Calverton argues that aesthetic judgments are necessarily relative, conditioned as they are by the experiences, circumstances, and age of the reader. "Since man's customs and ideas—which include his tastes and inclinations—vary with every change in his environment, there can be no judgment passed upon a work of art or science except in strict sociological terms. Esthetic criticism, then, must be sociological in fundament, or fail utterly of its purpose."

It is only through the relation of the work to its environment, by the genetic method, that the work can be judged at all. "The genesis or environment of a piece of art is indispensable to an understanding of its effect upon its observers. Knowledge of origins affects immediately, not remotely, our esthetic experience. And finally the entire problem of values is so knit into the texture of society that no judgment of an art-object can be made except in terms of the social-structure, and the permanency of that judgment is dependent upon the permanency of the social structure from which the judgment arose. In no other way can the oscillation and relativity of esthetic values be explained."

Although Calverton later modified his views, admitting technique or "craft" as a factor distinct from ideas, he continued to stress the importance of environment for the understanding of literature. His major effort to apply this Marxist concept is *The Liberation of American Literature* (1932), a study which he took pains to identify with a tradition of social history rather than literary criticism, and in which he attempts to explain the whole development of American literature in terms of social forces, especially class conflict. The "colonial complex" and the "puritan myth," sources of the Philistinism and materialism of the petty bourgeois class, received their first opposition from the frontier spirit of the dynamic West, with which Calverton identifies Whitman, despite his Eastern origin, and Mark Twain. These two were prophets of a frontier democracy that confidently asserted the freedom of the individual and rejected the idea of subservience to caste or privilege.

Its rebellious, individualistic spirit was defeated, however, with the rise of exploitative monopolistic industries, a development that contributed to the growth of realism and naturalism. Writers like Sherwood Anderson and Theodore Dreiser rebelled against the repressiveness of the new bourgeois society, its falseness and hypocrisy, without finding new collective values to save themselves from pessimism and disillusion. Thus, for Calverton, the "liberation" of American literature is still to be achieved: "While American literature, then, has been plunged from optimism into pessimism and from order into chaos, it has at the same time liberated itself from two handicaps, namely, the colonial complex and the petty bourgeois censor, which combined weighed down upon it so heavily in the past that it was almost impossible for it to soar. Its pessimism and its chaos are the products of the passing of an old tradition, and old faith, and the failure on the part of its writers to discover a new tradition and a new faith. The liberation from that pessimism and chaos can only follow when that new tradition and faith are found."

Although the revolution is not yet in sight, the change in attitudes brought about by the depression encourages Calverton. He points to individual writers and critics who have identified themselves with the working class: John Dos Passos, Michael Gold, Theodore Dreiser, Edmund Wilson, Newton Arvin, Waldo Frank, Granville Hicks—only a few of the many writers shifting toward some sort of commitment, however qualified, to Marxist objectives. What is needed, and what seems to be developing, is a new faith in the masses like that expressed by Whitman and Emerson in the years of nineteenth century expansion, but a collectivist rather than an individualistic faith.

In one important respect the temper of Calverton's work differs from that of orthodox Marxist critics of the mid-Thirties. Lacking an absolute faith in the god of history, he is free from the compulsive Messianic tone of later critics and is less rigidly dogmatic in his judgments. In a remarkably restrained conclusion he suggests that with a renewal of social faith on a collectivistic basis it is possible, but not inevitable, that the twentieth century proletariat can "remake the modern world."

As literary criticism, *The Liberation of American Literature* suffers from the narrowness of its concepts and the breadth of its coverage. To describe Twain's work as the embodiment of the "frontier force" is to simplify so drastically as to rob the generalization of meaning. Although Calverton wished his book to be viewed in the context of social history rather than criticism, it is questionable whether any literary history, which interprets and passes judgment upon literature, can be so distinguished, except in terms of emphasis. Calverton's treatment certainly contributed to the reorientation of critical attitudes during the 1930's, and his broad analysis of economic themes inspired more detailed critical studies.

4

The journal that best represents the development of orthodox sentiment is the *New Masses.* Established in 1926 with a board of editors including Egmont Arens, Joseph Freeman, Hugo Gellert, Michael Gold, James Rorty, and John Sloan, the journal at first continued the liberal tradition of the old *Masses* and *The Liberator.* Early issues contained fiction and verse by D. H. Lawrence, Whittaker Chambers, William Ellery Leonard, and John Dos Passos—essays and reviews by Leon Trotsky, Joseph Freeman, Ezra Pound, Floyd Dell, Max Eastman, V. F. Calverton, Michael Gold, and Bernard Smith. In the second issue, John Dos

Passos appeals for freedom from domination by Russian ideology and terminology in an article entitled "The New Masses I'd Like": "I don't think there should be any more phrases, badges, opinions, banners, imported from Russia or anywhere else. . . . Why not develop our own brand?" He hopes that the magazine will be receptive to contributions free from doctrinaire limitations.

In the same issue Michael Gold answers this plea for tolerance and freedom of inquiry. While agreeing with Dos Passos' suggestion that an exploration of the American scene is needed, he is sharply critical of American writers who ignore pressing social problems by developing escapist creeds: Eugene O'Neill has "strayed into a queer mystic universe of his own"; Waldo Frank is "discovering tragic 'beauty' in the bullfight and in parlor Zionism"; Sherwood Anderson is "still mumbling prayers before the ancient phallic gods"; and Carl Sandburg has "suddenly become a sentimental American nationalist." Hoping for a discovery of "the world of revolutionary labor," Gold would like "the *New Masses* to be the bridge to this world for American artists and writers, which means it will not be a magazine of Communism or Moscow, but a magazine of American experiment," as long as the experimenting is not in the "minor esthetic cults."

Gold's reply was an augury of the future of the *New Masses.* Although as yet it did not acknowledge full commitment to the Moscow Party line, it disapproved of literature which was not directly concerned with the problem of the class struggle from an international Marxist viewpoint.

After Gold became editor in 1928, the magazine moved rapidly toward an identification with official Stalinist Communism, and many of the earlier contributors were no longer welcomed, although there were still occasions on which tolerance was professed. In recognizing Dreiser's sixtieth birthday in September 1931, the *New Masses* began with the statement, "Let us not split hairs. It is, at the moment, not important that Dreiser is not a Marxist, that he does not believe many things which Communists do, and believes in many things which they do not. It is more important that at the height of his career he had the vision and the courage—like Bernard Shaw and Romain Rolland in Europe—to take sides openly with the world revolutionary movement of the working class." The same leniency was not extended to critics who had been closely identified with the revolutionary movement. When Floyd Dell resigned as a contributing editor in 1929, announcing that he was no longer in sympathy with what the magazine represented, Gold retorted that Dell was a victim of the money he had earned from his popular novels and sex treatises, that he was a Greenwich Village playboy whose primary interest lay in female anatomy, and that he had never been a real revolutionary.

The times favored the increasingly doctrinaire position of the *New Masses* under Gold's editorship. The growing gulf between the have's and the have-not's in the early Thirties made the idea of solving a hopeless economic problem by revolutionary means attractive to increasing numbers of workers and intellectuals. The ranks of the writers within the party were being swelled not only by younger men who were coming of age in a depression world, but also by writers of the individualistic war generation, many of whom had expatriated themselves during the Twenties and were now returning, after the collapse of the bubble, to find their places in American society. (Their story has been well told by Malcolm Cowley in *Exile's Return* [1934].) Writers from both of these groups responded eagerly to Michael Gold's slogan, "Go Left, Young Writers," and to his insistence on the need for total commitment. "The old *Masses* was a more brilliant but a more upper class affair," he wrote. "The *New Masses* is working in a different field."

One of the younger men who tried to develop a critical theory in support of orthodox Marxism was Philip Rahv, later co-editor of the *Partisan Review.* In an article entitled "The Literary Class War" (August 1932), Rahv argues that the critic should be a pathfinder for the proletarian writer; he stresses the need for criteria that will establish a more "definite frontier between the proletarian and the bourgeois in letters." In an effort to supply suitable standards he revises the Aristotelian theory of catharsis by adding to the emotions of pity and fear the quality of militancy and by asserting that "the proletarian Katharsis is a release through action." "No Katharsis can be effected by a writer who is not consciously up in arms against capitalism, who does not visualize the free, rational society of the future." Considering the attitude that should be taken toward literary fellow-travellers, Rahv recommends an initial leniency. He warns, however, that the liberal who fails to integrate is to be distrusted and that if he does not move forward (i.e., commit himself unreservedly to the dogma of the Party) the orthodox will "go forward," in Lenin's words, "without him, and over his body."

Ironically, Rahv himself was not exempt from inquisition. In December, his essay was attacked for its unorthodoxy in an article entitled "Pity and Terror": "Comrade Rahv's modernized version of the Aristotelian concept of Catharsis," the author, A. B. Magie, solemnly asserts, "has something of the quality of a historical joke." By quoting and applying the statements of both Lenin and Aristotle out of their historical contexts, Rahv is guilty of an "idealist scholasticism." In the light of the historical materialism of Marxist theory, his error lies chiefly in his "tendency to consider the problems of proletarian literature in a vacuum of abstract aesthetics without relation to the concrete class struggle and the needs of the working masses." And even within his approach, dubious as it is, he errs in accepting the Aristotelian formula of pity and terror in any context, since terror is an emotion "absolutely alien to the revolutionary proletariat." (The standards of purity required by dogmatic theory are difficult for even Caesar's wife.)

An older critic who had begun his career in the Twenties and who became a convert to Communism during the depression, was Granville Hicks, who has told the story of his progress through the party in *Where We Came Out* (1954). Hicks wrote extensively, in articles and books, in an attempt to formulate and apply principles of Marxist criticism. His history of American literature, *The Great Tradition,* first appeared in 1933 (revised, 1935); he also helped to edit the anthology, *Proletarian Literature in the United States* (1935).

"Literary Criticism and the Marxian Method," one of Hicks's early articles, was published in Calverton's *Modern Quarterly* in 1932. Hicks says, rather tolerantly, that the Marxist critic must use his political views as a "compass rather than a yardstick," and that he must employ such aesthetic standards as economy of organization, plausibility of character, effectiveness of style, and verisimilitude. He must also recognize that "the correctness of a person's social theories is no guarantee of literary achievement, which depends on the power of perception rather than ideological soundness." However, it would seem that the odds are in favor of the superior perception of the proletarian writer, because "the person who looks at life from the point of view of the exploiting class inevitably distorts it, whereas the person who regards it from the proletarian point of view is capable of accurate and clarifying interpretation."

More arbitrary criteria were set forth in "The Crisis in American Criticism." In this 1933 *New Masses* essay Hicks stresses the idea that the proletarian point of view is an index of reality and formulates what he calls a "theory of effect," according to which the critic will judge a book "not by its direct effect upon himself, but by the qualities that contribute to its possible effect upon a certain class of reader," namely the proletariat. The work must meet three fixed requirements. First, there must be "centrality of subject matter"; that is, a novel must deal with the class struggle, since, "according to Marxism, that is central in life, and no novel that disregarded it could give an adequate portrayal of life." Second, the critic must insist upon intensity, a quality dependent upon class consciousness. And third, the critic must demand "that the author's point of view be that of the vanguard of the proletariat."

These standards are clear enough. They are, however, extremely limited, and even within these limits specific applications are lacking. The closest approach to an illustration—and it certainly does not satisfy the reader's desire for specificity—occurs in a brief discussion of Proust's *Remembrance of Things Past,* which Hicks praises as a good novel of decay. However, because it does not "carry us forward with a surge of determination and hope," it is not so good as the imperfect proletarian novel, for that, despite its failure, looks to the future. But, decadent though it is, Proust's work is better than the work of "the avowed revolutionary who cannot give us an intense perception of either the character of the proletariat or of the character of the bourgeoisie."

Hicks's most ambitious Marxist study is *The Great Tradition.* Because it begins with the writers of the "Golden Day," he is able to treat individual authors in greater detail than Calverton was. His interpretation takes into account the author's awareness of the socioeconomic forces at work in his society. Partly for this reason his discussion of the post-symbolist realists and naturalists is more satisfactory than his treatment of the romantics. Hawthorne's work suffered from his isolation and his inability to come to terms with his generation. Emerson, despite his criticism of contemporary commercialism, was essentially a child of his time. Thoreau must be admired for his devotion to his principles, but these principles are irrelevant and meaningless to us in an industrial society. The greater the individualism of these writers, the less their value for Hicks. Whitman is treated more sympathetically as a prophet of the masses who saw, though vaguely, the implications of his message for an industrial age. But because he lacked mastery over his materials, his poems are chaotic.

In the end, however, Hicks finds in these major nineteenth century figures the source of the "great tradition" beginning to flower in twentieth century proletarian literature. In a tone inconsistent with his harsh earlier judgments, Hicks praises Emerson for "his confidence in the common man" (Emerson said that he was interested in the uncommon man), Thoreau for his rebellion against shams and oppressions, and Whitman for his "kinship with workers and farmers." This literary tradition—which continued through Howells and Twain, Garland and Norris, to Sinclair and London—represents a "passion for brotherhood, justice, and intellectual honesty."

In a final chapter, "Direction," added to the revised edition, Hicks surveys current proletarian fiction, poetry, and drama —much of which has since faded away—and prophesies that the burgeoning revolutionary literature, which represents a new sensibility in western literature, will "grow into a richer and fuller expression of the proletariat." With the accomplishment of the revolution and the shift to a classless society, proletarian literature will slowly "ripen into something finer and nobler than itself," representing the fulfillment of the spirit of all American writers who have contributed to the "great tradition."

Except in this finale, which reads like one of his hortatory *New Masses* articles, Hicks avoids the terminology of Marxism, even though he is dealing with his subject from the point of view of a social revolutionary. Whatever the reason for the use of lay language rather than a technical Marxist vocabulary, Hicks's argument is nonetheless revolutionary. Despite the inadequacy of the treatment of numerous major figures not really in the "tradition" (Hawthorne, Melville, and James are instances) and the lack of competence in discussing poetic form (Sandburg is praised for his revolutionary sentiment; Pound's revolutionary form is ignored), the book remains—like Calverton's *Liberation of American Literature*—a landmark in Marxist literary study.

5

The breakdown of the orthodoxy of the mid-Thirties can be seen in the history of *Partisan Review,* established in 1934 as a publication of the John Reed Club of New York, under the editorship of Philip Rahv and William Phillips. The first issue announced the magazine's intention of representing the viewpoint of the revolutionary proletariat, of working toward the abolition of the system that breeds "imperialist war, fascism, national and racial oppression," and of defending the Soviet Union. The appearance of the new magazine, which was to concentrate on creative and critical writing, coincided with the transformation of the *New Masses* into a weekly journal increasingly devoted to economic and political questions.

Many of the early numbers of the *Partisan Review* stressed its Communist commitment. An editorial on "Problems and Perspectives in Revolutionary Literature" (1934) defines the responsibility of the revolutionary critic as the leader and ideologist of the proletarian literary movement, even though the movement is divided by two opposing tendencies, both deviations, described as a professional "leftism" which substitutes a "verbal revolutionism" for a genuine commitment and a right-wing tendency among half-hearted revolutionaries who make only sporadic use of Marxist philosophy. The editors mention Dos Passos' novels as examples of the right-wing tendency and censure younger poets of the left for adopting the "obscurantism of the verse in the bourgeois-esthetic little magazines."

However, in the same period, other articles indicate a sympathy with avant-garde tendencies and allow for latitude in working toward revolutionary objectives. In a review of Hemingway's *Winner Take Nothing,* in the first issue, Philip Rahv remarks that much American proletarian writing is marred by a "mawkish idealization and sentimentality" and that one might well study Hemingway, despite his intellectual limitations, because of his "supple precision and impersonality of method." In a symposium, "What Is Americanism?" (1936), the participants were invited to consider whether Marxism is compatible with American traditions, whether "our revolutionary literature reflects and integrates the American spirit or is in conflict with it," and whether "the very premises of revolutionary writing prevent the organic integration of the two." Most of the contributors, including Theodore Dreiser, sought to link the proletarian cause with native American revolutionary and radical traditions and to revise Marxist ideology into, in Dreiser's words, an "adaptable form," a noteworthy divergence from an orthodox position like Rahv's in his *New Masses* article on the "Literary Class War" four years earlier. But there were limits to tolerance. William Carlos Williams provoked censure for his opinion that the American democratic tradition is "completely opposed to Marxism" and "that our revolutionary literature is merely tolerated by most Americans, that it is definitely in conflict with our deep-seated ideals." Nevertheless, the very appearance of this statement in a revolutionary journal was a straw in the wind.

After a year's suspension the *Partisan Review* reappeared in December 1937 with an editorial declaration of independence: the magazine will no longer support the Communist Party, which the editors distrust because of its totalitarian tendencies; it will remain free from any party or organizational identification. While still committed to the cause of revolutionary literature, the editors acknowledge a value in the nonpolitical aesthetic revolt; they speak of the "forms of literary editorship, at once exacting and adventurous, which characterized the magazines of the aesthetic revolt," as having a definite cultural value, and express a wish to adapt these forms to the literature of the "new period."

This emphasis set the *Partisan Review* apart from most journals of radical opinion; its editors had obviously tired of the too simplified versions of life in much proletarian fiction. Although their social and political preoccupation was still apparent, they encouraged essays on writers of greater complexity. From the end of 1937 through 1938, articles appeared on Flaubert, Zola, D. H. Lawrence, Dostoevsky, Henry James, Thomas Mann, and Franz Kafka. Edmund Wilson, in "Flaubert's Politics" (1937), sees the bourgeois as the villain in Flaubert's novels and *L'Education sentimentale* as a work in which the author's analysis of society comes close to socialist theory. In "Dostoevski and Politics" (1938), Philip Rahv concludes that Dostoevsky's art is "radical in sensibility and subversive in performance," even though the author has been judged an enemy of socialism because of the reactionary nature of his abstract ideas. In "The Last Phase of Henry James" (1938), Wilson argues that James, far from being detached from his society, was finally moving, after his 1904 visit to America, in the direction of a new realism acutely critical of life in capitalist America, a development seen most fully in his uncompleted last novel, *The Ivory Tower.* William Troy's essay, "The D. H. Lawrence Myth" (1938), anticipates later myth criticism by isolating as a basic motif in Lawrence's novels the author's projection of himself as a "suffering hero" or sacrificial god.

During the 1940's the growing aesthetic and formalist emphasis of the magazine drew it to accept the work of conservative critics and creative writers. Although Auden and Spender were often featured, George Orwell was writing a regular "London letter," and new liberal and radical American critics were appearing as contributors, so also were poets and critics who had been associated with the Southern Agrarian movement—Cleanth Brooks, Allen Tate, Robert Penn Warren. In some cases, the views of new contributors were far to the right of the magazine's early position. For example, T. S. Eliot had been branded as an extreme reactionary by the leftist critics of the mid-Thirties. A reviewer in the second issue of *Partisan Review* had described him as "rubbing shoulders with every myth and dogma which is used by capitalism to maintain itself" and had added that Eliot's deities in *After Strange Gods* were "the caricatures and monsters of fascism." Yet two of the *Four Quartets* appeared in *Partisan Review* in 1940 and 1941 ("East Coker" and "The Dry Salvages") and the "Notes towards the Definition of Culture" in 1944. In 1934 the editors had deplored the obscurantism of much of the verse in the "bourgeois-esthetic little magazines," but in 1942 they printed Dylan Thomas's "Ballad of the Long-legged Bait."

In 1946, when William Barrett joined the staff as an associate editor, the magazine began giving space and attention to contemporary existentialism, a subject introduced through translations of Sartre and Camus and an article by Hannah Arendt entitled "What is Existenz Philosophy?"

The immediate postwar period was a time of assessment and reorientation for the *Partisan Review.* In contributing to a 1947 discussion of the future of socialism, Granville Hicks, who had been a confident prophet ten years earlier, views with a disillusioned eye the problem of realizing socialist goals through Marxism: the three basic Marxist assumptions —the inevitable collapse of capitalism, the transfer of power to the proletariat, and the establishment of a classless society by the proletariat—he can no longer affirm. In the face of a dangerous trend toward totalitarianism, he counsels, "To begin with we must get rid of any remnants of belief in progress." We must also be skeptical of any socialist plans. Rejecting the attitude of *intransigent liberalism,* with which he identifies Dwight MacDonald, he recommends a *critical liberalism,* which would work toward the achievement of the possible even though it would fall short of the ideal. In a time when a clarification of attitudes is needed, he would like to see a new party, "unqualifiedly democratic, unsparingly critical of the evils of capitalism but not committed to socialist dogmas, genuinely imaginative in its plans for social reorganization." Lacking such a party, the disillusioned Marxist remained an unaffiliated liberal.

Hicks's skepticism toward revolutionary programs was typical of the New Liberalism of the postwar period. Among *Partisan Review* contributors supporting this position were Richard Chase and Lionel Trilling. In *Herman Melville: A Critical Study* (1949), Chase, like Hicks, emphasizes the complexity of human nature and social problems. The reputation of Melville, together with that of Hawthorne, rose tremendously in the postwar period. For the disillusioned, the "tragic vision" and awareness of the baffling contradictions of life by these writers were marks of a deeper insight than that of the prophets of the democratic American dream. Chase describes his work as a contribution to the New Liberalism of the "dark center of the twentieth century" which is to "ransom liberalism from the ruinous sellouts, failures, and defeats of the thirties." Trilling's *The Liberal Imagination* (1950) also recommends a critical skepticism, suggesting that the job of criticism should be "to recall liberalism to its first essential imagination of variousness and possibility, which implies the awareness of complexity and difficulty."

This is a far cry from the assurance of earlier Marxist critics that literature could be efficiently interpreted and used as an instrument for achieving clearly defined social goals. Accompanying this new attitude is the shift from a cursory view of the literary work as an illustration of a social or political principle, to a closer examination of the text in an effort to probe its complexities. In a *Partisan Review* article entitled "James T. Farrell, the Critic Calcified" (1947) Irving Howe writes, "I think there is a need today for social criticism; but it will have to be both social *and* criticism. That is, it will have to make the leap from sociology into the work of art itself."

6

The shift of emphasis in the articles appearing in the *Partisan Review,* a paradigm of a larger trend, was accompanied by a questioning of the value of Marxist theory for criticism. In "The Esthetics of the Founding Fathers" (1938), the *Partisan* editor William Phillips denies the existence of an adequate theoretical foundation for Marxist criticism and charges the Communist Party with making use of its official organs to circulate "the myth that there exists a ready-made set of esthetic principles, fashioned by the hand of Marx himself, and known as 'Marxist criticism.' "

Even earlier, in 1936, James T. Farrell discusses the problem in *A Note on Literary Criticism.* He points out the impossibility of establishing a doctrinaire critical theory when the concept of proletarian literature, the object of such criticism, cannot be exactly defined. Farrell objects chiefly to the fact that, because of the current economic crisis, Marxist critics have focused upon the objective and functional aspects of literature to the exclusion of the subjective and aesthetic. It is desirable, he believes, to transcend the purely functional approach and to recognize that literature, which is ultimately a matter of taste, represents a pluralism of values.

In "Marxism and Literature," first published in the *Atlantic Monthly* in 1937, Edmund Wilson remarks that Marx and Engels, and Trotsky after them, never attempted to "furnish social-economic formulas by which the validity of works of art might be tested." Like Farrell, Wilson stresses the standard of subjective taste and declares that "Marxism by itself can tell us nothing whatever about the goodness or badness of a work of art." Without imagination and taste, the most exemplary Marxist is unable to discriminate between two more and less admirable works which may be equally sound ideologically. What Marxism can do, and more satisfactorily than the bourgeois criticism of Taine, is to provide a perspective for considering "the origins and social significance of works of art." But before Marxist principles can be brought into play, the critic must understand that the meaning of literature is not a "simple message but a complex vision of things, which itself is not explicit but implicit." (In this observation Wilson anticipates the postwar emphasis on complexity.) *

7

During the Thirties numerous critics sympathized with revolutionary socialism and made use of social and political ideas in their criticism, but resisted conformity to Marxism in both critical language and method.

One of these was Newton Arvin. At the second American Writers' Congress of 1937, when a popular front was being

* A bibliography of Marxian aesthetic theory in the United States is provided in the excellent group study, *Socialism and American Life* (2 vols., 1952), edited by D. D. Egbert and Stow Persons; the work also contains a chapter, "American Writers on the Left," by Willard Thorp.

fostered, Arvin read a paper, "The Democratic Tradition in American Letters," recommending that writers "on the Left and on the Center that bends toward the Left" make the most of the democratic tradition in support of a revolutionary program. This tradition—from its beginnings in the Puritan nonconformists like Hooker and Williams, through the revolutionary fathers and the writers of the Golden Day like Emerson and Whitman, to Howells, Sinclair, and Dreiser—is in its spirit sympathetic to progress toward democratic goals. As the more recent writers have come to understand, "the good democrat cannot hope to rest on his oars . . . in an industrial society torn apart by conflicting interests. To make real the whole purport of the democratic plan—its social, its economic, its ethical, its cultural purport—is not . . . idly to accept its partial conquests in the past but to work for its full achievement in the future."

Arvin also appeals to native democratic tradition in his *Whitman* (1938), which opens with the question of whether Whitman can can be called a "socialist poet." While recognizing the conservatism of many of Whitman's ideas, Arvin sees him as pointing toward collectivist democratic ideals through his emphasis on brotherhood and the solidarity of the mass of men. Although Whitman is not the poet of an "international social democracy," *Leaves of Grass,* with its stress on growth, solidarity, and progress, reaches out beyond its own time. Whitman can fortify "the writers and the men of our time in their struggles against a dark barbarian reaction" by holding before them a brave anticipatory statement of a "democratic and fraternal humanism."

Arvin's book is like much of the less orthodox criticism of the Thirties. While defining the qualities of Whitman's work that belong to his time, Arvin is aware of its relevance to the problems of a later age. He affirms the instrumental or propaganda values of literature, and the responsibilities of the critic and writer. But he avoids Marxist terms and invokes traditional democratic ideals. Arvin's stress upon the theme of progress toward social goals in his treatment of Whitman is closer to the tradition of evolutionary democratic socialism than to revolutionary Marxism. There is no suggestion that "socialist" literature must explicitly support the ideology of any party.

Kenneth Burke's first volume of criticism, *Counter-Statement* (1931), published during the early depression, presents a "program" demonstrating the political and social implications of his critical theory. In a "Curriculum Criticum" appended to the second edition (1953), Burke looks back over his work and recognizes a shift at that time from an individualistic "Aestheticist" period to a concern for the "interdependent, social, or collective" aspects of literature. Like all of Burke's writing, *Counter-Statement* moves toward a synthesis of shifting critical methods. "Psychology and Form," which had first appeared in *The Dial* in 1925, defines form, in terms of a "psychology of the audience," as "an arousing and fulfillment of desires." Burke thus locates the formal matrix of the work in the collective social consciousness of the audience rather than the private consciousness of the writer.

Burke opposes the Marxist position in his hostility to science and technology, which he considers responsible for much of the derangement of taste in modern society, and in his distinction between the truth of science, which is based on a revelation of facts, and aesthetic truth, which emerges when the revelation of science is "ritualized," or converted into a symbolic process which expresses metaphorical truth. His ideas are more characteristic of the romantic idealist than of the dialectical materialist, and his reference to the ritualization of art points to the later myth interpretation that he himself employed in his rebirth-ritual analysis of Keats's "Ode on a Grecian Urn."

Burke sees art as necessarily implicated in the social process. The program he recommends would oppose the bourgeois-practical world, not with a proletarian revolutionary attitude, but with a bohemian or aesthetic negativism. Against the totalitarian or facist tendency of industrialized society, he urges not a revolutionary Marxism but a negativist democracy, with a system of checks and balances, the inefficiency of which would be a guard against the centralization of power. Burke's plan, for which he hopes to find support among the farmers, is remarkable not so much for its radicalism as for its likenesses to the conservative agrarianism of the Southern writers. A "Lexicon Rhetoricae" included in *Counter-Statement* extends Burke's discussion of form as stimulating and controlling the desires of the audience through devices which appeal to recurrent patterns of experience. It also shows his concern for the language of criticism: he discusses the five aspects of form under such headings as "progressive form (subdivided into syllogistic and qualitative progression), repetitive form, conventional form, and minor or incidental forms." Burke's terminology is more elaborate than that of either the Humanist or the Marxist critics. Poetics and rhetoric are the principal source of his vocabulary here. The words that he is at pains to define precisely include—besides *form*—*rhythm, rhyme, eloquence, symbol, manner,* and *style.* His penchant for categorization is a trait he shares with the Aristotelian genre critic.

In his subsequent criticism of the 1930's Burke professed a commitment to Marxism, but it was a commitment curiously qualified and perhaps neutralized. In *Permanence and Change: An Anatomy of Purpose* (1935), he insists that only communism, under one name or another, can provide the solution for existing social maladjustment. He plays throughout on the words *communism, communicant,* and *communication,* to indicate the interrelationship of political, religious, and aesthetic processes. In the interest of promoting social reorganization he employs the strategy of deliberately scrambling "magical, religious, poetic, theological, philosophical, mystic, and scientific lore." The constant for these various rationalizations of human existence is not the historical development of the means of production but man's neurological structure, which has supplied a permanent basis that underlies changes and differences in environment (hence the title *Permanence and Change*).

Burke's "communism" has a distinctly un-Marxian foundation. In a section entitled "Towards a Philosophy of Being," Burke rejects Hegel and Marx, the promoters of a *historical* approach to human problems through philosophies of *becoming,* and turns "through symbolism to a philosophy of *being,* the Spinozistic concern with man *sub specie aeternitatis.*" The metaphor of progress he would replace by the metaphor of a *norm,* the basis of which is the notion that "at bottom the aims and genius of man have remained the same."

Although this view is heretical in its denial of the upward progress of the forms of social organization and its neglect of environmental factors, Burke continued to profess a commitment to Marxism and to think of criticism as a revolutionary activity. In *Attitudes Toward History* (1937), he speaks of the critic as a "propagandist and craftsman" and of his own program as the integration of "technical criticism with social criticism (propaganda, the didactic)": "Since works of art, as 'equipment for living,' are formed with authoritative structures as their basis of reference, we also move automatically into the field of technical criticism (the 'tactics' of writers). And since the whole purpose of a 'revolutionary' critic is to contribute to a change in allegiance to the symbols of authority, we maintain our role as 'propagandist' by keeping this subject forever uppermost in our concerns." The transference of allegiance is from capitalistic and patriarchal symbols to communal and matriarchal ones. Since these identifications are bound up with traditional religious attitudes, as well as with psychological processes, Burke insists that "such matters as 'authority symbols,' 'identification,' 'acceptance and rejection,' 'rituals of purification and rebirth,' 'transcendence upward,' 'transcendence downward,' 'character-building by secular prayer,' 'the collective poems of socio-economic organization,' 'bureaucratization of the imaginative,' 'alienation,' and 'repossession' are at the very basis of both esthetic and moralistic strategy." Discussions of these terms—together with such others as *clusters, communion, imagery, perspective by incongruity, secular prayer, symbolic mergers,* and *transcendence*—are included in the "Dictionary of Pivotal Terms" with which Burke ends *Attitudes Toward History.* At one point in the dictionary, under "Lexicological," Burke describes his intention to develop a "tripartite vocabulary" of interrelated religious, capitalist, and aesthetic elements.

Burke's interest in drama is everywhere evident. In the *Philosophy of Literary Form* (1941) he combines dramatic with religious and psychological terms to analyze verbal art as a "symbolic action," the hub of which is "ritual drama," the *ur*-form in any dramatic theory. For Burke, drama supplies a perspective for the analysis of social processes since its dynamic depends upon oppositions comparable to the dialectic of history. Glancing back at the earlier *Attitudes,* the reader can see that the rebirth ritual is a central feature of drama because it deals with a *conversion* of social attitudes involving a *transference* of allegiance from one *authority symbol* to another (capitalism to communism). At one point Burke describes the difference between symbolic drama and the drama of real living as a difference between "imaginary obstacles and real obstacles." But, he goes on to say, "the imaginary obstacles of symbolic drama must, to have the relevance necessary for the producing of effects upon audiences, reflect the real obstacles of living drama."

Having been reading with admiration Caroline Spurgeon's *Shakespeare's Imagery and What It Tells Us* (1935), Burke introduces the technique of analyzing image clusters in his discussion of Clifford Odets' *Golden Boy,* in which the complex of values associated with the *violin* is opposed to that surrounding the *prizefight.* Burke's use of dramatic techniques and image patterns—together with his concern for ritual and myth—places him closer to the emerging formalist and myth than to Marxist criticism. But in *Philosophy of Literary Form* Burke calls his approach to art " 'sociological,' in that it can usefully employ coördinates bearing upon social acts in general." He does not consider it sociological in the sense that "one treats a book as a kind of unmethodical report on a given subject matter."

Although Burke thought of his work as a contribution to the revolutionary Marxist movement, it is difficult to judge it in this light. His theory encouraged analytical criticism sensitive to the social values of literature. But the remoteness of most of his vocabulary from the language of politics tends to obscure its revolutionary implications. This indirection is a mark, not of duplicity in the critic, but of an awareness of the multiplicity of literary meanings. It is also, however, in keeping with Burke's conscious "strategy," for in *Attitudes Toward History* he speaks of the critic's receiving guidance from his audience through "the kind of resistance and acceptance that his terms encounter." The critic, that is, will "convert" the language of politics to that of religion or psychology partly in the interest of "converting" his reader. This technique may have made Burke's ideas more palatable. But he may also have alienated readers by discussing revolutionary themes in the language of rebirth rituals rather than more directly. Aside from this problem, which cannot easily be settled, there remains the question of whether Burke's criticism, despite its intelligence and sensitivity, may not be self-defeating in distracting attention from literature to the developing theoretical apparatus of the critic, a mechanism that has come to have a kind of autonomy of its own. This possibility does not lessen his importance as a seminal theorist who has contributed to the vocabularies and influenced the practice of many other critics.

Edmund Wilson's criticism has shown from the beginning a concern for the relation of literature to social forces and problems. In dedicating *Axel's Castle* (1931) to his Princeton teacher, Christian Gauss, Wilson acknowledged a debt for his "idea of what literary criticism ought to be—a history of man's ideas and imaginings in the setting of the conditions which have shaped them." Despite changes in the climate of opinion and in his own thinking, Wilson has over the years tended to discuss literature from a socialist point of view.

Because from early youth he had felt at odds with the "broker's world" in which he was educated, at F. Scott Fitzgerald's Princeton, it was easy for Wilson to become a supporter of revolutionary Marxism in the early 1930's. He visited Russia in 1935 and gave his view of the Communist experiment, sympathetically though not without reservations, in *Travels in Two Democracies* (1936). An admirer of Lenin, he became increasingly disenchanted with the Stalinist regime and finally with Marxism as a revolutionary program, particularly as in its Soviet development it took on ever more strongly the autocratic features of the Czarist rule it had displaced. *To the Finland Station* (1940), begun in enthusiasm and finished in disillusion, is a historical study tracing the European revolutionary tradition from its beginnings in Vico and Michelet, through the development of socialist theory by Marx and Engels and their forerunners, to its activist phase in Lenin and Trotsky. Wilson is aware of the errors and abuses of Marxist theory and application, but he values the tradition as a manifestation of a collective human wish for progress toward a more just social order. The dialectic which Marx and Engels converted from its Hegelian formulation into a form of religious myth expresses the historical truth that, although "we can no longer depend on God to give us laws that transcend human limitations," we have in Marxism "a new science of social change," imperfect but important because developed in reaction to "a situation in which it has finally become apparent that if society is to survive at all, it must be reorganized on new principles of equality." Although the revolution has not borne out its promise, Wilson in his conclusion sees Lenin at the Finland Station in April 1917, upon his return to Russia to lead the

Bolshevik revolution, as a symbolic figure pausing at a milestone on the road toward the fulfillment of humanistic socialist ideals. At this moment, Wilson says, Western man "can be seen to have made some definite progress in mastering the greeds and the fears, the bewilderments, in which he has lived."

In a "Summary as of 1940," Wilson reviews the weaknesses of Marxism in the perspective of history and considers what heritage it may have for us. He comments on its technique, "which we can still use with profit . . . , of analyzing political phenomena in social-economic terms," and on its aims and ideals. He endorses the Marxists' "desire to get rid of class privilege based on birth and on difference of income; the will to establish a society in which the superior development of some is not paid for by the exploitation, that is, by the deliberate degradation of others—a society which will be homogeneous and coöperative as our commercial society is not, and directed, to the best of their ability, by the conscious creative minds of its members." But this goal must be worked toward not through the application of a doctrinaire program (the Marxist dogma is no more a Holy Writ than the formulas of other creeds), but "in the light of one's own imagination and with the help of one's own common sense."

Axel's Castle: A Study of the Imaginative Literature of 1870 to 1930, Wilson's most influential critical work, traces the development of the modern symbolist movement through essays on Yeats, Valéry, Eliot, Proust, Joyce, and Gertrude Stein. It explains the French symbolist movement as a reaction against naturalism, with its mechanistic world view and documentary method, and against rationalism, with its logical precision and conventional language patterns. The technique of symbolism is defined by Wilson as "an attempt by carefully-studied means—a complicated association of ideas represented by a medley of metaphors—to communicate unique personal feelings."

In the essays, Wilson follows his professed intention of considering works in "the setting of the conditions that have shaped them," especially their literary and social traditions. The poetry of T. S. Eliot is discussed against the background of French symbolism, seventeenth century English metaphysical poetry, and American Puritanism. In relating Eliot to the present, Wilson recognizes, particularly since his profession of classicism, Anglo-Catholicism, and royalism in 1928, "a kind of reactionary point of view which had already been becoming fashionable among certain sorts of literary people—a point of view which has much in common with that of the neo-Thomists in France and that of the Humanists in America."

In his essay on Joyce, Wilson focuses upon *Ulysses.* After explaining its parallels with the Homeric story, he notes that in developing a symbolistic stream-of-consciousness technique Joyce transcends the method of naturalism, which has tended to emphasize man's insignificance and the sordidness of the modern world. He endows the world with poetic beauty by presenting it through the subjective vision of the artist, or dreamer; and by penetrating the minds of his characters he individualizes them and invests them with dignity, justifying their existence as human beings, if not as children of the gods.

The concluding essay, "Axel and Rimbaud," presents the hero of the poem "Axel," by Villiers de l'Isle-Adam, as the image of extreme symbolist withdrawal from the world, the type of the heroes of Pater, Laforgue, Mallarmé, and

Eliot, and the example of one type of escape in modern literature. Another, that taken by Rimbaud in life, is primitivism, represented by D. H. Lawrence, with his mornings in Mexico, and Hemingway, with his bullfights and safaris. Wilson considers neither tendency appropriate for current literature. He does not believe that the writers who dominated the literary world during the Twenties can serve as guides, although they may continue to be admired as masters. With the end of the Twenties, during which Americans accepted the pessimism and resignation of modern literature, both Americans and Europeans are looking toward Russia, as a country "where a central social-political idealism has been able to use and to inspire the artist as well as the engineer."

Out of this new spirit (which was to animate both creative writers and critics during the 1930's), Wilson feels that a literature might arise to displace such symbolists as Valéry, Eliot, and Proust, just as H. G. Wells, Anatole France, and G. B. Shaw had earlier been displaced, although certain innovations of the symbolists would be incorporated in further technical advances. The "revolution of the word," to which the symbolists contributed, had made possible the economical expression of complex ideas and could bring about a revolution in syntax comparable to developments in the fields of philosophy and science. While helping to break down the materialism of the naturalistic tradition, symbolism reveals to the imagination "a new flexibility and freedom" which may help "wake us to the hope and exaltation of the untried, unsuspected possibilities of human thought and art."

For a decade or more after its publication *Axel's Castle* served as an introduction to the tradition of symbolism and to the work of some of the more difficult modern writers for a new generation of American readers, chiefly in the colleges and universities. Despite Wilson's judgment that many of the modern symbolists were decadent and belonged, because of their social outlook, to a dying order, their reputations prospered. Younger novelists and poets were influenced by Eliot, Joyce, and Yeats, who survived, as many of the militant, socially conscious writers did not, the passing of the decade and the coming of the war years. During the Thirties, symbolism received increasing attention; in the postwar years it emerged as a dominant emphasis.

Clarity of style has helped to make Wilson one of the most readable of modern critics. He has not devoted himself so closely to the text as recent formalist critics and has had less need of rhetorical and linguistic terms. But he has not ignored the task of textual analysis; in fact, his elucidations of literary works have served as guides to later readings. He has thus in a sense anticipated the practice of the New Critics. He is dissociated from them not so much because he does not share their interest in analysis as because he has always kept in sight the social relevance of literature.

8

A helpful perspective for the literary criticism of the 1930's is supplied by two works, one published on the eve of the decade and the other just after its end, each marking a turning point in the methods of literary study in America. They are V. L. Parrington's *Main Currents in American Thought* (3 vols., 1927-30) and F. O. Matthiessen's *American Renaissance* (1941).

Parrington's work, left unfinished at his death in 1929, treats American literature from its beginnings to 1920 in three volumes entitled *The Colonial Mind, The Romantic*

Revolution in America, and *The Beginnings of Critical Realism.* Inspired by Taine and more immediately by Charles A. Beard's *Economic Interpretation of the Constitution* (1913), Parrington attempts to explain the development of American literary culture in relation to the intellectual traditions and economic forces that shaped it. Committed to Jeffersonian ideals and to economic determinism—a somewhat troublesome combination—he traces the growth of native liberalism and considers its prospects.

In his introduction Parrington says that he has chosen to follow "the broad path of our political, economic, and social development, rather than the narrower belletristic." Simply to say this, however, does not relieve him from the responsibilities of his critical judgments. Parrington's discussions are sometimes admirable, as when he writes about the New England Brahmins, Howells, and the younger naturalists. But he often slights individual figures, dismissing Poe as outside the main stream of American thought, a case for the psychologist and the "belletrist" rather than the historian, and writing off Hawthorne and Melville as, respectively, a skeptic and a pessimist. In the treatment of certain figures, particularly those whom he wishes to enlist in the cause of liberalism, he is sometimes guilty of distortion.

Parrington identifies Emersonian transcendentalism with the social idealism of the eighteenth century. Although he recognizes that Emerson was a mystic and that transcendentalism was a faith rather than a philosophy, he draws upon Emerson's social criticism to characterize him as a Jeffersonian liberal: Emerson was like Jefferson in asserting the moral independence of the individual and opposing the Federalist-Whig stake-in-society theory, and his essay "Politics" is critical of the institution of property.

But Emerson was hardly a Jeffersonian liberal; he was the promulgator of a philosophic anarchy that bore little resemblance to Jefferson's idea of the democratic state. Although opposed to the stake-in-society principle, Emerson believed that "property will always follow persons." Like the Puritans, he thought that the beneficiary of God's grace, or, in his terms, the higher moral law, would also enjoy material rewards. Like Jefferson in favoring an agrarian order and minimal state, he was, on the other hand, a religious rather than a social idealist, and his basically mystical and other-worldly orientation, like that of the Hindu sages he admired, made him largely indifferent to the problems of democratic reform and progress that absorbed Jefferson's mind and energies.

In "A Chapter in American Liberalism" of his unfinished third volume, Parrington reviews the progress and prospects of liberalism. The years before 1917 had been a period of renewal in which the Muckrakers, the young critics, and the eclectic radicals who supported the old *Masses* were revitalizing liberal thought. The doctrine of economic determinism was spreading. Accepting it, "liberalism still clung to the older democratic teleology, convinced that somehow economic determinism would turn out to be a fairy godmother to the proletariat and that from the imperious drift of industrial expansion must eventually issue social justice." Instead, the war came, and in its wake a cynicism that blighted liberal assumptions and hopes. The army intelligence tests established the moron as the typical American, and followers of Nietzsche arose to proclaim that the moron needed a master. In psychology the behaviorists simplified human nature by explaining it in terms of belly and sex needs. Parrington's disillusioned view of these recent developments, with their denial of the efficacy of reason and moral choice upon which the idea of democracy depends, helps explain the attraction of Emerson's conception of the divinely self-sufficient individual. Democratic liberalism seemed to be, for the time at least, defeated, and its future lay "on the knees of the gods."

Although Parrington's work remained influential, particularly during the 1930's, there is a sense in which he is the last champion, in literary study, of the old democratic liberalism. His voice, speaking confidently across three decades, in spite of some misgivings, is a voice from another era. Rhetorical in the manner of an earlier and more expansive age, it sometimes sacrifices critical distinctions to sweeping generalizations. But it speaks in a language supported by a democratic heritage. Parrington's interpretation of American literary and cultural history has an integrity rooted in a long tradition, although it is one that has suffered eclipse in recent years. *Main Currents in American Thought* will remain a landmark in a field of study not greatly distinguished by liberal or democratic views.

In *American Renaissance,* published at the beginning of the Forties, F. O. Matthiessen acknowledged Parrington's influence even though he was reacting against it. *Main Currents* appeared at a time when the economic interpretation of literature and history flourished; *American Renaissance* was written during the accession of the New Criticism. Early in his career, during the 1930's, Matthiessen contributed to the movement toward formalist criticism. In *The Achievement of T. S. Eliot* (1935), he opposed the "increasing tendency to treat poetry as a social document and to forget that it is an art." Yet he retained his early sympathy for Parrington's outlook.

Like Parrington, Matthiessen was loyal to the native liberal and radical tradition. He shared Parrington's admiration for Whitman's democratic idealism, his magnanimous conception of man in the open air, and his gravitation toward socialism in the latter decades of the nineteenth century. But Matthiessen's literary interests were more diversified, as can be seen in his work on Sarah Orne Jewett, his study of Elizabethan translation, his association with I. A. Richards in the early 1930's, his pioneering work on T. S. Eliot, and his later studies of Henry James and Theodore Dreiser. He responded to Eliot's sense of the wealth of literary tradition and the complex relationships of the individual work to the established order of literature.

Matthiessen's growing preoccupation with myth and tragedy, apparent in *American Renaissance,* could earlier be seen in the study of Eliot, for which Yeats's statement that "we begin to live when we have conceived life as a tragedy" served as an epigraph. The values of suffering and tragic insight that Matthiessen found in Eliot deepened in his own work, as C. L. Barber has noted, through the *American Renaissance* to the study of Henry James completed during World War II. A consciousness of evil distinguished him from the older liberal literary historian and explains his elevation of Hawthorne and Melville, whom Parrington had regarded as sterile pessimists, over Emerson, whom Parrington had exalted as a prophet of liberalism. To Matthiessen, Emerson's bland optimism was a defect of sensibility.

In *American Renaissance,* Matthiessen remarks that while his reading in American literature had been done in the era of Van Wyck Brooks and Parrington, the critics who most helped him to define his subject were Coleridge and Eliot. More selective and intensive in his coverage than Parrington, Matthiessen discusses the work of the five major figures of the Golden Day—Emerson, Thoreau, Hawthorne, Melville, Whitman—in the light of their theories of literature, their relationships to each other, their debt to the literature of the past, and the parallels between their work and other arts. His concern for the older liberal tradition out of which these writers came appears in his statement that one thing they possessed in common was a "devotion to the possibilities of democracy" and that we can derive a literature for our democracy from their total achievement "if we will make the effort to repossess it."

Although *American Renaissance* is rich in sensitive interpretation supported by textual analysis, its organization is complicated and sometimes obscure. One main line of development is the exposition of Emerson's theory of symbolic expression as something "on which Thoreau built, to which Whitman gave extension, and to which Hawthorne and Melville were indebted by being forced to react against its philosophical assumptions." Other themes include the individual's place in society, the nature of good and evil, and the relation of literary technique to the tradition of oratory and to the stress on vision of the nineteenth century—that is, its identification of the poet or artist with the seer.

In concentrating upon Emerson's organic theory, Matthiessen extends the modern study of symbolism to which Edmund Wilson had earlier contributed. Matthiessen had already been following the line of inquiry opened by *Axel's Castle* when he wrote *The Achievement of T. S. Eliot: An Essay on the Nature of Poetry* (1935; revised 1947, 1958), which explored Eliot's relationships with not only the symbolist and metaphysical poets, but also Arnold, Browning, Dante, Dryden, and others. Matthiessen recognized in Wilson "the rare quality of persevering honesty, the determination to state exactly what he has perceived, which makes him the most valuable of contemporary critics in this country."

In *American Renaissance* Matthiessen considers the reactions of Hawthorne and Melville against Emerson's optimistic idealism. In their work the symbol derived from nature represents evil as well as goodness. In a section entitled "The Vision of Evil," Matthiessen presents his idea of tragedy: the tragic hero is never simply an individual; "he is a man in action, in conflict with other individuals in a definite social order." Tragedy assumes "the mixed nature of life" and the radical imperfection of man, but recognizes that man, "pitiful as he may be in his finite weakness, is still capable of apprehending perfection, and of becoming transfigured by that vision. But not only must the author of tragedy have accepted the inevitable co-existence of good and evil in man's nature, he must also possess the power to envisage some reconciliation between such opposites, and the control to hold an inexorable balance. He must be as far from the chaos of despair as he is from ill-founded optimism." In Hawthorne's *The Scarlet Letter,* the dramatic irony of the tragic vision embraces the opposition of the supernaturalistic and naturalistic world views represented by the characters of Dimmesdale and Hester Prynne. In Melville's work the conflict between transcendental and naturalistic attitudes is paralleled by another: the affirmation of democratic values in the face of their denial by society. For the liberal critic the idea of tragedy provides a way of coping with this seemingly hopeless problem; Matthiessen's interpretation of Melville anticipates the criticism of Richard Chase and other representatives of the "New Liberalism."

One of the contributions of the age of Emerson and Whitman was its discovery of myth and of the idea of the poet as myth maker—both reactions against rationalism. In his last chapter, Matthiessen considers the "need for a mythology" in his own age, burdened as it is by "the accretions of another century of the historical method." He commends modern writers like Lawrence, Joyce, and Mann for valuing the timeless order of myth amid the disorder and flux of history. Myths suited to the needs of modern America should have as their protagonists not supermen but representative Americans, close to the common life, having a kinship with such folk heroes as Davy Crockett and Johnny Appleseed and Sut Lovingood. But there is a negative and critical as well as a positive value in literary myth. Melville's story of Ahab and Moby-Dick reveals the "tragedy of extreme individualism and the disasters of a selfish will, the agony of a spirit so walled within itself that it seemed cut off from any possibility of salvation."

An interest in myth had been fostered by *The Waste Land* and by the anthropologists upon whose work Eliot had depended. Its appeal to Matthiessen and his contemporaries can be understood as one symptom of a disillusionment deepened by such events as the Spanish Civil War and the Moscow purges. For many critics of liberal and radical sympathies, cherished political ideals of equality and international brotherhood seemed hopeless in a world in which the regnant powers were nationalistic and increasingly totalitarian. It is therefore not surprising that they turned to the conservative traditions of myth and tragedy with their unintellectual and unprogressive rationales of human existence. For the disillusioned liberal critic, tragedy supplied a formula by which counterpoised ideals and destructive forces could be "contained," and the "tragic equation" provided an aesthetically satisfying rationalization of defeat.

Matthiessen's work helped to elevate the level of American criticism and to increase the understanding of native literary traditions. In participating in the general reaction against a historical approach that tended to view literature primarily as supporting documentation for fixed social and political views, he combined historical intelligence with literary sensitivity in his interpretations of the writings not only of the American romantics, but also of Henry James, T. S. Eliot, and Theodore Dreiser. His *American Renaissance* has helped to revolutionize the teaching of American literature through its illuminating discussions of classic writers and its definition of a historically conditioned American aesthetic.

◆ 5 ◆

THE NEW CRITICISM

1—Origins; 2—T. S. Eliot; 3—John Crowe Ransom; 4—Cleanth Brooks; 5—Allen Tate; 6—Yvor Winters; 7—R. P. Blackmur; 8—The language of the New Criticism

1

Within the universities the New Criticism rose to prominence as the liberal and radical criticism of the Thirties declined. By the early 1940's the movement had begun a revolution in teaching and scholarship that was consolidated with the support of younger men in the postwar period. Devoted to close textual analysis rather than historical scholarship, the New Critics strengthened their position with theories of poetic language and structure and extended their influence through textbooks and journals. In the 1940's they controlled such literary quarterlies as *The Kenyon Review* and *The Sewanee Review,* and during the 1950's they gained acceptance in the more conservative scholarly journals. By the end of the decade, however, reactions to the New Criticism and further developments in theory were displacing or modifying many of its principles.

There has been considerable disagreement about the name and nature of the movement. "What is the New Criticism?" is a question that has been more frequently than fruitfully discussed. Such designations as *aesthetic formalism* and *analytical criticism* have sometimes been urged as preferable because they more closely describe the practice of the New Critics. But these titles do not take into account certain attitudes and theoretical assumptions that distinguish the New Criticism as something other than simply a formalist movement. It seems best to limit the term *New Critics* to several men associated with John Crowe Ransom from the early 1920's and to others who share their common outlook. Besides their practice of close textual analysis, the members of this group have been bound by the conservatism of their literary, social, and political views. They have been hostile toward the physical and social sciences and have avoided ideas and terms from these disciplines, depending rather upon traditional rhetorical and literary sources and their own coinages. As defenders of literature, some of the New Critics have attempted to establish standards by which the language of poetry might be distinguished from that of science. On the basis of such distinctions, they have argued that poetry or imaginative literature provides knowledge or truth different from that supplied by science. With this idea of "two truths" they have contributed to an aesthetic mystique, according to which the truth of art is apprehended immediately through the contemplation of the aesthetic symbol or icon.

Although the term *the New Criticism* had been introduced by Joel Spingarn in 1910, the more immediate source of the name of the later movement was the title of a collection of essays by J. C. Ransom published in 1941. In the last of these, "Wanted: an Ontological Critic," Ransom notes the wide reception of the contextualist criticism of I. A. Richards and his pupil William Empson and announces, "I think it is time to identify a powerful intellectual movement that deserves to be called a new criticism."

Looking to T. S. Eliot and I. A. Richards as their guides, the New Critics came to include—besides Ransom—Allen Tate, Cleanth Brooks, R. P. Blackmur, Yvor Winters, and R. P. Warren—although distinctions would have to be made about their individual ideas. (Kenneth Burke, who might be considered a fellow traveler of the New Critics, stands apart from them in his professed Marxism and his use of terms from many disciplines, including the social sciences.) A number of contemporaries and younger followers have also been associated with the group.

With its formalism, the new movement attempted to develop an "ontological" theory establishing poetry as a unique mode of apprehending reality. As Ransom announced in *The New Criticism,* "I suggest that the differentia of poetry as a discourse is an ontological one. It treats an order of existence, a grade of objectivity, which cannot be treated in scientific discourse. . . . Poetry intends to recover the denser and more refractory original world which we know loosely through our perceptions and memories. By this supposition it is a kind of knowledge which is radically or ontologically distinct."

The core of the New Criticism was formed during the Twenties, when Ransom, a professor at Vanderbilt University, began editing the poetry magazine *The Fugitive* (1922-25) with the assistance of Donald Davidson, Merrill Moore, Allen Tate, Robert Penn Warren, and others. Criticism was confined to brief reviews and editorials, usually by Ransom or Tate. Unlike many other little magazines of the period, *The Fugitive* was conservative in temper, and most of the verse appearing in its pages was traditional in form. The one editor sympathetic to experiment, Allen Tate, had early come under the influence of T. S. Eliot, whose ideas he transmitted to the other Fugitives. Tate carried on a gentlemanly feud with Ransom in the columns of the magazine, contending, in a sympathetic review of *The Waste Land,* that "aberrant versification" is sometimes a necessity for the modern poet.

Tate's argument opposed Ransom's insistence on regular rhyme and meter. More specifically, it was a reaction against Ransom's attack on *The Waste Land* in "The Literary Review" of the New York *Evening Post* (July 14, 1923). Ransom denounces Eliot's work as "one of the most insubordinate poems in the language," objecting to its fragmentation and its negative philosophy. The imaginative vision of the true artist fuses the discrete elements of experience, and "it is to be suspected that the author who holds his elements apart is not using his imagination, but using a formula, like a scientist anxious to make out a 'case.'" In art, however, refractory elements in experience are brought to an imaginative "higher synthesis." In closing, Ransom solaces himself with the reflection that, since it is unlikely that the language can for long continue to accommodate "two such incompatibles" as Wordsworth and Eliot, "any realist must admit that what happens to be the prior tenure of the mansion in this case is likely to be stubbornly defended."

2

In spite of Ransom's poor opinion of *The Waste Land,* there is little doubt that Eliot was the most important early influence upon the theory and practice of the New Critics, even though they did not accept all of his ideas. His name was often linked with those of Ransom, Tate, and their associates during the late Twenties and the 1930's. Before these men were known as "New Critics" they were recognized by both the New Humanists and the Marxist critics as "the classicists." And when Ransom said, in *The World's Body* (1938), that he desired a program that would be "in manners, aristocratic; in religion, ritualistic; in art, traditional," he was echoing, in Southern Agrarian terms, Eliot's description of himself as "classicist in literature, royalist in politics, and Anglo-Catholic in religion." Eliot's early career was a model for the New Critics. In his desire to focus upon technique and in his concern for critical language and method, Eliot was an effective leader, carrying forward a program already launched by T. E. Hulme and Ezra Pound, and later taken over from Eliot by the New Critics.

In his first collection, *The Sacred Wood: Essays on Poetry and Criticism* (1920), Eliot reacted against the extremes of impressionism and moralism in favor of a technical criticism. "The Perfect Critic" sets forth the idea that a fine mind tends to perceive a work in structural terms. "Criticism is the statement in language of this structure; it is a development of sensibility." Bad criticism is simply an expression of emotion. In "Imperfect Critics," Eliot calls Irving Babbitt, his old Harvard teacher, and Paul Elmer More victims of moralism and didacticism, besetting weaknesses of American criticism. It is too bad, Eliot remarks, that "the culture of ideas has only been able to survive in America in the unfavorable atmosphere of the university."

Two of the essays in *The Sacred Wood* have been especially influential. "Tradition and the Individual Talent" develops Eliot's idea of past literature as a historical order and sketches the outline of his impersonal theory of art. According to this theory, "classical" in its reaction against romantic subjectivism, an individual poem must be judged, not on its own terms, as a unique expression, but by the standards of the "tradition" in which it takes its place. The poem is not "self-expression," the direct statement of the personal emotions of the writer, but rather an impersonal formulation of common feelings and emotions. In this process, emotions which the poet has never experienced "will serve his turn as well as those familiar to him." Poetry is thus "not a turning loose of emotion, but an escape from emotion; it is not the expression of personality but an escape from personality." Consistent with these ideas is Eliot's preference for dramatic rather than lyric poetry. Many of the early essays deal appreciatively with the renaissance dramatists, while the romantic poets, especially the rebellious and atheistic Shelley, are given short shrift.

"Hamlet and His Problems" introduces a term that was to become widely adopted by the supporters of the impersonal theory: "The only way of expressing emotion in the form of art is by finding an 'objective correlative'; in other words, a set of objects, a situation, a chain of events which shall be the formula of that *particular* emotion; such that when the external facts, which must terminate in sensory experience, are given, the emotion is immediately evoked." Even when the term itself was not used, the idea of the objective correlative was adopted by the New Critics, and by midcentury the standard of impersonality was usually taken for granted as a test for poetry. Although Eliot himself later modified his views, most of his followers adhered rigidly to these early principles.

In the years following, Eliot turned his attention to seventeenth century poets like John Donne and during the 1920's helped to establish the vogue of the metaphysical school. At this time he was also undergoing his conversion to Anglicanism. During the 1930's he became increasingly preoccupied with social problems, and in 1939, on the eve of the second World War, he issued *The Idea of a Christian Society,* a tract advocating a return to a class-stratified social order monitored by the hierarchy of an established church.

Eliot has at various times considered the relation between literature and religious dogma and the extent to which belief is involved in criticism. In "Poetry and Propaganda" (1930), he cites two opposing views. One, attributed to Montgomery Belgion, considers the artist inevitably an "irresponsible propagandist" whose work always tends to *persuade* the reader to accept the writer's point of view, however capricious that may be. The other, identified with I. A. Richards, supports the ideal of a "pure" reaction in which the reader practices a willing suspension of disbelief while regarding any stated beliefs simply as art.

Accepting neither extreme, Eliot rejects more strongly the purist idea, arguing that no art, and particularly no literary art, can exist in a vacuum and that a man's beliefs are to a greater or lesser extent affected by his reading. As for Belgion's idea of literature as propaganda, Eliot distinguishes among "responsible propagandists" like Lucretius and Dante, who speak for established philosophies or world views; a conscious but "irresponsible" propagandist like Milton, whose viewpoint is that of an eccentric heretic; and a poet like Shakespeare, who affects his readers' views, but in such diverse ways that he can hardly be thought of as propagandizing. Although he rejects the idea of poetry *as* knowledge, Eliot concludes that the quality of a poet's belief or philosophy is a factor in the criticism of his work: "We can hardly doubt that the 'truest' philosophy is the best material for the greatest poet; so that a poet must be rated in the end both by the philosophy he realizes in poetry and by the fullness and adequacy of the realization."

The treatment of this subject in "Religion and Literature" (1935) is unequivocal in its insistence that orthodox Christian standards be applied in criticism. The essay begins with several propositions elaborated by dogmatic assertions: "Literary criticism should be completed by criticism from a definite ethical and theological standpoint. In so far as in any age there is common agreement on ethical and theological matters, so far can literary criticism be substantive. In ages like our own, when there is no such common agreement, it is the more necessary for Christian readers to scrutinize their reading, especially of works of the imagination, with explicit ethical and theological standards; although we must remember that whether it is literature or not can be determined only by literary standards."

Eliot suggests that while aesthetic or technical analysis is the necessary foundation of criticism, it is not sufficient for final judgment of a work—a final judgment which would approve or censor its ideas and values on the basis of their conformity to orthodox Christian ethics and beliefs. A problem arises, however, when one considers that even within the Christian faith there is a considerable range of opinion on these matters, involving such important questions as the freedom of the will and man's moral nature. Although Eliot does not say so explicitly, his standards would undoubtedly be the doctrines of the Church of England.

To those who are not orthodox Christians but who are interested in the innumerable ways in which literature treats values, Eliot's pronouncement may seem confining. Most of our "greatest" Western literature derives power and interest from the ways in which it reacts against orthodoxy and generally accepted conventions. If a "common agreement on ethical and theological matters" could be achieved, there would be little occasion for literature as a free inquiry into the conditions of human life.

Eliot's moralistic and authoritarian tone is like that of the New Humanists. So also is his assumption of an enlightened minority, or Christian elite, responsible for the moral regeneration of society. ("What I believe to be incumbent upon all Christians is the duty of maintaining consciously certain standards and criteria of criticism over and above those applied by the rest of the world. . . .") So also is his hostility to modern literature, which he considers "corrupted" by "Secularism." ("So long as we are conscious of the gulf fixed between ourselves [Christians] and the greater part of contemporary literature, we are more or less protected from being harmed by it, and are in a position to extract from it what good it has to offer us.") Secularism means evidently not only the naturalistic view that denies the "primacy of the supernatural over the natural life" but the belief that human life and morality can be decisively improved through social and economic changes. Eliot's comment expresses most immediately a rejection of Marxism, but it also implies a distrust of science, industrialism, and the idea of social progress—a distrust shared by both the New Humanists and the New Critics.

3

In 1930, when Eliot, an established international figure, described himself poetically as an "aged eagle," his close contemporary John Crowe Ransom was just beginning to try his critic's wings. Ransom's first prose work, *God Without Thunder: An Unorthodox Defense of Orthodoxy,* published in that year, reflects many of Eliot's views, which are, however, more baldly stated by Ransom in the role of an unabashed Southern fundamentalist. He expresses a dislike of science, which is both abstract and "predatory," and defends myth as a mode of concrete presentation that respects the particularity of nature. (The tendency to personify abstractions, attributing will and morality to them, is typical of Ransom's theory.) While there are many orders of myth, the fundamentalist chooses one preferred dogma ("the simplification of myth") and commits himself to it unswervingly. For Ransom, as for Eliot, the choice is the Christian myth, with emphasis, however, upon the Old Testament religion of wrath. Thus, the myth of the fall of man is interpreted by Ransom in a chapter entitled "Satan as Science." The Hebrew Satan, or Lucifer, is equated with the Greek Prometheus and as the "light-bearer" is identified with the "scientific Enlightenment." Progress, from the garden state to agrarianism to industrialism, has involved an increasing exploitation of man and nature and is accursed. Science, which has provided the basis for industrialism, "is an order of experience in which we mutilate and prey upon nature."

It is difficult to reconcile Ransom's view of science with the commonly accepted idea of a disciplined and disinterested inquiry directed not toward exploitation or self-aggrandizement but toward an understanding of nature and man.

Ransom, like Eliot, feels the need of a sustaining orthodoxy, but, unlike Eliot, he can find no institutional support for his ideas. His conclusion considers possible alternatives. Within the Christian fold, orthodoxy seems strongest in the

Greek church, but it is too remote. He would find it abhorrent to go outside his own tribe and join with strangers. The same inhibition rules out the synagogue, where the God of Israel is to be found "in his greatest purity." Anglicanism, though closer home, is also unacceptable for both social and "inherited" reasons. The other Protestant sects cannot be endorsed because they are too unorthodox.

What is left for the churchless modern devotee of orthodoxy? Only this position:

"With whatever religious institution a modern man may be connected, let him try to turn it back towards orthodoxy.

"Let him insist on a virile and concrete God, and accept no Principle as a substitute.

"Let him restore to God the thunder.

"Let him resist the usurpation of the God head by the soft modern version of the Christ [compare the New Humanist attitude toward 'humanitarianism'], *and try to keep the Christ for what he professed to be: the Demigod who came to do honor to the God."*

Ransom's tract was characterized by Yvor Winters as "Thunder Without God," because it could find no supernatural center or sanction for the orthodoxy it professed. Its social and religious attitudes were, however, not peculiar to Ransom but typical of many of the Southern Agrarians with whom he was identified at this time.

Twelve of these men, including Tate and several other "Fugitives," banded together to bring out *I'll Take My Stand: The South and the Agrarian Tradition* (1930). The immediate cause of the symposium was the plight of the nation's economy generally and that of the South particularly in the wake of the 1929 crash. The Agrarians took for granted the failure of the system, just as the Marxists did.

Unlike the Marxists and like the Humanists, they believed in property as the foundation of social order. Consequently, the evil to attack was not capitalism but industrialism, and the opposition of the farmers and the industrialists took the place of the Marxists' class struggle. The Agrarians saw the spread of industrialism in the "New South" as destroying an older, leisurely society. They consequently tended to idealize the plantation culture of the Old South, ignoring or justifying the fact that it had rested upon a system of human slavery. They wished to recapture the virtues of the vanished past through a program that called for de-industrialization and the encouragement of widely diffused small property holdings as a basis for social stability and order. The Agrarians were doubly unfortunate. For one thing, the stable, cultured old order to which they looked back nostalgically never existed except in the realm of fantasy, as Wilbur J. Cash has pointed out in *The Mind of the South* (1941). For another, the Agrarians had no place to take their stand, politically, except in the Democratic Party, which was for industrial growth as well as for Dixie. Although the group could really do nothing to help the South, the new Democratic administration which took over in 1933 managed to bring about some improvement in the conditions of life for large numbers of Southerners through the instruments of science and technology, which the Agrarians loathed, in such projects as the T.V.A.

The chief outlet for the political interests of the Agrarians was in writing. Besides contributing to the 1930 symposium, most of the Southern group associated with Ransom (Tate, Brooks, R. P. Warren, Donald Davidson) also wrote articles for *The American Review* (1933-1937), the successor to *The Bookman.* This magazine was founded, as its editor

Seward Collins explained, to provide a forum for the "Radicals of the Right" or "Revolutionary Conservatives." The four groups that supported the magazine included—besides the Agrarians—the English "Distributionists," led by Hilaire Belloc and G. K. Chesterton; the American New Humanists, represented by G. R. Elliott, H. H. Clark, Norman Foerster, and Robert Shafer; and neoscholastics like Christopher Dawson and Father D'Arcy of Oxford, the men carrying on the "Aristotelico-Thomistic tradition in philosophy and applying it to modern problems." Among other contributors were T. S. Eliot, Douglas Jerrold, Eric Gill, Wyndham Lewis, and Yvor Winters. "The corporate state" and the "restoration of property" were recurrent themes; and Italian and Spanish fascism and German Nazism were sympathetically discussed in several articles. The history of the magazine has been very well told in "Seward Collins and the *American Review:* Experiment in Pro-Fascism, 1933-37," by Albert E. Stone, Jr. (*American Quarterly,* 1960).

Although Ransom and his fellow Agrarians had no church and no party through which to extend their influence, their cause was not lost. There remained the field of literature and criticism, and here a victory was won, and a decisive one, for many of their ideas and attitudes.

The World's Body (1938) continues Ransom's attack against science, but in the name of poetry rather than religion, and with a shift of emphasis from dogma to ritual: "It is my idea that religion is an institution existing for the sake of its ritual, rather than, as I have heard, for the sake of its doctrines. . . ." Its value is thus primarily aesthetic. In a world in which political and economic and religious problems seem insoluble, the only possible resolution of issues is aesthetic. For Ransom poetry is a source of order and knowledge. It also serves a redemptive or at least restorative function, since through its sensuous particularity it re-establishes the "body" of the world that science has skeletonized through its abstractions: "What we cannot know constitutionally as scientists is the world which is made of whole and indefeasible objects, and this is the world which poetry recovers for us," a world representing a "new kind of knowledge," so radical that the scientist cannot recognize it as such.

In an essay on I. A. Richards, "A Psychologist Looks at Poetry," Ransom takes account of Richards' efforts to apply scientific methods to the study of poetry. He is not pleased by Richards' behavioristic tendency to explain human motives in terms of such hypothetical mental data as impulses. He also dislikes Richards' early distinction between the verifiable propositions of science and the pseudostatements of poetry because it denies the validity of the knowledge presented through the concrete images of poetry. Ransom notes with approval that Richards, since *Coleridge on Imagination* (1935), recognizes that all modes of expression, including the scientific, are mythic. But Richards' altered view does not satisfy Ransom because it does not sufficiently distinguish the fullness and creativeness of the poetic spirit from the meager abstractness of science. (Ransom's reservation is not entirely just to Richards, who gave poetry precedence over science as the inexhaustible "utterance of the whole soul of man" and as a "necessary channel for the reconstitution of order.")

In his concluding essay, "Criticism, Inc.," Ransom regrets that the university professors of literature, who should provide the best criticism, do not because their departments are dominated by old line historical and philological scholars unconcerned with formal analysis or aesthetic values. He believes that a revolution in methods is needed and expresses the opinion that criticism should become more "scientific" (his use of the term is surprising) and precise and that the proper place for this development is the university. The question of what criticism is or should be Ransom eschews for the easier question of what it is not. It is *not* subjective impressionism, historical or linguistic studies, moral studies (whether New Humanist or Marxist), or "any other special studies which deal with some abstract or prose content taken out of the work."

Ransom's pessimism about the future of criticism in the university now seems exaggerated. *The World's Body* was published in the same year as Cleanth Brooks and R. P. Warren's *Understanding Poetry,* a textbook that helped to bring about the revolution Ransom desired.

By 1941, when *The New Criticism* appeared, the movement was already becoming established in the universities. This work renews the theme of the *Dinglichkeit,* or sensuous particularity of poetry, developed in *The World's Body.* In stressing the concreteness of poetic language, Ransom pushes his theory to the extreme of iconicism. Speaking of Charles W. Morris's division of sign functioning into three separate categories, the *semantic, syntactic,* and *pragmatic* (corresponding to the spheres of science, art, and technology), Ransom takes exception to Morris's qualification that "the aesthetic sign, in common with all signs, has all three dimensions of sign functioning." Ransom believes that Morris does not sufficiently distinguish art from science on the grounds of the difference between *symbol* and *icon.* The difference is "that the object symbolized by a scientific sign would seem to be abstract, as, for example, a single property or aspect of objects, whereas the object symbolized by an iconic or aesthetic sign must be a whole object. . . . In brief, under the iconic sign the abstract item is restored to the body from which it was taken."

Of course, Ransom's pronouncement ignores the fact that all art and all language are the products of abstraction and that any distinctions made between modes of discourse can be only provisional and a matter of emphasis. The image, whether in poetry or visual art, can refer only to a selection of the qualities of experienced events. To identify the iconic sign with an object in nature, as Ransom wishes to do, suggests a magical view of language. For Ransom, the world that we know in its vibrant immediacy as children and that dims for us as we grow older and our perceptions become conventionalized by "science," can be "reconstituted" through the iconic language of poetry.

Ransom's distinction between the language of science and that of art or poetry is summarized in these words: "Science deals exclusively in pure symbols, but art deals essentially, though not exclusively, in iconic signs." But this statement, which establishes the iconic sign as the distinguishing feature of poetry, is not consistent with Ransom's own conception of the poem, which he develops in considerable detail. The escape clause lies in the words "though not exclusively." According to Ransom's definition, the poem is distinguished by something more than sensuous particularity. "A beautiful poem is one which proceeds to the completion of a logical structure, but not without attention to the local particularity of its components." In other words, abstract logic, for Ransom the identifying characteristic of scientific language, seems also to be a necessary feature of poetry. Though the logic of the poem may not be so close or so rigorous as that of science, it is there: "What is the value of a structure which (a) is not so tight and precise on its logical side as a scientific or technical prose structure generally is; and (b) imports and carries along a great deal of irrelevant or foreign matter which is clearly not structural but even obstructive? This *a-* and *b-* formulation is what we inevitably come to if we take the analysis our best critics offer. We sum it up by saying that the poem is a loose logical structure with an irrelevant local texture."

Ransom further describes texture as "adventitious" and a "curious increment of riches" that cannot be contained by any statement of argument, or logical paraphrase. In other words, it is the stuff upon which the logic feeds, so to speak; it supplies the basis for any logical definition of structure. Yet it eludes logic and remains an object of pleasure and refreshment in itself, and it is, for Ransom, the essential poetry of the poem. It is not accessible, however, except through the rational structure, which acts as a necessary guide to the reader.

In Ransom's traditionalistic view structure includes conventional rhyme and meter and a rationally developed argument with a beginning, a middle, and an end, and with properly developed transitions from stage to stage of the argument. The lack of this kind of order provoked his dislike of modern experimentalist verse, demonstrated as early as 1923 in his attack on *The Waste Land.* The same bias is apparent in *The New Criticism* in his discussion of "the moderns," among whom he includes Pound, Eliot, Tate, Stevens, and perhaps Auden. These poets broke from convention, he believes, because of their feeling that the old tradition had become trite and its ontology inadequate. But he would prefer renovation rather than rejection of established conventions, thinking it best to "work by taking liberties with the old practice and irregularize and desystematize it, without denying it." He sees in most of the moderns, except for an occasional "perfect poetic phrase," the impression of decadence or "spent energies" that may explain their surrender of the principle of order.

Because of his distinction between structure and texture, Ransom's theory rests upon a dualism comparable to the ancient form-content dichotomy. The useful feature of the distinction is that it takes account of the apparently "irrational" elements of the work of art—also of the wealth of details which are an inexhaustible source of new insights. But all these details are formally organized and interrelated in numerous ways even though their relationship may not be immediately apparent.

Although Ransom discusses the "concrete universal" (borrowed from Hegel) as a concept which helps to explain the nature of poetry, he does not believe that the poetic statement achieves a "synthesis" of the general and the particular. Rather, he uses the term—in "Criticism as Pure Speculation" (1941)—to describe the fact that the poem contains two kinds of elements, the general and the particular, the structure and the texture. The interest of the critic, he thinks, is a speculative one focused on the structure and the texture and the relation between them.

In his dualism and his concern for rational structure, Ransom stands apart from the other New Critics. Except for Yvor Winters, most of them consider the structure of poetry to be un- or anti-logical and the poem itself to be a unified whole. They tend to agree with Ransom, however, that poetic language provides a knowledge distinct from that of science. It does so not so much through its iconic nature, however, as through its contextual quality, the way in which it functions as a unified complex or symbol to express, metaphorically, a knowledge or truth like that of myth or religion.

4

The contextualist point of view, which derives from Coleridge through I. A. Richards, is best illustrated by the theory and practice of Cleanth Brooks, who was Ransom's student at Vanderbilt in the late 1920's.

Brooks has been influential as an editor and an author of textbooks and critical essays that have reached a wide audience. In preparing textbooks, he has most often collaborated with R. P. Warren, their joint works including *An Approach to Literature* (1936), *Understanding Poetry* (1938; revised, 1950, 1960), and *Understanding Fiction* (1943). Of these the second is best known. Its quick acceptance and widespread use helped to consolidate the strength of the New Criticism in colleges and universities.

The first edition of the anthology *Understanding Poetry* includes model analyses and questions to assist the student. In a "Letter to the Teacher," the editors reject such substitutes for the study of the poem as "paraphrase of logical and narrative content," "study of biographical and historical materials," and "inspirational and didactic interpretation." They recommend instead that "emphasis should be kept on the poem," "the treatment should be concrete and inductive," and "a poem should always be treated as an organic system of relationships, and the poetic qualities should never be understood as inhering in one or more factors taken in isolation."

The grouping of the poems under such headings as narrative, objective description, metrics, tone and attitude, imagery, and theme insures the discussion of subjects necessary to formal analysis. The avoidance of chronological listing or of arrangement by country of origin or literary type works against any historical plan for the presentation of material. The development within sections and for the book as a whole is from relatively simple to complex poems, a good pedagogical arrangement, but one that places a premium upon complexity.

One of the useful features of the book is an appended glossary of terms needed for the discussion of theme and technique. The last entry, on "Verse," presents in eleven pages a concise coverage of conventional English metrical patterns. The explanations of terms like *abstract, dramatic,* and *imagery* emphasize concreteness as a characteristic of poetic language. For the most part, however, the discussion of terms is not markedly "New Critical," except in its formalist emphasis. Words like *irony, paradox, structure,* and *texture* are included, but they are not given the special meaning and importance they receive in the later theory of the New Criticism. The glossary contains no entry for *myth,* and *symbol* is discussed only under *imagery* as a "metaphor from which the first term has been removed."

Helpful as *Understanding Poetry* has been, and it is difficult to overestimate the extent to which it has stimulated an intelligent interest in literature, the book is not without its defects. Its most important shortcomings result from the editors' biases. Their questions and analyses, which are often excellent, reveal a preference for the work of seventeenth century poets like Marvell and Donne over the romantics and even over Shakespeare. Among the romantics, Keats, because of his sensuousness and concreteness, is favored over Shelley, who receives particularly harsh treatment on grounds of abstractness and a lack of a logical integration of his images (the latter a common basis for New Critical censure of Shakespeare, as well).

Another feature of the analyses is a predominant concern for tone and conceptual meaning. Despite the editors' statement that "poetic qualities should never be understood as inhering in one or more factors taken in isolation," there is relatively little attention paid to the interrelation of metrics, syntax, and emotive qualities as dimensions of form which may offset a relatively slight development of conceptual meaning. This emphasis may help to explain the slighting of the modern free verse tradition. Although *vers libre* selections are included in the collection, neither the analyses nor the glossary section on verse discusses the problem of free verse metrics.

In *Modern Poetry and the Tradition* (1939) Brooks extends Eliot's discussion of the metaphysical and symbolist poets to the "moderns" and helps to establish the New Critical canon. In his preface—which expresses his debt to Eliot, Richards, and his own American contemporaries—Brooks sees himself as participating in a revolution against a romantic theory that had relegated wit and complex metaphor to the level of "fancy," inferior to the truly poetic imagination for both Wordsworth and Coleridge; that had elevated the standard of "high seriousness," in Arnold's phrase, as a hallmark of great poetry; and that had through its didacticism encouraged the use of discursive and sententious language rather than concise, sensuous imagery.

Brooks argues that the concrete metaphor is the essence of

poetic expression and that the mingling of intellectual and emotional qualities in the paradoxical conceits of the metaphysical school achieves an insight into reality that meets the requirement of "high seriousness" more effectively than any other technique. Quoting Richards to the effect that irony is a constant characteristic of poetry of the highest order, Brooks finds it most fully present in metaphysical poetry. The French symbolist poets were like the metaphysicals in their search for private and often obscure "objective correlatives" for the experience they wished to communicate; in this sense all poetry is, for Brooks, symbolist poetry.

The idea of the personal conceit or private myth serves as a link between a metaphysical poet like Donne and a modern like Yeats, "the poet as myth-maker." Yeats's private system of myth is explained as a reaction against "the impingement of science upon the poet's world," and his determination to create a poetic myth to compensate for the loss of the religion of his childhood is sympathetically discussed. Brooks quotes Richards' *Coleridge on Imagination* to the effect that "the saner and greater mythologies are not fancies; they are the utterances of the whole soul of man, and, as such, inexhaustible to meditation."

Besides Yeats and Eliot, other modern poets embraced by the "tradition" are J. C. Ransom, Allen Tate, and R. P. Warren, whose work, discussed in some detail, is found to possess the requisite concreteness, irony, and tension. Others considered, and accepted to a greater or lesser degree, are W. H. Auden, in his best poems, and Robert Frost, when he does not philosophize and when his "anecdote is absorbed into symbol." Archibald MacLeish, who might seem a fitter candidate for admission than Frost, is examined but found wanting in "dramatic tension." Even a poem like *Conquistador,* concerned as it is with heroic action, is "essentially reverie, not drama; the final effect pathos, not tragedy."

In *The Well Wrought Urn: Studies in the Structure of Poetry* (1947), Brooks further develops his theory in several skillful and well-written essays on individual poems. While the focus is in each case upon the work at hand, the analysis is conducted so as to elucidate and support Brooks's idea of the nature of structure, particularly as it rests upon the principle of "paradox," a word that echoes through the book. The poets range from Shakespeare and Milton to Yeats, and the discussion extends the application of the techniques of paradox and ambiguity to the romantic and Victorian poets, Wordsworth, Keats, and Tennyson. In the first essay, Brooks asserts that "the language of poetry is the language of paradox" and demonstrates that this principle applies *even* to Wordsworth.

One of the best known and most representative of the essays is "Keats's Sylvan Historian," an analysis of the "Ode on a Grecian Urn." After observing that the poem violates the "doctrine of the objective correlative" by ending with the sententious statement that beauty is truth and truth beauty and that this is the sum of mortal knowledge, Brooks justifies the device by arguing that "it is a speech 'in character' and supported by a dramatic context." The paradox of the "speaking urn" stressed throughout the poem achieves a climax and resolution in the enigmatic final utterance. "The assertions made in a poem are to be taken as part of an organic context." Whatever "truth" the poem conveys is only the truth of the *"poem as a whole,"* presented through metaphor, rather than the truth of "some statement of theme abstracted from it by paraphrase."

This conclusion anticipates the theme of the final essay, "The Heresy of Paraphrase," in which Brooks defines poetic structure as "a structure of meanings, evaluations and interpretations," while "the principle of unity which informs it seems to be one of balancing and harmonizing connotations, attitudes, and meanings." The "structure," a union of opposed elements, is primarily a structure of meaning, "something far more internal than the metrical pattern, say, or than the sequence of images," and more complex than any statement that can be abstracted from it. Poetry is a form of myth, and Keats's urn bears witness that this myth is truer than history. The poetic statement, in its complexity, is inviolable to analysis. Thus the poem is invulnerable to criticism which would analyze poetic meaning by abstraction, a process that would leave the "full poem" untouched. The principal weakness of most criticism results from what Brooks calls the "heresy of paraphrase," in which a rational statement is substituted for "the real core of meaning which constitutes the essence of the poem." Its "essential structure," unlike that of a statement abstracted from it, is not logical; it is rather "a pattern of resolved stresses," or of "resolutions and balances and harmonizations, developed through a temporal scheme."

This total structure of meaning, which is kept in balance by paradox, ambiguity, and irony, cannot be translated into discursive terms subject to the test of consistency and verification by experience. But as a poetic symbol, or myth, it communicates "knowledge." What kind of knowledge this may be is a question that Brooks treats without complete explicitness in an appended essay entitled "The Problem of Belief and the Problem of Cognition." While poetry "does not compete with science and philosophy," it involves a "coming to terms with situations," and thus provides "wisdom," although it "indulges in no ethical generalizations." Brooks quotes, as a view close to his own, W. M. Urban's assertion that the "poetic symbol gives cognition," even though the poem is untranslatable. The only other inkling of the nature of this knowledge appears in an approving reference to Allen Tate's claim that literature gives a "complete knowledge of man's experience," in contrast apparently to the narrower knowledge of science, which Tate has elsewhere described as concerned with the "verification of limited techniques."

The contextualist critic like Brooks is himself the victim of an ironic dilemma in asserting the cognitive function of poetry while denying that statements of truth can be abstracted from it. His idea that the poetic symbol provides an order of truth or knowledge distinct from that of science is not a new one. In romantic theory, the higher knowledge is spiritual enlightenment. The various attempts by modern critics to define a higher truth in aesthetic terms as a "complete knowledge," or a "felt reality," or the "truth of myth" are substitutes for earlier supernaturalistic notions. Literature may or may not be true. It represents *knowledge* to the extent that it is productive of verifiable statements. These, like any other element of the work, can be abstracted by the critic, who must take into account the extent to which they are modified and qualified by their context. (The contextualist critics themselves succeed in conveying an idea of the complexity of a poem by abstracting and interrelating representative formal aspects.) The truth statements of literature may be expressed metaphorically, in figurative language, or they may exist in the form of explicit generalizations within a poem. In either case, like scientific statements, they are true only as they are verifiable. The "two truths" theory which exists in many sophisticated versions in modern criticism is an archaic survival of supernaturalism.

5

The ideas of Allen Tate about the cognitive function of poetry resemble those of Ransom and Brooks, his long-time associates. In "Literature as Knowledge" (1941) he opposes the efforts of positivist linguists to reduce poetic statements to meaninglessness. Taking Richards' description of poetry as the "completest mode of utterance," Tate insists that attention must be focused on the poem itself, "in which we get knowledge of a whole object"—a statement reminiscent of Ransom's idea of the reconstitution in poetry of the world of "whole and indefeasible objects." Tate is closer to Brooks, however, in his emphasis on the total structure of the poem as a device for uniting and resolving discordant qualities. In "Longinus and the 'New Criticism' " (1948), he finds an early prophet of contextualism in the pseudonymous first century author of "On the Sublime." Longinus's discussion of a composition in which contraries are united and which affects us by its total impact anticipates the organic theory of Coleridge and the later New Critics.

In describing the organization of the poem, Tate has made use of the word *tension* in a manner complementing Brooks's use of *irony* and *paradox.* "Tension in Poetry" (1938) explains the word as originating in the logical terms *extension* and *intension,* which refer to the abstract and denotative meanings of poetic language on the one hand and its concrete and connotative values on the other. The principle of tension supports the poem's structure of meaning and is the most important formal element for the New Critic: "The meaning of poetry is its 'tension,' the full organized body of all the extension and intension that we can find in it." It also supplies a standard of value, for, to Tate, "good" poetry is a "unity of all the meanings from the furthest extremes of intension and extension." In illustration, Tate describes metaphysical and romantic or symbolist poets as using different strategies, one beginning with the extensive or denoting end of the line, the other with the intensive, although "each by a straining feat of the imagination tries to push his meanings as far as he can toward the opposite end, so as to occupy the entire scale."

The apprehension of a poem's unity depends upon its confrontation as a Gestalt, the values of which abide in its "total quality." Although contextualist critics have usually not drawn attention to the fact that their theory, developed to its logical conclusion, is incompatible with practical criticism, Tate has considered the problem of criticism on several occasions. In an essay entitled "The Present Function of Criticism" (1941), he hopefully held that the role of criticism should be "to maintain and demonstrate the special, unique, and complete knowledge which the great forms of literature afford us." Ten years later his outlook was much less confident.

In "Is Literary Criticism Possible?" (1950-51), Tate discusses the problem of the teaching and practice of criticism. Discouraged in his efforts to define criticism, he concludes that "in teaching criticism we do not know what we are teaching" and that this unknowable subject cannot be taught.

Although he provisionally accepts the idea of three kinds of critical discourse (acts of evaluation; the communication of insights; rhetorical study), Tate believes that only rhetoric as the study of the art of language is pertinent to criticism.

But we really do not believe in the uses of rhetoric "because we do not believe that the full language of the human situation can be the vehicle of truth." It seems to Tate that the modern critic is languishing in a "pragmatic vortex" for want of absolute values, and he questions whether we can "believe in the language of humane truth without believing in the possibility of a higher unity of truth, which we must posit as *there,* even if it must remain beyond our powers of understanding." Concluding that literary criticism is both "perpetually necessary" and "perpetually impossible," he again raises the question of whether it can exist "without a criterion of absolute truth."

For some critics the literary work itself supplies the desired value, but for Tate the aesthetic absolute cannot satisfy religious and philosophical needs. Perhaps for this reason he has often seemed more concerned with the problems of "The Man of Letters in the Modern World" (the title of a 1952 essay and a 1955 collection of his essays) than with the problems of literary criticism alone. His traditionalism and his distrust of reason are reflected in the titles of some of the collections of his essays: *Reactionary Essays on Poetry and Ideas* (1936), *Reason in Madness* (1941), *On the Limits of Poetry* (1948), and *The Forlorn Demon* (1955). (His *Collected Essays* appeared in 1959.)

Given Tate's interest in absolute values, his admiration for the virtues of a traditional society, and his concern for the lack of moral unity in modern society, it is not surprising that he should have entered the Roman Catholic Church. The specific pressures and motives that brought him over the threshold Ransom could not cross are not indicated, but his conversion was completed in 1951. In "The Man of Letters in the Modern World" (1952) he speaks of the "dehumanized society of secularism," which because of its "intractable Manicheeism" cannot be redeemed.

Like Eliot, Tate considers that a chief cause of modern secularism was the "dissociation of sensibility" resulting from Descartes' isolation of thought from man's total being. Like Eliot again, he has committed himself to the "idea of a Christian society." In an address delivered in Italy before a congress for peace and Christian civilization, later published as "Christ and the Unicorn" (*Sewanee Review,* 1955), Tate speaks as an orthodox layman and a defender of the faith: "There can be no culture for us, in the true sense, without our unique Revelation." And further: "Either we are a Christian civilization or we are nothing."

The "unicorn" opposed to Christ is "utopian politics" whether it be in the form of "Gnosticism, or the belief in the omnipotence of reason in the political order" (the reference seems to be to democratic liberalism), or "Manicheeism," when in disillusionment with the idea of perfectability we go to the other extreme of viewing man as a "vicious imbecile" and call in "the kind of order represented by the omnicompetent state." These twin demons can be exorcised only by choosing the Christian society: "So our first battle must be with the ambiguous demon, the unicorn that at once flatters our intellectual pride and denies the good of nature by pillaging it. The task remains the same, whether the demon come from the East or within ourselves."

Tate's exhortation echoes earlier themes. The Agrarian's hatred of science and industrialism is here translated and expanded, on a global scale, into an authoritarian animus against both liberal democracy and Communism. Few modern American critics have made an accord with Rome, as Tate has done, but many have found substitute faiths in the aesthetic cult of the imagination or in the idea of literature as myth. Tate and those who found a surrogate religion in art, as he would not, have all followed in their own ways the path of Eliot, the model of the modern intellectual and artist who has not been able to accept a naturalistic world view.

6

In *The Function of Criticism* (1957) Yvor Winters, poet and scholar-critic, speaks of the critical revolution in college teaching which he—together with J. C. Ransom, Cleanth Brooks, Allen Tate, and R. P. Blackmur—had helped to bring about. Although his critical essays demonstrate the analytical technique of the New Critics, he differs from them in his emphasis upon the rational and moral nature of poetry. In a deliberate reaction against the antirationalism of Ransom and Tate, Winters published under the title *In Defense of Reason* (1947) a collection of his earlier volumes of criticism: *Primitivism and Decadence* (1937), *Maule's Curse* (1938), and *The Anatomy of Nonsense* (1943). In these works he has attempted to develop a systematic theory of poetry and criticism. From his own clearly defined position, Winters has conducted a running criticism of the theory of his fellow New Critics, sometimes to good effect.

Although close to the New Humanists in his concern for reason and morality in literature, Winters has disclaimed kinship with them: "I do not consider myself one of the Humanists: I disagree with Babbitt on too many counts to do so, though I admire him and have learned a good deal from him; and Babbitt's colleagues have always appeared to me to be worth very little indeed."

In the foreword to *In Defense of Reason,* Winters describes himself as an absolutist—one who "believes in the existence of absolute truths and values" and in the "duty of every man and of every society to endeavor as far as may be to approximate them." But the source of these values remains mysterious. Winters acknowledges that his absolutism implies a "theistic position" and that "there is only one place in which those absolute truths can be located." But he has elsewhere stated that he is not a Christian and that he permanently lacks, he fears, "the capacity to become one." Despite his protestation, Winters' position seems to be, as far as one can tell, close to that of the theistic Humanist. Like the Humanist, he views the university as "the intellectual and spiritual center of our world," the institution which can best sustain the continuity of human values.

Although he objects to the idea of literature as a substitute for religion or philosophy, Winters believes that poetry, like all art, provides a moral evaluation of experience in rational terms. He has defined a poem as "a statement in words" in verse, "in which special pains are taken with the expression of feeling." He describes the function of the poet:

"The poet deals with human experience in words. Words are symbols of concepts, which have acquired connotation of feeling in addition to their denotation of concept. The poet, then, as a result of the very nature of his medium, must make a rational statement about his experience, and as rationality is a part of the medium, the ultimate value of the poem will depend in a fair measure on the soundness of the rationality: it is possible, of course, to reason badly, just as it is possible to reason well. But the poet is deliberately employing the connotative content of language as well as the denotative: so that what he must do is to make a rational statement about an experience, at the same time employing his language in such a manner as to communicate the emotion which ought to be communicated by that rational understanding of the particular subject. In so far as he is able to do this, the poem will be good; in so far as the subject itself is important, the poem will be great."

He proceeds to a definition of the critical process: "It will consist (1) of the statement of such historical or biographical knowledge as may be necessary in order to understand the mind and method of the writer; (2) of such analysis of his literary theories as we may need to understand and evaluate what he is doing; (3) of a rational critique of the paraphrasable content (roughly, the motive) of the poem; (4) of a rational critique of the feeling motivated—that is, of the details of style, as seen in language and technique; and (5) of the final act of judgment, a unique act, the general nature of which can be indicated, but which cannot be communicated precisely, since it consists in receiving from the poet his own final and unique judgment of his matter and in judging the judgment. It should be noted that the purpose of the first four processes is to limit as narrowly as possible the region in which the final unique act is to occur." Winters sensibly adds that for various reasons a given task in criticism may not require all of these processes and that the extent to which particular processes are developed is a question to settle as occasion arises.

For Winters, the greatest of English critics was not Coleridge but Samuel Johnson, and he shares Johnson's lack of deference toward established types or genres. He views the commitment to the traditional order of forms as a weakness of the criticism of R. S. Crane, leader of the Chicago Aristotelian critics. Himself a lyric poet, Winters believes that the lyric or the short poem is the most viable form for the present age and most congenial to the modern sensibility. Such older genres as the epic and tragedy he considers unsuited to our age.

One of the weakest and most troublesome features of Winters' theory of criticism is the "final and unique" act of judgment, or evaluation, an act somehow related to absolute values and taking into account both the poet's mastery of technique and the quality of the moral truth to which the poem lays claim. If two poems demonstrate an equal mastery of technique, one is to be evaluated more highly than the other according to the magnitude of the moral problem or truth which it encompasses. Winters has said, "We regard as greatest those works which deal with experiences which affect human life most profoundly, and this criterion is not merely one of the intensity of the experience but of the generality or inclusiveness of the implications."

Winters' own standards of evaluation are not always clear, although he has attempted to illustrate his methods by comparing Racine's *Phèdre* and Shakespeare's *Macbeth*. Winters judges *Macbeth* the greater play because of the complexity of the hero as a moral agent and the larger implications of his sin. In many cases, however, his judgments do not inspire confidence. He has been inclined to excessive enthusiasm for the work of little-known poets whose verse agrees with his theory. One of the most celebrated of his unique acts was his singling out of Mrs. Elizabeth Daryush, the daughter of Robert Bridges, as "the finest British poet since T. Sturge Moore." Whatever the cause of such caprices, many of Winters' judgments have at least the virtue of revealing the hazards if not the futility of deliberately evaluative criticism.

Winters has often concentrated his censure on obscurantism and moral confusion as related phenomena. The chief example is *Maule's Curse: Seven Studies in the History of American Obscurantism.* In the essay which sets the key for the volume, Winters treats Hawthorne as an heir to the Puritan tradition of allegory and as a victim of confusion because he was cut off from his Puritan moral heritage. The plight of Hawthorne and his contemporaries was intensified by the anti-intellectualism and amoralism of the romantic tradition, reaching its crisis in Poe, who denied truth to poetry altogether and attempted to render states of pure feeling. The Puritan-romantic dissociated consciousness was transmitted to the twentieth century through such writers as Henry James and Henry Adams.

In a more recent essay, "Robert Frost, or the Spiritual Drifter as Poet" (1948), Winters sees Frost as an Emersonian romantic who believes in "the rightness of impulse" but who is without the pantheistic faith that sanctions impulse. The poem "The Road Not Taken," which seems to deny any moral or rational basis for choice, is the expression of a "spiritual drifter," who, because of his air of kindliness and wisdom, is actually a menace to "the general intelligence." In spite of Frost's serious defect in point of view, Winters acknowledges that many of his shorter lyrics, like "The Last Mowing" and "Spring Pools," are beautiful and effective poems.

Although Winters' criticism is sometimes keen, his view is too often a narrow one which fails to note compensating excellences and complexities that lie outside the scope of his interests. This deficiency is most apparent in the treatment of writers like Hawthorne and James. There is not a confusion of moral values in Hawthorne, but a controlled conflict developed in a manner quite distinct from that of simple allegory. The fiction of Henry James, despite its impressionistic surface, gives a much fuller sense of the grounding of moral problems in society than Winters recognizes.

Winters has been more generous in the attention paid to fellow critics than in his judgment of them. Of Eliot and Ransom, about whom he has written most, he has said, "They think as badly as possible, and it is curious that men of so much talent should think so badly, as it is likewise curious that they should so often impose their thought on other men of talent." Both Allen Tate and R. P. Blackmur he has treated only incidentally, explaining that "there is nothing in their thought which is not to be found in Eliot and Ransom." Winters has described Blackmur as a relativist unwilling to commit himself to any principles, but he admits that this opinion may be unjust to Blackmur, "for he has neglected the arts of syntax and organization to the point that it is almost impossible to understand him."

Cleanth Brooks's theory of irony as a principle of structure is faulty because it does not permit a fair estimate of work in which irony is not a dominant feature and because it blinds the critic to other defects in works which possess the qualities of irony and paradox. The chief weakness of Brooks's theory is the inadequacy of his one principle of structure as a standard for evaluation, to Winters "the primary function of criticism."

Winters' most extensive discussion is reserved for the theory of Ransom. "John Crowe Ransom, or Thunder Without God" (1943) considers Ransom's nominalist hatred of abstractions and his assertion that the essential feature of poetic language is its concreteness. Against this view, Winters argues that language is, after all, an abstraction, that words are "both conceptual and evocative, denotative and connotative, and that the feeling, evocation, or connotation is directly the result of the concept and dependent upon the concept for its existence." A poem about a tree does not present the tree in its concreteness but presents through words abstractions from the experience of a tree—its greenness, roughness, motion—which are evocative of feelings and values. Winters sees Ransom's theory as based on the idea of art as imitation of an object for its own sake. He points out, however, that this is not true to the nature of the poetic process, for it is concerned not so much with the object, which Ransom professes to love, as with the necessary evaluation of the object. Shakespeare presented Iago as he did not "because he loved him so sentimentally that he wished to render him in all his aspects" but in order to evaluate his actions.

Winters recognizes the anti-intellectual motive of Ransom's structure-texture distinction, by which the rational content of the poem is limited to a core about which the "irrelevant" texture is clustered. To Winters the rational content is not "a *core* to which irrelevancies are attached in a kind of nimbus; it is something which exists from moment to moment, in every word of the poem, just as does the feeling, and the value of the poem resides precisely in the relationship between these two elements, and not in qualities supposedly attaching to one of the partners in the relationship." Winters does not, however, think of the rational, emotive, and moral qualities of a poem as a rigid stratification or as separable elements any one of which can be isolated from the others. In *Primitivism and Decadence* he describes the poem as an "almost fluid complex, of relationships between words . . . involving rational content, cadences, rhymes, juxtapositions, literary and other connotations, inversions, and so on. . . . They partake of the fluidity and unpredictability of experience and so provide a means of treating experience with precision and freedom."

Despite its bias and eccentricity, Winters' criticism is extremely valuable as a foil and a corrective to the theory and practice of the critics with whom he has identified himself. He has indeed been a stout defender of reason in a period in which that faculty has been much traduced by many of the most respected and influential critic-teachers in American universities. To champion the intellectual and moral relevance of literature against such opposition has been a courageous action and one in which Winters has enjoyed slight aid and comfort.

Besides these virtues, Winters' work reflects a certain rigidity of mind that may help to explain his lack of a larger following. Despite his rationalism, he shares many of the attitudes of the traditionalist New Critics. He is as much an absolutist as Tate, although on less orthodox grounds. His advocacy of reason and moral values would be more cogent if he recognized that these are permanent but necessarily relative aspects of literary form.

Because of Winters' hostility to the theory of his fellow critics, it is not to be expected that he would make much use of their terminology. Nor has he developed other critical terms that have passed into current usage in the way that *irony, paradox,* and *texture* have. His early study of experimental poetry, *Primitivism and Decadence* (1937), introduces several terms for categorizing structural techniques. One of these, *pseudo-reference,* applies to a device by which the poet retains the "syntactic forms and much of the vocabulary of rational coherence" without any corresponding basis of coherent meaning in the poem. To designate two other structural methods, *repetition* and *qualitative progression*, Winters borrows and adapts from Burke's definition of the five aspects of form in *Counter-Statement* (1931).

7

Often cited as the model of the practicing New Critic, Richard Palmer Blackmur has devoted himself to the language of literature in an effort to understand and elucidate its effects. Unlike the critics with whom he is grouped, Blackmur has expressed a distaste for dogma and the doctrinaire mind. He thinks of himself as a relativist and an imaginative skeptic, and he admires "the early Plato and the whole Montaigne" as exemplars of undoctrinated thinking. A traditionalist in many of his attitudes, concerned about the lack of order in contemporary culture, he shares with Yvor Winters and most of the New Critics a preference for conventional poetic form, although he has on occasion appreciatively discussed the metrics of free verse.

While Ransom, Tate, and Brooks are Southerners—and Yvor Winters a Midwesterner who has long lived in California—Blackmur is a native of Massachusetts whose traditions are those of Harvard and New England. His ties with this past can be seen in his feeling of kinship for Henry Adams as an artist, a man of cultivation, and a skeptic.

The Hound and Horn (1927-34), a literary magazine that originated in Cambridge as "a Harvard Miscellany" and later moved to New York, provided an outlet for Blackmur's early work. Disclaiming a commitment to any special interest or dogma, the editors avowed that their standard of judgment was "technical." Blackmur was an editor (in

1929) and a contributor of poems and numerous reviews and essays. Other critics associated with the magazine included Kenneth Burke, T. S. Eliot, Francis Fergusson, Allen Tate, and Yvor Winters. After *The Hound and Horn* expired, in the depth of the depression, much of Blackmur's criticism appeared in *The Southern Review,* edited by Cleanth Brooks and R. P. Warren; *The Kenyon Review,* edited by J. C. Ransom; and the revived *Sewanee Review,* edited for some years by Allen Tate.

Blackmur's first collection, *The Double Agent: Essays in Craft and Elucidation* (1935), contained "The Critic's Job of Work," in which criticism is defined as an art, interdependent with the other arts, rather than a science. It is "the formal discourse of an amateur" which may deal with literature from any of a number of relative points of view. It is Blackmur's opinion that "any rational approach is valid to literature and may properly be called critical which fastens at any point upon the work itself." This disarmingly simple statement contains two terms, "rational approach" and "the work itself," that point to complicated questions in Blackmur's theory and practice.

Blackmur defines his approach as "primarily through the technique, in the widest sense of that word, of the examples handled; technique on the plane of words and even on linguistics in Mr. Richards' sense, but also technique on the plane of intellectual and emotional patterns in Mr. Burke's sense, and technique, too, in that there is a technique of securing and arranging and representing a fundamental view of life." The advantage of the "technical approach" is twofold: it is hospitable to other approaches and even "anxious to be complemented by them," and "it treats of nothing in literature except in its capacity of reduction to literary fact."

In this latter aspect it resembles traditional scholarship, except that it is closer to the heart of literature.

"Literary fact," like "the work itself," is a deceptive term. Blackmur admits that the *facts* of literature are not simple or easy to get at. Getting at them involves an apprehension of values which cannot even be said to be wholly logical, since the complexes of meaning and value evoked by language lie at deep levels. They can be explored through the adventures of the intuition in the preconscious, where swells "the living, expanding, *prescient* substance without the tags and handles of conscious form." The object of criticism is "the establishment and evaluation (comparison and contrast) of the modes of making the preconscious *consciously* available."

The use of psychological terms and concepts is not typical of Blackmur. But the preconscious need not be stressed, he feels, once it is recognized. The mind of the critic will operate on its own level, presumably a conscious one, "only a little sensitive to the tap roots below." Here the mind maintains an "attitude of provisional skepticism," where it scrutinizes and scrutinizes until the "inscrutable divination" is revealed, and where, finally, the critic stops with all the "facts" he can muster, having "indicated, surrounded, detached, somehow found the way demonstrably to get at, in pretty conscious terms which others may use," the substance of his case.

Blackmur's language in this passage is tentative and elaborately qualified, but appropriate to its subject. It is as though the covert values of literature, which exist in a subliminal realm, can be approached only indirectly and caught half-unaware by a technique through which the critic exploits the suggestive and almost incantatory resources of his own language. This style, Jamesian in its syntactic elaboration and qualification, has been criticized as obscurantist and even, by Winters, unintelligible. But such is hardly the case. Blackmur's style is the expression of a mind different from Winters': it is less rationalistic, and, while it is preoccupied with the problem of order, it is sensitive to the creative potential and fecundity of the irrational and the unconscious.

The language of Blackmur's criticism *is* intelligible—more so when he is confronting a literary work than when he is theorizing—and his essays are usually well organized on principles derived from a reading of the work und a consideration of the circumstances of its origin. Ample evidence appears in the essays of the 1930's, when Blackmur was a practicing New Critic before that term had come into use. "The Later Poetry of W. B. Yeats" (1936) explains Yeats's interest in magic as a provisional "imaginative faith" and interprets his poems in relation to his system of thought. Before discussing the earlier *Cantos* in "Masks of Ezra Pound" (1933), Blackmur considers two finished works, *Mauberley* and *Homage to Sextus Propertius,* one an "original" work and the other a translation, as points of departure and reference. He observes that the idiomatic translation, which takes the original Latin poem as its subject, is a better modern poem than *Mauberley,* in which Pound exercises his craft with a less coherent and substantial subject. Deciding that Pound is an accomplished poet without a real subject, Blackmur examines the *Cantos,* finding their narrative structure to be disconnected and anecdotal, whether the subject of the anecdote be contemporary experience or earlier history or literature. Although Pound demonstrates his skill within these limits, in individual passages of beauty, Blackmur concludes that the reader is cheated of the ordered narrative structure which he had been led to expect and thwarted by an anecdotal allusiveness to unexplained events outside the poem.

Blackmur's reading of Pound, like most of his other reading, is sensitive and acute, and his comments on the excellence of Pound's translations are discriminating. The only dubious feature of his analysis is his unquestioning use of the idea of a conventional narrative structure as a criterion for the *Cantos,* ignoring the possibility that discontinuity and references to events outside the poem may be necessary features of the open form considered appropriate to modern poetry by Pound and other experimental poets.

Two essays giving scope to Blackmur's flair for the detailed analysis of poetic language, the hallmark of his criticism, are those on Wallace Stevens and E. E. Cummings. In "Examples of Wallace Stevens" (1931), Blackmur explores the meanings and associations of words like *funest, fubbed,* and *girandoles* and finds Stevens' language not simply ornamental, as some readers have considered it, but precise in its poetic context even though it may sometimes seem to be elegantly nonsensical. The control lies, it seems, in the poet's mastery of rhetoric, "language used for its own sake," yet having an unusual "content of concrete experience." After considering, as foils, examples of the poetry of Eliot and Pound, Blackmur defines Stevens' distinctive manner as a "non-dramatic, meditative style" formally dependent on rhetoric.

The better-known "Notes on E. E. Cummings' Language" (1930) also undertakes a close examination of usage. But while Stevens is redeemed from nonsense by the concreteness of his language, Cummings is damned because the meanings of words like *flower, thrilling,* and *fragile* are private and abstract. The cause is Cummings' romantic egoism, and the result is not poetry but a sentimental expression of subjective feelings. Blackmur asserts, as a principle of poetic language, that "when a word is used in a poem it *should be* the sum of all its appropriate history made concrete and particular in the individual context." (Italics added.) This standard, or law, of language is supported by a distinction between poetry as the "communication" of abstract ideas, a view that Blackmur rejects, and poetry "as expression, as statement, as presentation of experience," with emphasis on "what is made known concretely." Cummings' poetry is finally condemned for unintelligibility and meaninglessness on the grounds that "true meaning (which is here to say knowledge) can exist only where some contact is preserved between the language, forms, or symbols in which it is given and something concrete, individual or sensual which inspired it; and the degree in which the meaning is seized will depend on the degree in which the particular concreteness is realized."

Many of Blackmur's comments on Cummings' poems are sound, and many readers share his feelings about their romantic egoism, anti-intellectualism, and sentimentality. The basis of his judgment is suspect, however, and a case for Cummings can be made if Blackmur's assumptions are challenged. Although a professed relativist and skeptic, he has accepted absolutely the ideas of his generation about poetic language. Despite his disavowals of dogmatism, his insistence upon the concreteness of poetic language sounds very much like Ransom's opposition of the aesthetic icon to the semantic symbol. But the language of poetry is necessarily more or less abstract, as Winters has pointed out, and to insist on sensuous particularity or concreteness is to deny the use of generalized imagery or the possibility of a poetry of statement. Cummings is a romantic for whom the basic reality behind the shifting phenomena of the world is the sensual life-force personified as "Spring." Given his point of view, which is in many ways like that of the romantic nature-mystic, it is not surprising that his imagery of the physical world should be generalized. For the critic to be prescriptive about the nature of poetic language or poetic structure is to foreclose the possibilities of new modes of expression.

A later statement of Blackmur's idea of the nature of criticism is provided by "A Burden for Critics" (1948), reprinted in *The Lion and the Honeycomb: Essays in Solicitude and Critique* (1955). Blackmur begins by playing on the word *burden,* as something that the critic carries and also that carries him along, the burden of his momentum. In one sense the burden is the raw forces of reality "which operate in the arts" and which "are greater than ourselves and come from beyond and under ourselves." This reality, this primal force, is more inscrutable and mysterious than the preconscious realm of art discussed at the end of "A Critic's Job of Work." Although Blackmur does not describe it as supernatural or divine, one feels in the presence of a mystery—of that from which everything that we are has come. The psychological viewpoint of the earlier essay has given way to an attitude that more closely resembles the mystical.

The burden that the critic bears is also the burden of the writer, who in a modern society in which traditions are largely submerged has almost complete responsibility for "the whole job of culture." In this world, in which there is an "attrition of law and rational wisdom and general craft," it is the burden of the critic to "make bridges between the society and the arts: to prepare the audience for its art and to prepare the arts for their artists."

This function has not been performed by the "New Criticism," as defined by J. C. Ransom. What is needed in a world in which the culture has broken down is a reintegration of values and a judgment of the culture (Arnold is recalled) that can be achieved only through an enlarged critical aesthetic and an instruction of the public in "the lost skill of symbolic thinking." To achieve this end, criticism needs first to get rid of the contributions to aesthetics of both the sciences and the social sciences and turn to the techniques of literature itself. Blackmur suggests provisionally that "for the literary critic aesthetics comprises the study of superficial and mechanical executive techniques, partly in themselves but also and mainly in relation to the ulterior techniques of conceptual form and of symbolic form."

By symbolic techniques Blackmur means "what gets into the arts" in terms of the "invokable forces" of reality and of the cultural values bound up with them. Thus, through a judgment of the techniques of art, criticism would produce "a sequence of rational critical judgments upon the art of our time as an aid in determining the identity, the meaning in itself, of present society." "What I want to evangelize in the arts is rational intent, rational statement, and rational technique, and I want to do it through technical judgment, clarifying judgment, and the judgment of discovery, which together I call rational judgment."

In contrast to the position outlined in "The Critic's Job of Work," this statement is distinguished by its concern for culture and its emphasis on reason. The social responsibility of the writer and critic is stressed in a number of essays occasioned by Blackmur's travels to Europe and the Middle East in the early 1950's. "Toward a Modus Vivendi" (1954) discusses the cultural leveling which has resulted from the spread of universal education of an elementary order in countries undergoing rapid industrial development. This development has introduced a "New Illiteracy" in culture, Blackmur feels. He recommends a utilization of the remnants of the old elite to maintain a continuity of cultural values. His fear of deculturization helps to explain his desire to broaden the social base of criticism and to restore through an aesthetic mode "the lost skill of symbolic thinking."

The concept of reason in "A Burden for Critics" is more difficult to understand. The broadness of Blackmur's usage, which seems to take in everything involved in the whole "rationale" of art, suggests that he is using *reason* almost as a synonym for *form.* However, since the forces of reality that are beyond reason express themselves through symbolic forms, it may be that the word has for him something of the aura of the "higher reason" of the romantic transcendentalist. It is hard to know.

The problem is intensified rather than eased by a more recent essay, "Between the Numen and the Moha, Notes toward a Theory of Literature" (1954), collected in *The Lion and the Honeycomb.* Here Blackmur is concerned with the relation of literature to morals and of criticism to moral philosophy, although the subject is not technically treated. Criticism, which depends upon the exercise of reason, tends to become "unconscious" and "crowded with intuition" in the presence of literature. It is then the business of moral philosophy to bring "back across the threshold of consciousness, back into the story of the whole mind, the reflective power that had thickened into habit." Blackmur's conception of "rational art" is represented by a mandala-like chart or diagram in the form of a square. At the center are the twinned pair of the Numen and the Moha. The *Numen,* or *numinosus,* is aspiration or that power within that moves us. The *Moha* (a Sanskrit word for cow) represents our animal behavior and will. At the four corners of the chart are philosophy (including science), lore, myth, and poetry—all attracted by each other and all attracted and repelled and related by the Numen and the Moha in the center. Between these two stands reason, "either as art or as the reflective faculty—acknowledging, ministering to, and representing both in the names of memory and hope. Reason is in this sense the whole mind, the residual form of all we have been, and the conceiving matrix of all that we may become. Reason is a servant, the housekeeper who keeps things going by criticism, by philosophy, by art."

But the companion of poetry is "the grand, heaving figure of the unconscious," and criticism itself tends to be unconscious until it is reclaimed by moral philosophy. The presence of the unconscious and the irrational in art makes for a dynamic freedom and variability as we see in literature the possibility of ever-renewed forms of order. Although the relation of the unconscious to literary form is interestingly developed, I must admit that after reading "Between the Numen and the Moha" I do not clearly understand what Blackmur means by "rational" art or criticism. The essay, which is more qualified and elaborated than this brief summary indicates, is really a kind of prose poem, rather than an exposition. Within the poem, the figures of the Numen and the Moha and the four-sided chart function as an elaborate metaphor without, however, any firm basis in common experience. If we were to judge this poem by Blackmur's own standard, we would have to damn it for its abstractness, its lack of contact with something "concrete, individual or sensual." This poetic technique can be productive of effective criticism when it is brought to bear upon a literary work and avails itself of its resources. It is less effective when it is exercised in the interests of theory. A virtue of most of Blackmur's practical criticism, in contrast to that of some of the other New Critics, is that the principles upon which an essay is organized are usually drawn from a disinterested view of the subject rather than from an a priori theory.

Blackmur's dissatisfactions with the limitations and the rhetorical preoccupations of the movement with which he is associated have been expressed on several occasions. In "The Lion and the Honeycomb" (1950), collected in the book of the same title, Blackmur speaks of the need of a more complete criticism which will combine the poetical, the dialectical, and the rhetorical modes of understanding. The "sacred books" upon which this fuller criticism could be based would include not only Coleridge, the spiritual father of the New Critics, but also Aristotle, whom they have slighted. The two are complementary and should be brought together, Blackmur feels. The heart of Coleridge's contribution lies in three words, all of which relate to the contextual function of language. They are *esemplastic,* "which means forming, shaping at a rhetorical level"; *coadunative,* "which means having to do with the union of dissimilar substances, at a dialectical level"; and *synergical,* "which means having to do with working together, operative action where the total effect is greater than the sum of the effects taken separately, and all this done, of course, at the level of poetics." In Aristotle, Blackmur is especially concerned with the meaning of six terms: "*Praxis,* or action; *Mimesis,* or the imitation of action;

Mythos, or plot, which is the soul of the work; *Ethos,* or the operation of character; *Pathos,* or the tragic incident through which action is felt; *Katharsis,* or the purging, cleansing, purifying of the *mythos* subject to *mimesis.*"

Of these, *mimesis,* or imitation, is central because in it the three functions of poetic, rhetoric, and dialectic are commingled. It supplies the bridge to reality, and to culture, that Blackmur seeks and that most contexualist New Critics will not acknowledge. Blackmur speaks of the mimetic act as "the incarnation into actuality of what we can grasp of reality." This sentiment is not opposed to the idea of the relation of art to reality held by most of the New Critics. But the principle is. The contextualist would say that art gives access to reality, not through imitation but through the work as a symbolic whole or icon.

In contemplating these key terms for a more complete criticism, the reader may be struck by the fact that with one possible exception (*synergical*) they are words that Blackmur himself has rarely used in his own criticism. He is in his element when he is working with the interplay and manifold meaning of words in their poetic context, where they act upon each other in ways that he has delighted in making clear. In this process he has incidentally but not habitually made use of rhetorical terms, but he has contributed little to the working vocabulary of the New Criticism. In *A Glossary of the New Criticism* (1949), prepared by William Elton, Blackmur's name appears in discussions of only four of 114 entries. These are *symbolic action,* which Blackmur has accepted and used, with acknowledgment to Kenneth Burke; *expressive form,* which he applies to Lawrence and which Yvor Winters also uses; *trope,* a rhetorical term which he distinguishes from *image* in "Notes on Four Categories in Criticism" (1946); and *sensibility,* a favorite word that represents the poetic mind's faculty of imposing a qualitative subjective order on experience and also that mind's resistance to rigidly limited categorical thinking.

Nor has Blackmur accepted to any extent the vocabulary of his colleagues, possibly because it represents a limited view of poetry. He has described the theory of Brooks as a "rhetoric of Irony and Paradox, with subtypes of Ambiguity, Attitude, Tone, and Belief." While recognizing that irony is a necessary feature of much modern poetry in the "school of Donne," for which he has no great enthusiasm, Blackmur has observed that paradox and irony are "forms of arrogance and self-distrust." He is at odds with other aspects of the New Criticism. He does not share Ransom's "ontological" preoccupations, and—although he has made some dogmatic statements about the nature of poetic language, as in his essay on Cummings—he has not devoted himself, as have Ransom, Brooks, and Tate, to establishing distinctions between the language of poetry and the language of science. He has on the contrary said that "literature is the bearer . . . of all the modes of understanding of which *words* are capable." Blackmur distrusts the current emphasis on unity and wholeness, recognizing that each reading of a work is a new experience of form. Unity he prizes as an essential ordering principle, but to him unity is necessarily provisional. In discussing Pound's *Mauberley,* he remarks that "wholeness, preconceived, is a prison into which the mind is not compelled to thrust itself."

8

Although collectively the New Critics have probably contributed more terms to the language of criticism than any other group, they have also helped to confuse it. This confusion inspired, among numerous reactions, William Elton's *Glossary of the New Criticism* (1949). Since no attempt had been made to define the language of the New Criticism, Elton discussed many of the key terms against the background of the theories of individual critics. His hope was to prepare the way for "an accepted critical vocabulary and a more orderly approach to the problems of poetic criticism." Although opponents of the New Criticism seized upon it as evidence of hopeless confusion within the enemy camp, the *Glossary* helps to clarify meanings as well as to reveal confusion.

It is not necessary to consult the *Glossary* to understand some of the sources of confusion. One is that any kind of uniformity of terminology is lacking. Even among critics whose idea of the nature of poetry and of poetic language is much the same, there is a tendency for each to develop his own specialized vocabulary, rather than to pool terms and ideas. Furthermore, because many of the terms have been developed to support a biased and limited theory, they often have no reference to the experience of literature and no meaning except in relation to the theory they are intended to serve, a natural result of theory based on apologetics rather than disinterested inquiry. Examples include Ransom's *ontology* and *texture,* Tate's *complete knowledge* (a self-contradictory expression), and such terms as *absolute* or *total form.*

It is not surprising that a limited and prescriptive aesthetic should also be sensitive to "heresies" and zealous to outlaw ideas in conflict with its special views. Terms of disapprobation coined by the New Critics or by critics influenced by them include *heresy of paraphrase, intentional fallacy,* and *affective fallacy.* They are reminiscent of an earlier defender of pure poetry who buttressed his position by the same tactics and who contributed terms like *epic mania* and *heresy of the didactic* to the criticism of his time. "Our Cousin, Mr. Poe," as Allen Tate calls him, is akin to the New Critics in more ways than Tate allows for in his essay.

The problem of language has been aggravated by the increasing tendency of critics, since Richards' *Coleridge on Imagination* (1935), to identify poetry or imaginative literature with myth. To make use of myth—in the form of primitive plot patterns with supernatural associations—as a way of interpreting one aspect of poetic form is often enlightening. But to *equate* poetry with myth is another matter. When Richards subscribed to Coleridge's idea of the poem as the "complete utterance of the whole soul of man," he theoretically severed his lines of communication with anyone interested in the poem as an object of criticism. It is possible to understand Coleridge's statement as the expression of a nineteenth century romantic view of art. But for twentieth century criticism the word *soul* needs definition and translation, while the idea of completeness or wholeness is ruled out both by the necessary abstractness of art and by the limitations of the reader's perception of form. The statement itself is "emotive," in Richards' own terms.

The view of poetry as myth has encouraged the use of a language that can best be described as incantatory rather than analytical, discursive, or even communicative. In practical criticism it has led to a technique by which the critic makes a statement, poetic in its metaphorical density, that conveys the complex idea of the poem, including its affective qualities, derived from the critic's immediate response. When this strategy is used by a critic like Blackmur, who usually maintains a firm contact with the poem and a respect for its integrity, the result can be intensive criticism of a high order, illuminating the distinctive formal characteristics of a poem or novel. When the technique is employed by a critic who accepts the idea of literature *as* myth and who is more concerned for his own theory or private feelings than for the work itself, the criticism is less responsible. And when this manner is carried over from practical criticism to theory the result can be completely meaningless.

The language of incantation can be seen in a discussion of the nature of form by R. P. Warren, who is identified with the New Critics although he has been most active as a writer of verse and fiction. In "Knowledge and the Image of Man" (*Sewanee Review,* 1955), Warren defines the knowledge provided by poetry, in contrast to that of science, as a "knowledge *of* form." After posing the question, "How does the knowledge of form give man an image of himself?" he supplies the answer in these words: "It does so insofar as it gives the image of experience being brought to order and harmony, the image of a dance on the high wire over an abyss. The rhythm is, as it were, a myth of order, or fulfillment, an affirmation that our being may move in its totality toward meaning. The soul faces some potentiality of experience, drawn from actuality, and the form is the flowing vibration of the soul, the abstraction of experience by imagination. The form gives man an image of himself, for it gives him his mode of experiencing, a paradigm of his inner life, his rhythm of destiny, his tonality of fate. And this evocation, confrontation, and definition of our deepest life gives us, in new self-awareness, a yet deeper life to live."

The effect of criticism or theory of this kind, in which terms like *rhythm* and *myth* and *form* and *soul* and *man's image of himself* are interchangeable, is to blur distinctions so thoroughly that no understanding of the ostensible subject is communicated. What is apparent is that the writer is giving expression to his own feelings of tension and exaltation in the presence of literature. What is lacking is any clear indication of the nature of poetry or form.

In short, writing of this kind is impressionistic, and it is an irony of the New Criticism—to use one of its own terms—that it should fall victim, particularly in its theory, to a weakness of nineteenth century criticism that it had originally reacted against.

Yet in spite of the confusion of their language and the narrowness of their theories of knowledge and poetic structure, the New Critics have greatly advanced the interests of literary criticism and the understanding of literary form. The discussion of their work presented in this chapter has focused upon theory and terminology. It has not fully indicated the quality of much of their practical criticism that has been less restricted by theoretical preoccupations. Their sophistication, intelligence, and informed sensibilities are apparent in many excellent and stimulating essays. When achievements are set against limitations, one is impressed by the thought of what the New Criticism might have accomplished with a less hermetic theory. The task of the present is to develop a criticism of form resting upon a theory that fully acknowledges and explores, as the New Critics have not, the social and historical dimensions of literature.

6

THE NEO-ARISTOTELIANS

1—R. S. Crane and the Chicago group; 2—Richard McKeon; 3—Elder Olson; 4—Critiques of the New Critics; 5—W. R. Keast on Johnson's theory; 6—R. S. Crane's analysis of the plot of Tom Jones; *7—R. S. Crane's* The Languages of Criticism and the Structure of Poetry; *8—Summary—the treatment of language and metaphor*

The rhetorical preoccupations of the New Critics and their desire to establish an "ontological" status for poetry that would protect it from the incursions of the physical sciences or other kinds of knowledge provoked reactions from many quarters. Within the university, where the New Criticism had risen to a position of prestige, opposition came primarily from those committed to historical and literary traditions of one kind or another.

I

In 1948, one of the more influential scholar critics declared that recent theoretical efforts to develop an anti-science definition of poetic language had led only to a blind alley. What was needed, he felt, was a "newer" criticism which "will not worry so much about saving poetry—this, after all, has been with us a very long time, and, besides, contains within itself powerful springs of human interest, surely not yet exhausted—but will devote itself to a scholarly and philosophically comprehensive study of poetry calculated to refine our instinctive response to poems by giving us an adequately sensitive critical apparatus for discriminating among them."

The writer was Ronald S. Crane, a leader of the group which came to be known as the neo-Aristotelians, or the Chicago Aristotelians. Like the New Critics, who had recognized him as an early collaborator, Crane had reacted against the dominance of the social and historical emphasis in scholarship and had campaigned vigorously to establish criticism as a recognized discipline. He disapproved of the New Critics, however, because of their neglect of traditional poetics as a basis for their theory and practice. It seemed to Crane that the *Poetics* of Aristotle was the most valuable traditional source upon which modern criticism could draw to develop a badly needed theoretical foundation. During the 1930's he was associated at the University of Chicago with men in the fields of English, philosophy, and romance languages who shared his outlook. He collected essays they wrote during the late Thirties and the Forties into a volume entitled *Critics and Criticism: Ancient and Modern* (1952). The authors of the twenty essays include, in addition to Crane, W. R. Keast, Richard McKeon, Norman Maclean, Elder Olson, and Bernard Weinberg.

Because of its strongly polemic quality the collection is an anti-New Critical symposium, comparable to *The Critique of Humanism* edited by C. H. Grattan in 1930, with the difference that *Critics and Criticism* has a positive as well as a negative function. In the introduction Crane says that he and his colleagues wish to advance the interests not only of literary criticism but of the humanities generally. These studies, he feels, are liable "to lapse from time to time into contentment with simple and easy procedures and a narrow range of questions and distinctions, to substitute rhetoric or sectarian polemic for disinterested inquiry, to break with the past and make new starts by struggling afresh with problems long since solved, or (as in much contemporary linguistics, philosophy, and criticism) to seek renovation, unhumanistically, by assimilating themselves to the sciences of nature and society." The sentiment reveals not only an implicit judgment of the limitations of the New Criticism but also an attitude, shared by the New Critics and the New Humanists, of hostility toward the physical and social sciences.

The function of the Chicago critics should be, in Crane's opinion, to examine current critical principles and investigate the possibilities of "particular methods in the different arts which either have not been developed in the past or have been neglected in modern times." Although the critique is directed primarily against the New Critics, Crane begins with the insistence that any critical statement is relative to the critic's methodological principles, whether stated or not, and that the only reasonable view to take of a field permitting a wide variation of response is one that recognizes a "plurality of distinct critical methods," each "valid or partially valid within its proper sphere." But even from this pluralistic point of view, it is possible to "discriminate between critical systems, no matter how different their foundations, which permit a reasonably many-sided or comprehensive discussion of literary phenomena—i.e., which abound in pertinent and usable distinctions—and other systems, unfortunately more numerous, which content themselves with partial views while pretending to omit nothing essential."

It is on these grounds that the attack upon New Critical

theory is conducted by Crane and his colleagues. As a limited point of view, the New Criticism is not even granted a distinctive modernity, since Crane sees its remote beginnings in "the new critical methods developed in Alexandria and later in Rome after the decline of the philosophic criticism of the classical Greeks," and its more immediate origins in "the profound reorientation of criticism, beginning in the eighteenth century, from an emphasis on poetic genres and their rules (considered usually in rhetorical terms) to an emphasis on common poetic qualities, no matter in what kinds of works they appear." It is therefore not surprising that modern criticism lacks a sufficient theoretical base for considering poetic works as various kinds of artistic wholes. It is also not surprising that the New Critics, thinking of poetry as a kind of discourse, should read all poems as though they had been constructed on the same principles, "confusing . . . mimetic forms with didactic, and treating lyrics and novels, tragedies and essays, by means of the same distinctions."

The remedy can be found in Aristotle, who established a systematic method for dealing with poetic works as "synola, or concrete artistic wholes, and made available, though only in outline sketch, hypotheses and analytical devices for defining literally and inductively, and with a maxiumum degree of differentiation, the multiple causes operative in the construction of poetic wholes of various kinds and the criteria of excellence appropriate to each." Unlike the New Criticism, which is restricted to diction in terms of discoverable "meanings," the method of Aristotle treats the work as a developed whole which can be discussed in relation to its parts and to other kinds of wholes. The poem is not conceived as discourse but as an *imitation* or "representation of humanly significant or moving actions, characters, or thoughts [each of which may be isolated for discussion], to the end of achieving a particular over-all effect, mimetic or didactic."

Of course, the modern critic must recognize that Aristotle's theory, valuable though it is as a foundation, is sketchy and incomplete and needs to be developed further "through extension and refinement of its basic concepts" and supplemented by other approaches that can deal with aspects of poetry for which Aristotelian terminology makes no provision. These would include some of the useful though limited techniques of the New Criticism. It is desirable to have a plurality of critical methods, Crane believes, and to distinguish among them. The advantage of Aristotle's method is that it supplies a controlling point of view and uniform procedures and standards of judgment. The method also supplies, through its genre system, a historical perspective for the individual work lacking in the New Criticism.

2

The most extensive discussion of theory is Richard McKeon's "The Philosophic Bases of Art and Criticism," an essay first published in 1943-44. Like Crane, McKeon recognizes the necessary relativity of any critical approach and recommends the encouragement of a variety of methods. As a philosopher, he stresses the importance of systematic theory not only as a support for the artist and the critic but also as an active influence upon literature: "Even though principles do not achieve finality and universal adherence in philosophy, they do serve to state the purposes of the artist and the criteria of the critic. The shifts of artistic styles, critical evaluations, and philosophic principles illustrate the importance of standards and principles, and the alternations of advocacy of a set of principles and attack upon them do not constitute evidence for those who think to avoid the discussion of principles as stultifying in art, futile in criticism, and fantastic in philosophy."

McKeon's essay is divided into three sections dealing with "the objects of criticism, criticism itself, and the terms of criticism." In the first two parts, in which the treatment is primarily historical, McKeon discusses the changing views of the nature of the art object (as imitation, by Plato and Aristotle; as imagination, by Kant and Bacon; and as operations, by Horace and Tolstoy) and the development of ideas of the function of criticism. The third section, on critical terminology, is more strongly theoretical and presents a classification of six modes of criticism—one "dialectical" and five "literal"—which can be used to order and distinguish the various kinds of aesthetic analysis that have been used in criticism.

"Dialectical" criticism, the largest and most amorphous of these classes, was used first by Plato. Its terms, according to McKeon, reflect the two constant features of the method: "The differentiation of terms in application to subjects and their reduction in the solution of problems." (This is extremely general and not very clear.) There have been shifts in the nature of the art work. In Plato, the method is a "dialectic of things," and his analysis requires "the differentiation of object of imitation (which itself has a quality or value), the imitation (whose value depends on its correctness and the value of its object), and the execution of the imitation (which adds considerations of skill and medium to the previous two criteria)." The most distinctive features of this method, in the eyes of a modern reader, are the apparently objective source of criteria and the very slight attention paid to language as the medium. The first big shift in the nature of the dialectic, corresponding to the development of the idea of art as imagination, was to a "dialectic of knowledge," as represented by the theory of Kant, while the next shift was to a "dialectic of processes and relations," as in the aesthetics of Tolstoy and Dewey. New and changing types of dialectical criticism arise from emerging historical developments. As examples of three modern types of dialectical criticism, McKeon cites Humanist, Marxist, and Tolstoyan criticism as dependent upon cultural, economic, and moral and religious data respectively. The chief weakness and danger of the dialectical method is "a loss of balance consequent on the dogmatic freezing of the dialectic in defense of an unexamined faith." As a result, "the consideration of art or of any other subject may be submerged in other concerns or become itself the ruling principle of other considerations."

There are five literal modes that are more limited and sharply separated from each other and from the dialectical mode. The second (of the six) is Aristotle's "scientific" criticism, which balances Plato's dialectical mode. The third is "poetic" criticism, which proceeds from the conception of the author as a lofty and universal spirit to an examination of the language in which he expresses himself. It takes the ideas and utterances of great authors and uses them as touchstones and standards; Longinus is mentioned as a practitioner in this mode. "Scholarly" criticism, the fourth class, employs a reversed procedure as it "attempts to reconstruct the peculiar character and significance of an author from the corpus and development of his work." It makes use of the devices of the historical sciences to explain and interpret works of art. The fifth mode, "technical" criticism, is, like poetic criticism, concerned with expressive language, not, however, in relation to the poet, but rather to devices which are designed to secure a favorable or sympathetic audience response. The focus is upon style and technique as they relate to a desired effect of decorum; the names of Horace and Boileau are associated with this mode. The sixth and last type is "formal" criticism, which focuses upon the work and analyzes its language in terms of its figures of speech and rhetorical strategies; the semantic analysis of I. A. Richards is an obvious example of the method.

According to McKeon's classification, the New Humanists, the Marxists, and the psychological critics, whether Freudian or Jungian, fall under the dialectical mode. The Chicago critics would presumably come under the second listing as Aristotelian "scientific" critics. The New Critics, as close textual analysts, would be "formal" critics, although their theory might place them with the dialectical critics also. The latter classification would apply to all of the modern groups, including the neo-Aristotelians, to the extent that they are concerned with polemics and an interested advocacy of their special viewpoints.

The categories established by McKeon are not just a device for classifying modes of criticism. They also supply a perspective in which five less exact or more limited types serve as foils to Aristotelian criticism, which is more scientific in that it is concerned with the "work itself" as an artificial rather than an eternal or even natural object. In tragedy, for example, Aristotle provides a model of "scientific" analysis of a whole consisting of six parts: "plot, character, and thought arising from the object, diction and melody arising from the means, and spectacle from the manner of imitation." By observing this classification of parts and by recognizing the first of them, plot, as the primary organizing principle to which the others must be adjusted, the critic achieves a "criterion of unity and structure." Upon this, "the possibility of a poetic science depends, for otherwise the analysis of an object must reduce the diversity of concepts that might be included under Aristotle's six terms to two broad analytic elements—form and matter—and must go for its criteria directly to the intention of the artist, or the reaction of the audience, or the technical achievement of the structure."

If McKeon's argument is considered as the expression of a "scientific" critical attitude, several troubling questions arise. In analyzing tragedy, why is it incumbent upon the modern critic to recognize the six parts—not five or seven—that Aristotle defined after a presumably inductive analysis of the tragedy of his age? Why should not the latter-day critic just as effectively concern himself with the four elements of theme, character, plot, and setting as with the traditional six parts of the *Poetics,* especially since "melody" and "spectacle" have less apparent relevance to the staging of modern nonpoetic tragic drama? Also, why need the only alternative to Aristotle's *six* parts be the *two* elements of form and matter? A formal analysis would not recognize these two as separable, and it might be concerned with any one aspect or combination of aspects of form. As for the source of criteria, a question that deserves more attention, both the intention of the artist and the response of the audience (the latter more than the former) might, together with the technical aspects of form, supply standards as valid as those provided by Aristotle's six-part scheme.

These objections are not meant to suggest that Aristotle does not provide a useful critical method for those who find his poetics congenial. It should be recognized, however, that the method is no more "scientific" and no closer to the "work itself" than other methods. When it is dogmatically presented, it is less scientific. Any critical method, including the neo-Aristotelian, is limited by its theoretical definition and its vocabulary; and in dealing with a literary work it inevitably restricts itself to qualities that are conceptually reducible to its particular terms. This principle applies to the Freudian critic's use of the concept of the "dream symbol," with its overt and covert meanings; to the New Humanist's idea of the "dualism" of human nature as a thematic problem; to the Marxist's dependence upon "class struggle" as an explanation of literary conflict; to the New Critic's concern for "irony" and "paradox" as determinants of form; and to the Aristotelian critic's interest in "plot" and "character" as "parts" of the artistic whole. All of these terms offer valid means of interpreting the form of a literary work, and, as necessarily abstract interpretive devices, no one is closer to the "work itself" than another. It is regrettable that any one group should advance its method as "objective" or "scientific" to the derogation of others, when the most disinterested and scientific procedure, in view of the inexhaustible interest of the literary work, would be to adopt a genuinely pluralistic point of view and to try to develop a theory that would accommodate all modes of criticism without classifying them hierarchically.

3

A briefer essay supporting McKeon's position and offering some further ideas is "An Outline of Poetic Theory" by Elder Olson. Beginning with the observation that criticism in our time is a linguistic and methodological tower of Babel, Olson proceeds to a discussion of the advantages of Aristotle's system as offering a regulating point of view and method. Like McKeon, he recognizes that it is one of a possible plurality of methods and that it has a scientific foundation in Aristotle's scheme of knowledge. He recommends, humanistically, that modern critics build their theory upon the foundations provided by the past.

In applying the principle of Aristotle's part analysis to Yeats's "Sailing to Byzantium" as an example of lyric poetry, Olson omits melody and spectacle, which apply to tragedy alone. For "plot" he substitutes "choice" as the principal part, analogous to the action of tragedy. The poem thus consists of four parts, which are, in the order of their importance, choice, character, thought, and diction. In a note Olson attempts to counter the natural assumption that one should begin with the recognition that poetry is, after all, made of words. He argues that "poetry is not words but verbal," in the sense that the medium is shaped toward a preconceived end; analogously he says that "a chair is not wood but wooden." While acknowledging that diction is important in poetry, he insists that there is a sense in which the words are the least important part because "they are governed and determined by every other element in the poem." Olson does not take account of the fact that such other elements as plot, character, and thought can be determined only in the light of the way in which language is used. His deliberate neglect of language is typical of the modern Aristotelians.

4

Olson's ideas about poetic language are developed further in "William Empson, Contemporary Criticism, and Poetic Diction." Olson attacks Empson's work as an example of the New Criticism's exaggerated interest in language and in irony and ambiguity as structural principles. He denies that ambiguity is the "essence" or even a necessary feature of poetry. Arguing that language is always "merely a medium, a material, never a form," he contends that the ends of poetry are best served by language which is "as concise and clear as possible." Olson's standard has not enjoyed much repute in romantic and modern theory. A felicitous simplicity and clarity are qualities of much excellent poetry that lies outside the "tradition" of the New Critic. But though it may be true that language is, as Olson argues, "merely a medium, a material," form can be perceived only through this medium, the uses of which also determine form.

Olson characterizes Empson as a "tropist" whose method of analysis boils down to a "puzzling" over possible meanings with the aid of the *Oxford English Dictionary* and without respect to limitations imposed by the poem itself. In his preoccupation with the meanings of words, Empson is confining himself to only one part of the poem, and that the least important. At this point, Olson makes the rather incredible statement that, "strictly speaking, a *mimetic* poem, an imitation . . . , has no meaning at all" because "it is a certain kind of product, like a picture, a symphony or a statue; like an ax, a bed, a chair; it has no more meaning *as a poem* than these have."

Olson's motive is clear. He wishes to distinguish between *lexis* and *praxis,* "between speech as meaningful and speech as action," and to subordinate diction to the other formal elements, the "parts," as an antidote to the hyperanalytical dissections of word meanings by the New Critics. But the denial of "meaning" to literature cannot be entertained seriously. Words have meanings, both conceptual and emotive, and language is an instrument for the communication of meaning. Poetry and imaginative literature are language products. Literature necessarily communicates meanings both in relation to the events of a work (as in its plot) and in relation to events in the reader's experience. It is no more justifiable for the Aristotelian to limit the sphere of poetic language to the actions of a poem, to the exclusion of other meanings, than it is for the New Critic to limit the meanings of poetic language to the context of the work, to the exclusion of external references.

The essay on Empson is one of five in *Critics and Criticism* that concentrate on the limitations and defects of the practice of individual contemporary critics. "A Symbolic Reading of the *Ancient Mariner,*" also by Olson, attacks R. P. Warren's introductory essay to a 1946 edition of Coleridge's poem. Another hostile essay is W. R. Keast's "The 'New Criticism' and *King Lear,*" which discusses R. B. Heilman's *This Great Stage: Image and Structure in "King Lear"* (1948) and concludes that an intensive analysis of symbolic "meaning" has had the effect of reducing a great and complex drama to a few commonplace and trivial platitudes. R. S. Crane's rather early (1939) essay on I. A. Richards is concerned with the limitations of Richards' earlier theory and concludes that Richards had nothing to offer but a universal method for the reading of indiscriminate texts.

A later essay by Crane—"The Critical Monism of Cleanth Brooks" (1948), which first appeared in *Modern Philology*—is one of the most systematic and effective of several refutations of Brooks's theory. Crane goes to Brooks's acknowledged authority, the *Biographia Literaria,* to show that Brooks distorted Coleridge's theory, particularly his distinction between "poetry" and "poems." While poetry manifests the synthesizing power of the creative imagination, which reveals itself in "the balance or reconciliation of opposite or discordant qualities," Coleridge acknowledged that this power animates not only the poetic, but the philosophic (and presumably the scientific) genius as well. For Coleridge not "poetry" but the "poem" is opposed to works of science "by proposing for its *immediate* object pleasure, not truth; and from all other species (having *this* object in common with it) it is discriminated by proposing to itself such delight from the *whole,* as is compatible with a distinct gratification from each component *part.*" Ignoring Coleridge's distinction between "poetry" and the "poem" and his extension of the principle of the synthesizing imagination to science, Brooks applied the term *irony* to the poetic reconciliation of opposites and proclaimed it a distinguishing feature of poetic language that set it off against the language of science.

Poetic language cannot be differentiated in this way without false assumptions. Crane points out that in scientific statements, as in any other, words are modified and changed by the "pressure of the context" (Brooks's explanation of the way in which poetic words are ironically loaded). The syntheses of science reveal the same qualities as poetic syntheses. As for the reconciliation of opposites, Crane refers to the formula through which Einstein unified "the hitherto 'discordant' qualities of mass and energy." Observing Brooks's criteria for poetic structure, Crane offers the equation $E = mc^2$ as "the greatest 'ironical' poem written so far in the twentieth century."

Crane recognizes that one of the motives of Brooks and other critics like Richards and Ransom, who wish to establish differentiae for poetic language, is a "morbid obsession with the problem of justifying and preserving poetry in an age of science." But this kind of theory has led only to a dead end. What is needed is a newer criticism that will place the work in a larger perspective, preferably Aristotelian, and substitute an a posteriori for an a priori approach.

5

Some of the essays dealing with the criticism of the past treat the historical development and modification of Aristotle's ideas from the classical period through the renaissance. One, however, on the leading figure of eighteenth century literature, has no direct reference to Aristotle although it does have implications for both the New Criticism and neo-Aristotelian criticism. In "The Theoretical Foundations of Johnson's Criticism," W. R. Keast points out, by reference largely to the *Rambler* papers and the *Preface to Shakespeare,* that a consistent theoretical position underlies the critical opinions of Samuel Johnson, even though he has been most favorably regarded by many modern scholars for his lack of systematic principles and his distrust of general theory. Keast quotes from the *Rambler* Johnson's opinion that it is "the task of criticism to establish principles; to improve opinion into knowledge" and that criticism "reduces those regions of literature under the dominion of science, which have hitherto known only the anarchy of ignorance, the caprices of fancy, and the tyranny of prescription." Johnson expressed contempt for the free-floating sensibilities of impressionistic aesthetic critics: "The ambition of superior sensibility and superior eloquence disposes the lovers of arts to receive rapture at one time and communicate it at another; and each labours first to impose upon himself, and then to propagate the imposture."

Johnson is often regarded as an opponent of theory because he was an enemy of accepted dogmas and sought to free literature from prescriptive criticism. His method subverted established rules, such as that comedy must deal with low characters. In each case he would challenge the dictum and argue that other devices might just as well serve the desired end. In this way he resisted the idea of traditional literary genres, feeling that most of the distinctions relating to them were artificial and meaningless. The critics of pastoral had "entangled themselves with unnecessary difficulties by advancing principles, which, having no foundation in the nature of things, are to be wholly rejected from a species of composition, in which, above all others, mere nature is to be regarded." Johnson's concern for nature as a basis of criticism applied not only to pastoral, but to literature in general. For this reason he distrusted traditional terms, drawing his own from the characteristics of the work itself, the nature of the subject represented, and the particular qualities of the author.

Johnson saw literature, in Keast's words, "as a natural process, set in the context of other natural processes such as social behavior, and thus amenable to treatment in relation to its psychological causes and effects, its natural materials, and its circumstantial determinants." Literature was not "prescribed and limited" for Johnson. The poem or literary work he considered "inconstant" and "an object so mutable that it is always changing under our eye, and has already lost its form while we are labouring to conceive it." Aspects of literary form are thus shifting and relative, and the test of excellence lies in the response of readers over an extended period. Human nature, though variable and often unpredictable, is a constant, and the standard of judgment for literature, as for all human activities, must be found in "the general sense or experience of mankind." To Johnson, mankind meant the "common reader," for whose "pleasure and instruction" the work of literature was intended. He was not interested in a literary elite or an aristocracy of taste, but looked rather to what he called "the common voice of the multitude, uninstructed by precept, and unprejudiced by authority."

With this view of human nature, Johnson was opposed to the idea of genius as the distinguishable trait of a privileged few—the conception that was soon to be seized upon and magnified by the romantics. He also thought that both religion and mythology were poor subjects for poetry because neither is "level with common life."

Johnson's characteristic approach to literature, which Keast calls his "circumstantial method," appears in the *Preface to Shakespeare* and, more fully, in the *Lives of the Poets,* in which "external circumstances, the intellectual character of the writer, and the qualities of his works are successively treated" and through which the work is placed in a social and biographical perspective.

Most of Johnson's principles conflict with those of the later New Criticism: his idea of a shifting variable form, his opposition to religion and myth as literary subjects, and his reliance on biographical and historical information. But his opinions also run counter to neo-Aristotelian criticism in certain respects, particularly in his attitude toward the genres and proper terminology. It is surprising how many of Johnson's theoretical principles have relevance for contemporary criticism. His idea of relative form and his empirical approach suggest possibilities for broadening critical theory to accommodate more points of view. His concern for the common reader is a reminder of the need for a fuller recognition of the social base of criticism.

6

The third and final section of *Critics and Criticism,* devoted primarily to problems of theory, includes two essays in which the neo-Aristotelians apply their methods to practical criticism. One is Norman Maclean's "Episode, Scene, Speech, and Word: The Madness of Lear." The other is R. S. Crane's "The Concept of Plot and the Plot of *Tom Jones.*" Both attempt "part-whole" analyses in terms of Aristotle's theory. Maclean discusses the way in which the qualities of *Lear* as a poetic whole are represented in such constituent units as episodes, scenes, speeches, and individual phrases and words. Crane attempts to establish a concept of plot as the most important and inclusive of the parts of a work. He rejects the idea of plot as a skeletal framework of actions in favor of the idea of an architectonic unifying device. He defines the plot of a novel or drama as "the particular temporal synthesis effected by the writer of the elements of action, character, and thought that constitute the matter of his invention," a synthesis which accommodates ethical qualities and emotions, as well as actions and thought.

Using this broad concept of plot as a key, Crane turns to the text of *Tom Jones* and interprets its events, finding the unity of the complex plot to consist in nothing less than its "total system of actions, moving by probable or necessary connections from beginning, through middle, to end." Although the events of the plot are interrelated, they do not constitute an absolutely unified whole. Taking note of such faults as *longueurs* and inconsistencies of tone, Crane observes that "there are no perfect works of art." After analyzing the events of the novel and the relationships of its characters, he acknowledges that his discussion has not done full justice to the subject of plot and that there are many other aspects (functions of minor characters, moral quality of the "world" of the novel, supporting functions of diction and imagery) that might have been considered.

Crane's interpretation is quite detailed, within the limits permitted by his essay. If it were not for his whole-and-part framework, it would almost seem as though he were conducting a New Critical textual analysis, particularly since his concept of plot is so broad as to suggest the idea of the work as a "contextual whole." At least, there are no elements which he excludes from the plot.

7

Besides *Critics and Criticism,* which has been reprinted in an abridged paperback edition (1957), the most important work produced by the neo-Aristotelian movement is R. S. Crane's *The Languages of Criticism and the Structure of Poetry* (1953), a revised version of lectures given at the University of Toronto. In a closely reasoned and persuasive argument, Crane considers the multiplicity of critical languages and the advantages of an Aristotelian vocabulary and theory of poetic structure over those of other groups, especially the New Critics.

In keeping with his view of the New Criticism as *semantic,* Crane points out that most of its key terms relate in one way or another to the problem of meaning. These include *theme, statement, evocation, vision, total meaning, tension, attitude, denotation, connotation, ambiguity, metaphor, paradox, irony, symbol,* and *myth.* (Most of these, however, relate not simply to the problem of meaning, but also to the ideas of structure developed by the New Critics.) Another limitation of New Critical procedure is its use of "reduction terms" geared to its idea of structure as the balance of opposing elements. The variability and complexity of literature are often sacrificed to the isolation, through the analysis of symbolic imagery, of a set of relatively simple polarities like good and evil, love and hate, light and dark, chaos and order. The procedure, Crane observes, can be extended almost indefinitely without the introduction of any moving principles of formal development or unity. The weaknesses of present terminology can be offset, he believes, by building upon the vocabulary provided by Aristotle, who alone has developed a language that takes into account the structure of literary works as artistic wholes rather than merely as systems of language.

Crane recognizes that all critical methods have their corruptions in the hands of incompetents. The historical critic may be guilty of "antiquarian irrelevance," and the Aristotelian may lapse into mere formalism. The New Critic may be more concerned with language and rhetoric and with "generic figurations and techniques" than with the forms of literary works. These figurations often refer to supposedly antecedent patterns of myth (archetypes); yet the only evidence of myth we have is historical. Crane objects to the specious mystical basis of myth criticism. His objection is sound, but it is strange that he should contrast "generic figurations" and "forms." Some figurations or patterns of meaning may be less acceptable, intellectually, than others, and they may be more arbitrarily applied. But all definitions of form, including the Aristotelians' part specifications, depend to a certain extent upon pre-existing patterns. Our very recognition of the forms of literary works, or any objects, depends upon our conventionalized patterns of responses. Thus what Crane calls "generic figurations" cannot be ruled out as formal elements even though they may often be applied unjustifiably or with an undue literalness.

While Crane does not presume to advance his as the only proper critical method, he argues that it is best for the consideration of structural characteristics. But other kinds of criticism are needed, he thinks, since no one approach can ever have a "monopoly or even a distant approach to one," on the truth about literature. The multiplicity of critical languages is not to be deplored but rather approved, since it makes possible the fuller exploration of the complex literary work. Given the existence of diverse groups of critics, Crane feels that the chief obstacle to progress in the discipline of criticism is "the spirit of exclusive dogmatism which keeps them from learning what they might from one another." It would be better for each to recognize the claims of the other and to regard the various languages of criticism not as competing keys to the "truth" about literature, but rather as "tools of our trade—as so many distinct conceptual and logical means, each with its peculiar capacities and limitations, for solving truly the many distinct kinds of problems which poetry, in its magnificent variety of aspects, presents to our view."

8

The neo-Aristotelian position developed by Crane and his colleagues is valuable for its emphasis upon theory, historical perspective, and scholarly discipline. It has, however, stimulated very little practical criticism. The active movement that the leaders hoped for never developed, although their work undoubtedly encouraged a renewal of interest in genre criticism, shared by critics like Kenneth Burke and Northrop Frye in modified forms and by many other scholar critics within the universities.

One can only speculate upon the reasons why neo-Aristotelianism has not had a wider appeal. Aside from the inadequacy of its imitation theory, one of its liabilities is its genre approach, which sometimes leads to sterile categorization. Although the method can be sensitively handled, it often has a mechanical quality repellent to readers accustomed to more flexible analytical techniques. Although the Aristotelians have professed a "scientific" attitude, the application of their formulas to literature often seems to be in the deductive and a priori spirit they deplore in the New Critics.

The minimizing of language raises the important question of metaphor, to which the Aristotelians assign a subordinate rather than a central role. Metaphor is identified with the individual figurative expression and classified into such subtypes as "proportional," "correlative," and "subsumptive" (by Elder Olson), but it has the status of an added rather than an integral characteristic of literary language, and it is possible for the neo-Aristotelian critic to speak of nonmetaphoric literary language. Crane takes the New Critics to task for "preference for metaphorical over literal statement." To the extent that the New Critics overvalue the concrete conceits of the metaphysical tradition he has a point, but it is unfortunate that he should imply that direct statement in poetry is nonmetaphorical.

Elder Olson, at the close of his essay on William Empson, speaks of the use of words which, "while not constituting metaphor, have metaphorical suggestion." He gives an example: "The train glided out of a hole in the mountain and slid into a dark wood." This statement "suggests a serpent determinately, although without real metaphor, for these are perfectly literal attributes." It is possible to understand Olson's meaning since he had been speaking of metaphor as a scheme of figurative devices. But the limitations of his usage become apparent as we note that the images of gliding, of the hole, and of the dark wood contribute the connotative values that distinguish imaginative writing, whether expressed in the form of figurative association or in a more direct statement of feeling or thought. Olson's example is metaphorical if we recognize that metaphor exists in an interaction between experience and the valuation of experience in terms of thought and feeling. The tension between experience and ideas, whether conceptual or emotive, is a distinguishing feature of imaginative literature, and the poetic or metaphoric process is precisely this value-charging of literary language in the mind of the reader.

7

PSYCHOLOGICAL AND MYTH CRITICISM

1—The influence of Jung: Maud Bodkin's Archetypal Patterns in Poetry; *2—The problem of myth criticism: R. P. Warren; 3—Archetype and type-image; 4—The influence of Freud: F. J. Hoffman; 5—Freudian psychology and criticism: Edmund Wilson and Lionel Trilling;* 6—The American Imago; *7—Eclectic psychological criticism: Kenneth Burke and Leslie Fiedler; 8—Psychoanalysis and literary theory: S. O. Lesser's* Fiction and the Unconscious

From the theories of Freud and Jung have come two distinctive methods of literary study. The first effect of Freud's ideas was to focus attention upon the author and to consider his work primarily as a document through which his inner conflicts could be studied—hence the vogue of Freudian critical biographies in the 1920's. Subsequently there has been a modification of this concentration and an increase in attention paid to formal interpretation and to an exploration of the resources of Freudian thought for literary theory.

Freud's ideas were already widely known when Carl Jung, the Swiss analyst, attracted the attention of critics with his first publications in English on the relationship of literature and psychology, which appeared in the late Twenties and early Thirties. Jung's influence grew during the late Thirties and the 1940's, particularly in the development of myth and archetype criticism as a distinctive kind of modern literary study (sometimes classified as a subspecies of the New Criticism). The myth criticism he encouraged also drew support from modernized romantic theory like that of I. A. Richards in *Coleridge on Imagination* (1935), from Ernst Cassirer's philosophy of symbolic forms, and from Gestalt psychology as it provides an emphasis on the work of art as a perceptual configuration, or whole.

It is seldom that a critic proves to be a "pure" or orthodox disciple of either Freud or Jung. More often he is eclectic, drawing ideas from various sources as they meet his needs and interests. But myth and archetype critics are for the most part followers of Jung and share his mystical and religious inclinations, while critics attracted to Freud more often think of themselves as scientifically or historically oriented. Whether Freudian or Jungian, psychological theory has been most useful as it has supported criticism focused upon literature and its relations to common experience, rather than upon religious formulas or biographical considerations.

I

An important channel for the influence of Jung upon American criticism is the work of the English critic, Maud Bodkin, whose *Archetypal Patterns in Poetry* appeared in 1934. In early life a lecturer in psychology at an English training college, Miss Bodkin acknowledged Freud and Jung, especially Jung, together with Plato and Albert Schweitzer, as intellectual guides. She wrote her book as an exploration of the theory of "primordial images" or archetypes set forth in Jung's essay "On the Relation of Analytical Psychology to

Poetic Art," in *Contributions to Analytical Psychology* (1928). Jung had explained the special emotional appeal of some poems as resulting from the stimulation of unconscious forces in the reader's mind. These he identified with the primordial images, or archetypes, the "psychic residua of numberless experiences of the same type," experiences inherited by the individual in the structure of his brain and partaking of what Jung called the "collective unconscious" of the race.

Like most critics attracted to this theory, Miss Bodkin was skeptical of Jung's claim that archetypal patterns are biologically transmitted. But even though she doubted this basic assumption, she was drawn to accept the idea of archetypes because of their value as "symbols of a group tradition." It seemed to her that the archetype or poetic symbol might be able to fulfill the functions of "the images and dogma of institutional religion" in an earlier age. Miss Bodkin makes explicit her interest in the archetype as a necessary feature of a theory in which poetry may be considered the source of religious truth: "Where the development of individuality, and of sincerity in thought and feeling, has made impossible the acceptance of a dogmatic religion, while still a temperamental subjection to tidal changes of feeling enforces the need to find some stay in symbols of a collective tradition and supra-personal life, the function of poetry may be realized in its highest value."

For her this value is most fully expressed through the "rebirth archetype," in which we imaginatively participate in "the tidal ebb toward death followed by life renewal," an experience that "affords us a means of increased awareness, and of fuller expression and control, of our own lives in their secret and momentous obedience to universal rhythms." This interest in poetry as a substitute for ritual and dogma and in the rebirth pattern as a broader aesthetic and cultural support for the Christian story of the sacrificial death of Jesus is typical of modern myth and archetype critics.

The rebirth principle supplies the argument of the opening chapter, "Archetypal Patterns in Tragic Poetry." Considering *Hamlet* in relation to the problem of tragedy, Miss Bodkin recognizes the importance of Freud's theory of the Oedipus complex for an understanding of the hero's conflict. Especially pertinent is the idea, used by Ernest Jones in his study of the play, of the "splitting" of type figures. In this interpretation, both Claudius and the elder Hamlet are components of a single father image, and Hamlet's violently contrasted atittudes toward his father and the uncle who has married his mother represent the Oedipal situation and the son's ambivalent feelings toward his father.

This conflict of opposing emotions Miss Bodkin sees as the source of the necessary "inner tension" relieved by the death of the tragic hero. She goes further, however, and identifies the hero's inner conflict with an ambivalent attitude toward the self, involving a distinction between "a personal self—a limited ego, one among many—and a [suprapersonal] self that is free to range imaginatively through all human achievement." Tragedy thus expresses complementary motives toward self-assertion and toward the surrender of the ego to a greater power identified with the "community consciousness." The death of Hamlet—although it represents the sacrifice of the ego—is thus seen to be a kind of submission or sacrifice to the tribe, comparable to the sacrifice of the divine king or sacred animal that, through its shed blood, strengthens and renews the life of the group. The rebirth principle is illustrated by Hamlet's living on "in the story with which he charged Horatio" and us his readers.

The rebirth pattern is more fully explored in a chapter devoted to Coleridge's *Rime of the Ancient Mariner.* By drawing on personal associations, other literature, and Biblical parallels in imagery, Miss Bodkin discusses the shift from the stagnant calm, with its heat and parching thirst, to the renewed movement of the ship as the wind rises and the night storm brings an end to the drought. This change, which follows the Mariner's awakening of love for his fellow creatures the water snakes, is likened to the change which a poet or artist feels when, after a period of hopeless torpor, he experiences the renewal of creativity. In religious terms, it is the rebirth of faith after a period of alienation and despair.

These two states represent alternating rhythmic movements, one downward, toward disintegration and death, the other upward and outward—"an expansion or outburst of activity, a transition toward reintegration and life-renewal." The initial withdrawal, followed by return as in the night journey under the sea in the Book of Jonah, is a necessary feature of the rebirth archetype. In Jungian terms, Miss Bodkin identifies these movements as "introversion" and "extraversion," the inward and outward turning of the libido, both "necessary as alternations within a vital rhythm."

The downward movement Miss Bodkin recognizes as Freud's "death instinct" or "Nirvana principle." But for her it is more than balanced by the impulse toward life which she identifies with a creative impulse manifesting itself through one form or another of spiritual striving. Miss Bodkin does not *identify* the rebirth archetype in any work with a set religious belief or principle. She is rather, and frankly so, a seeker after common values which may provide a basis for moral community. Regardless of whether these come from religious tradition, literature, psychology, or politics (her quest had earlier led her into the Fabian Society), she considers them necessary for a sense of participation in a moral and psychological tradition. Access to this feeling is facilitated by "the great images of tragic poetry and of myth."

Miss Bodkin's final chapter considers patterns in sacred and contemporary literature. In the Gospels, which she treats from a literary and psychological, rather than an exclusively religious viewpoint, she regards the sacrifice of Jesus as having a poetic rather than a historical truth. His death, like that of the tragic hero with whom she identifies him, is a pledge, not of personal immortality, but of the continuing life of suprapersonal values. The image from modern literature that seems to her closest to that of Jesus in its "moral quality of love and compassion" is that of Shelley's Prometheus.

From more recent literature Miss Bodkin discusses the neglected subject of the male ideal (Jung's *animus*) in Virginia Woolf's *Orlando* and the rebirth archetype in Eliot's *The Waste Land,* making use of parallels from *The Rime of the Ancient Mariner* and the *Inferno.* Her reference to archetypes from Jessie Weston's *From Ritual to Romance* (1920) and her citations of Sir James Frazer's *The Golden Bough* are reminders of the influence of anthropology upon myth study even before Jung's theory was formulated.

One of the rewarding features of Miss Bodkin's work is her bringing together patterns of ideas and images from many different sources to illuminate a work—all toward the end, as she remarks in her conclusion, of defining in as full a way as possible the relations of the individual life to the larger life of the community. She is unlike many of the critics who have followed her in her belief that the process of definition and re-ordering requires a translation "from the terms of mystic and poetic faith into terms a psychologist can use." Freud's terms are not adequate, she feels, partly because of his preoccupation with the influence of the parent upon the child rather than with that of the parent as the representative of society and its stored values. While dependent upon Jung for her basic concept of the *archetype* (a term she later reconsidered) she attempts to enlarge and modify the vocabulary of her sources in order to study and illustrate "the environing larger life of the community, past and present, stored within the heritage of literary art, springing to creative activity within the minds of individual readers."

The assertion of the centrality of the rebirth archetype among mythic patterns points up one of the chief weaknesses of myth criticism, and a serious one. In the practice of many critics, the interpretation of literature becomes merely a search for archetypes. All literature is seen as myth and all mythic patterns are reduced to a *monomyth.* This term was introduced by Joseph Campbell, who got it from Joyce's *Finnegans Wake,* in *The Hero with a Thousand Faces* (1949), a study designed to reveal, behind the multiform myths and fragments of myths preserved in art and folklore and ritual, the *one* unifying rebirth myth of the hero involving "rites of passage," proceeding through the three stages of "the separation or departure," "the trials and victories of initiation," and "the return and reintegration with society." *The Hero* is convincing in its presentation of parallels among different systems of myth. But when the principle is applied to literature with the sole purpose of demonstrating a uniformity of pattern, as is often the habit with unimaginative critics who have seized upon the concept of the archetype as a convenient tool or gimmick, the process is stultifying rather than enlightening.

Maud Bodkin is aware of the hazard and imagines how her analysis of the rebirth archetype may strike a reader: "Here you are producing again your archetypes, your old labels. What can be more tedious?" Her first defense is that analysis need not be hard and reductive; it may be sensitive and pliant, adapting itself to the movement and complexity of the work as it explores its resources of thought and feeling. Certainly her own interpretations are not reductive. She places each poem in a context of appropriate personal, scientific, and poetic references and discusses it in such a way as to bring out its distinctive features. Like Eliot in "Tradition and the Individual Talent," she endorses the principle that a poetic work is to be appreciated, in her own words, "in its complete setting of national or world literature." Her emphasis on intellectual associations, in the form of a "music of ideas" realized in the reading of a poem, also distinguishes her from the many myth critics who believe that ideas destroy the wisdom of the heart or the "higher imagination."

2

Archetype criticism has often characterized the poet or artist as a hero who dies in his work but gains an aesthetic immortality through it. The idea of immortality through art is not new, as Shakespeare's sonnets remind us. It is one that has been particularly attractive to modern poets like Yeats, whose "Sailing to Byzantium" is a familiar example. Kenneth Burke's "Symbolic Action in a Poem by Keats," first published in an appendix to *A Grammar of Motives*

(1945), is a sophisticated archetypal interpretation of a romantic poem. Burke analyzes the "Ode on a Grecian Urn" "dramatistically," in accordance with his scheme for interpreting "symbolic action," and finds the poem to be a "viaticum" or sacrament through which the artist achieves immortality as the transitory passions of the living man are transmuted into the fixed and concretized "Cold Pastoral" of art.

The process of immortality, thus conceived, is itself a metaphor, one among many of which the critic may avail himself in interpreting literature. And the sophisticated reader, it is to be assumed, assents to the criticism on these terms.

But a question remains. While most modern critics do not accept the idea of spiritual rebirth in an orthodox religious sense, their use of the language of the rite, without adequate qualification or translation into contemporary language, implies at least a *wish* to accept the religious formula on its own terms. As a result such criticism propagates, somewhat irresponsibly, a mystique of literature that has received all too much support during the past twenty years.

The appeal of this mystique is understandable. It provides a sanction for contemporary interest in the religious patterns of meaning in literature. It also claims a place for literature as a substitute sacrament. But it does so at great cost because it formulates the values of literature in terms that provide too cheaply the luxury of a religious commitment as a "pure" aesthetic gesture, without the responsibility of defending or living a religious conviction or the struggle to express this conviction as a twentieth century experience. For this reason it would seem desirable that myth critics, and literary critics in general, make use of a language and a frame of reference that would give their work meaning in contemporary terms, whether religious or secular.

Most myth and archetype critics have failed to do so. In some cases their avoidance of a reference to contemporary experience may be the result of a historicist desire to treat a work in relation to the milieu of its composition. But it is often difficult to determine the extent to which the critic's treatment is partisan or disinterested.

Such a question is posed by Robert Penn Warren's "A Poem of Pure Imagination: An Experiment in Reading" (1945-46), first published as an introduction to an edition of *The Rime of the Ancient Mariner* and later collected, in slightly revised form, in his *Selected Essays* (1958). The revised essay elucidates Coleridge's references to his poem as a work of "pure imagination." The approach is "scholarly" in that Warren bases his interpretation, in part, on Coleridge's religious and aesthetic ideas at the time of the writing and revision of the poem. He also reviews and evaluates previous interpretations.

Following Maud Bodkin in seeing the poem as an example of "the archetypal story of Rebirth or the Night Journey," Warren accepts her explanation of some images. He is, however, primarily interested in interpreting two basic themes and explaining the relation between them. The first or "primary" theme is that of the "sacramental vision" or the "One Life," against which the Mariner sins by his wanton killing of the albatross, a fellow creature in the divine plan. Warren makes a point of explaining the killing as a manifestation of Original Sin and as a symbolic reenactment of the Fall of Man; and he supports this interpretation by quotations from Coleridge affirming his belief in Original Sin. The secondary theme is that of the imagination, through which spiritual truth is perceived; it is also the faculty through which the salvation of the sinful hero is effected.

The two themes are brought together, Warren believes, in an image cluster that assimilates the creative wind, the sacramental bird, and the moonlight of imagination. In contrast to this group is the linking of the images of the sun and the specter-bark, or ship of death. The light imagery thus has two poles, that of the moon, which represents the imagination, or the higher Reason, whereby man achieves the intuition of God, and that of the sun, which represents the world known through the understanding, a sense-bound death-in-life.

The two "lights" are the "two truths" of religion and science, which seemed to the romantic mind to be in deadly conflict and competition. Coleridge's resolution of this conflict was through the poetic imagination that reconciled the opposing claims of such contraries as body and spirit, science and religion, a solution that effected a synthesis of religious and aesthetic experience, as Warren points out. The Mariner's redemptive vision of beauty and love is a poetic vision, and the Mariner is identified with the figure of the poet in the spontaneity of his blessing of the snakes and in his compulsion to repeat his tale.

In following this line of interpretation, Warren refers to Coleridge's belief that a unifying truth is implicit in the symbolic poetic act and expresses the opinion that the poem is "central," not only for Coleridge but also for his age and that it is truly a work of "pure imagination." He suggests a further value for our own age in the idea of the poetic imagination expressed in the poem: "If poetry does anything for us, it reconciles, by its symbolical reading of experience (for by its very nature it is in itself a myth of the unity of being), the self-devisive internecine malices which arise at the superficial level on which we conduct most of our living."

Warren's interpretation explains the poem in terms of the romantic ideas and symbolic conventions of Coleridge's time. What it lacks is an indication of what the poem means in twentieth century terms. There is no suggestion that the romantic myth of Coleridge is not simply taken at its face value. When Warren acknowledges that the poem is, as Coleridge described it, a work of the "pure imagination," we know what the term meant to Coleridge. Warren has skillfully helped to make this meaning clear. But we do not know what the expression means to Warren, unless, of course, he accepts the romantic theory of the imagination. When his critique is placed beside Maud Bodkin's, it is apparent that his is more systematic and exhaustive within the limits he has established. But hers, which is more tentative and exploratory, has a richness of reference and a contemporary relevance lacking in his. By placing the work in a broad literary context and by attempting to interpret it in terms drawn largely from her twentieth century experience, Miss Bodkin produced criticism that, in its suggestiveness and flexibility, reaches beyond the limits of any one historically conditioned pattern.

3

The myth critic is usually a defender of the mythopoeic consciousness, a precious but vanishing heritage from the primitive past. In his eyes, this consciousness, which provided men with a common belief and with a sense of group solidarity, has in the questionable progress of the race given way to the rational, scientific mind, which abstracts rather than unifies; which separates subject and object, intellect and emotion; and which has brought man into the sterile and meaningless world of the laboratory and the machine.

A typical statement of this view appears in Philip Wheelwright's "Poetry, Myth, and Reality," collected by Allen Tate in a volume entitled *The Language of Poetry* (1942). Wheelwright sees the modern world as preoccupied with a "horizontal" scientific knowledge of "things, relations, and ideas" that make up our common-sense world. The needed perspective, he feels, is a "mytho-religious one" which will reach beyond the limits of "positivistic materialism" and restore man's sense of identity with his group and a higher Mystery. The mythic consciousness represents "man's primordial way of knowing, before the individual has separated himself with clear critical awareness from the group," and it is the necessary basis of his values and his faith. The secular, positivistic mind denies these values of myth and "ignores or deprecates that haunting awareness of transcendental forces peering through the cracks of the visible universe, that is the very essence of myth." As a result of the present bankruptcy of myth, the poet born into this age "will feel himself to be living in a cultural wasteland, his materials will be fragmentary and unpromising, and while he may prove an ingenious renovator of ruined monuments or a resourceful practitioner of metajournalism, his contribution as a poet —the contribution of a whole man who speaks powerfully to whole men—will be small." Because of our loss of a sense of "cyclical fullness and therewith of transcendental significance in human affairs," we have forfeited belief in the myth of tragedy, which might give meaning to our plight. In the midst of the general skepticism, Wheelwright looks forward to a "recrudescence of myth consciousness in America," although he cannot foresee what form it may take. (A fuller statement of Wheelwright's ideas about the mythic consciousness appears in *The Burning Fountain* [1954].)

The myth critic's preoccupation with two ways of knowing—through general concepts and immediate intuitions—creates a problem for archetype criticism. The question of the dual focus of myth—its "universality" and particularity—enters into any consideration of the usefulness of the concept of the archetype. Its helpfulness for establishing parallels or like patterns in works of different periods, and of thus ordering a body of literature, has been demonstrated by Miss Bodkin and others. But the term *archetype* is unfortunately a loose one, applying as it does to a whole class of experiences while pointing beyond experience to a metaphysical absolute.

Some of the difficulty can be seen in the work of Northrop Frye, who has based the theory of his *Anatomy of Criticism* (1957) upon the concept of the archetype, which he describes in one of several definitions as a "communicable symbol" and a tool of historical criticism which gives coherence and unity to an "existing order" of literature (to use Eliot's term) in relation to which individual works may be discussed. But Frye also thinks of the archetype as a "monad," or a "single infinite and eternal verbal symbol," through which the "literary universe" is revealed. Typical of religious myth criticism, this view considers literature not as something to be appreciated for its own sake in its relations with the world of experience but as an object to be transcended, a verbal springboard to the absolute. In this sense the term *archetype,* used without a communicable referent, is diffuse and indeterminate in meaning.

The dual nature of the archetype has been noted by other critics. Its social as against its universal or unconscious dimension has been discussed by Leslie Fiedler in an essay, "Archetype and Signature" (*Sewanee Review,* 1952). Discarding the term *myth* as so ambiguous as to have outlived its usefulness, Fiedler uses *archetype* to designate patterns of response that reside in "the Jungian Collective Unconscious or the Platonic world of ideas," thus representing, in its universal qualities, the "Community at its deepest preconscious levels of acceptance." Fiedler introduces *signature* as a complementary term to denote the individuating features of a work, "the sign of the Persona or Personality, through which the Archetype is rendered."

It is through the "signature," or personal dimension, that the archetypal work exists as a social or historical phenomenon since the signature is rooted in both the ego and the super-ego and thus represents the "social collectivity" on the conscious level, as well as the individual consciousness of the writer. But Fiedler is more interested in the usefulness of the archetype-signature idea for biographical than for social or historical criticism. And as a myth critic he is interested in the biographical approach for the means it affords, through the use of Jungian analysis, of penetrating beyond the personality of the writer to the communal unconscious that underlies it.

Fiedler's distinction between the conscious and unconscious dimensions of the archetype was anticipated by Maud Bodkin in a work that followed *Archetypal Patterns in Poetry* by more than fifteen years. In *Studies of Type-Images in Poetry, Religion and Philosophy* (1951), she recognizes in the archetype a "two-fold aspect" that Jung himself did not scrupulously distinguish: "The archetype is both a product of time, the shape in which it appears determined by past history, and also a creative energy, looking towards and helping determine the future." Although *archetype* as used by Jung is an "elusive term," Miss Bodkin goes on to say that it is possible to distinguish between a subjective and psychic and an objective and historical meaning of the word. It may refer mainly to "tendencies within the body-mind" or it may refer to "images handed down from one generation to another, and preserved in books and pictures": "When Jung speaks of 'psychic organs,' it is the disposition, the subjective factor that he has in mind. But when he names, for instance, 'the Wotan archetype,' it is of the more objective factor he is thinking. Here he can follow the cultural history of the archetypal image as tradition presents it in pictorial shapes and language symbols."

Miss Bodkin's misgivings stemmed largely from her distrust of Jung's theory that the archetypes are "psychic organs" inherited in the structure of the brain. She continued to use the term, despite its unsatisfactoriness, but she substituted another word in the title of her book, which she has described as a discussion of "type-images": "My own study of archetypes I have expressed in terms of 'type-images,' present in imaginative and religious writings, and of 'needs' corresponding to these, felt or latent in individual minds."

The word *type-image* might very well prove to be a more satisfactory term than *archetype* for the critic interested in the social and historical features of literary form. It implies uniformity and recurrence but is free of the mythic and Jungian associations of *archetype.* The idea of *a* type-image admits the possibility of a succession of types developing in a historical process, while *arche*type assumes a unique prototype underlying individuated forms and emphasizes the myth critic's desire to reduce this multiplicity (the many) to unity (the One) through the isolation of a universal monomyth. In contrast, the historical critic explores the variety of meanings and values of the type-image in a shifting time scheme. He thus contributes to the formal understanding of literature as culturally conditioned and valued not so much for its mythic uniformity as for its qualities of change and novelty, and its admission of the possibility of progress.

4

An interest in myth has not been confined to the Jungians. Freud and his followers in the psychoanalytic tradition have also studied traditional patterns of narrative and ritual. It was, after all, the Oedipus myth that supplied the basis for one of Freud's central theories, and both he and his followers have made use of myth in explaining the motives of literary works as well as the behavior patterns of individuals. But there is a basic difference in the attitude toward myth and literature of the two schools of psychology, a difference stemming from the contrasting orientation of their founders. Freud was deeply committed to the nineteenth century tradition of positivistic science, deriving from the Enlightenment, while Jung, the son of an Evangelical preacher, was steeped in the tradition of romantic idealism, in which man's dream consciousness and his intuition of spiritual reality are linked.

In an essay entitled "Freud and Jung—Contrasts" (*Modern Man in Search of a Soul* [1933]), Jung criticizes Freud for over-emphasizing the sexual principle and the pathological and negative aspects of human nature. For Jung sex is not the basic life force in man but one among many instinctive drives. Feeling that Freud erred in turning his back on philosophy and religion, Jung speaks of the need of modern man to rediscover the "life of the spirit," a goal best achieved through the archetypes, the universal symbols which give access to the racial unconscious, the East that lies within us but from which we are distracted by the "American tempo" of our outer, practical life. Freud, for his part, soon came to believe that Jung's method was unscientific and that his theory of archetypes was an irresponsible mysticism.

Although Jung's ideas won an acceptance among many critics during the 1940's, Freud's work has exerted a more pervasive influence over many years. It has affected both creative writing and criticism from the time of the early work on dream symbolism. Its effects were most immediately seen in the techniques of creative writers, although the analyst's interpretation of dream imagery was to influence the practice of criticism as well. Its most successful use did not appear, however, until the late 1930's and the following decade, by which time a competent technical criticism had been developed by the New Critics and their predecessors. For the past twenty years there has been a steady advance in the understanding of Freudian psychology and its relation to literature, which has brought about a corresponding refinement in the theory and techniques of pyschological criticism.

A work contributing to this understanding is Frederick J. Hoffman's *Freudianism and the Literary Mind* (1945), which traces the development of Freud's theories and the spread of their influence and distinguishes between Freud's ideas and popular conceptions of them. Hoffman considers the problem of Freud's influence on the work of six modern novelists: James Joyce, D. H. Lawrence, Sherwood Anderson, Waldo Frank, Franz Kafka, and Thomas Mann. (A revised edition of the book [1957] includes a discussion of F. Scott Fitzgerald's *Tender Is the Night.*)

He emphasizes the importance of Freud's early works like *The Interpretation of Dreams* (1900; American edition, 1913), which stimulated interest in dream symbolism and in language experiments designed to represent dream states, and the *Three Contributions to a Theory of Sex* (1905; American edition, 1910), which developed the idea of the Oedipus complex. Freud's work of this period introduced many now-familiar terms that have affected both creative writing and criticism. Among them are *ego, condensation, displacement, sublimation, repression, fixation, libido, father-image.*

Hoffman considers the influence of Freudianism upon writers whether they had a sophisticated knowledge of psychoanalytical theory—like Joyce, Mann, and Waldo Frank—or whether they were, like Sherwood Anderson, psychoanalysts "by default." Hoffman sees Joyce, who during his life abroad in Trieste, Zurich, and Paris was acquainted with psychoanalytic thought from its earliest years, as self-consciously making use of Freudian and Jungian ideas in *Ulysses* and *Finnegans Wake* (although Joyce insisted upon his independence). Hoffman believes that Sherwood Anderson, in contrast to Joyce, instinctively derived his themes of repression and frustration from his experience of midwestern American small-town life, even though he learned about some of Freud's ideas from the literary group he joined in Chicago in 1913.

The question of direct influence is perhaps less important than the fact that Anderson was responding to the same cultural pressures and emphasizing the same themes in his fiction that Freud was treating in psychoanalytical studies. Freud's importance is not diminished by the lack of direct influence of the psychology upon the literature or by the question of priority of insight. What is important is that both literature and psychology are complementary expressions of the consciousness of western man and that a carefully formulated psychology like Freud's exists as a resource for the writer or critic able to make use of its terms and concepts while pursuing his own ends.

Hoffman notes one of the appeals of Freudianism during the first third of the century: its recognition of the irrational forces in human nature undermined the prestige of reason and lent support to the modernist revolt against conventional morality. The leading prophet of irrationalism was D. H. Lawrence, who rejected Freud's ideal of the control of the id by the rational ego. To Lawrence the ego was the hated "white consciousness," hostile to the darker blood consciousness and inimical to its free expression.

The rationalistic and humanistic emphases of Freud's thought are reflected in the work of Thomas Mann, who felt that Freudian psychology permitted man to understand the unconscious without over-valuing it. Freud's effort to extend the dominion of the ego over the id won his sympathy and support, as did Freud's identification of progress with the "expression of reason and free will." Mann's endorsement of these Freudian ideas appears most fully in the Joseph novels, in which, Hoffman points out, Joseph is "the racial symbol of the ego, which will serve as a prototype of civilization."

5

Some leading critics have adapted features of Freud's theory without limiting themselves entirely to psychological interpretation.

Edmund Wilson's interest in Freudian psychology is best seen in his work of the late 1930's and early Forties. In *The Triple Thinkers* (1938; revised edition, 1948), Wilson begins his essay "The Ambiguity of Henry James" with a Freudian reading of *The Turn of the Screw* that explains the ghosts as projections of the neurotic consciousness of the genteel governess-narrator. Acknowledging an earlier analysis along these lines by Edna Kenton, he discusses James's ambiguity as a technique for dealing with covert themes comparable to the latent meanings of dreams. He also considers *The Sacred Fount*—perhaps the most baffling of James's novels, since the credibility of the narrator is even more in doubt than that of the governess in the ghost story—suggesting that its hidden theme may also relate to sex. Wilson characterizes the narrator as "a man shut out from love and doomed to barren speculation on human relations," a dramatic projection of James's conception of his own role as artist.

Wilson's analysis has been supported by subsequent criticism. What is surprising is that his essay on *The Turn of the Screw* should have provoked controversy. Perhaps the resistance to his interpretation can best be understood as the expression of an irrational but widespread hostility to Freud's psychology of the unconscious. Whatever the cause, one consequence is an unwillingness to accept the idea that literature, like other human enterprises, may represent hidden motives and meanings.

A slightly later collection of Wilson's essays, *The Wound and the Bow* (1941), also proved controversial, particularly because of its concluding essay, "Philoctetes: The Wound and the Bow," a discussion of Sophocles' play dealing with the legend of the wounded and suffering hero without whose unerring bow, the gift of the gods, the Greeks could not hope for victory at Troy. The fundamental theme of the legend lies, for Wilson, in "the conception of superior strength as inseparable from disability." Taking the idea from Gide's *Philoctete* of the hero as a literary genius, Wilson develops the implication that "genius and disease, like strength and mutilation, may be inextricably bound up together." To many critics, however, such a suggestion was anathema.

Although Wilson does not assert a cause and effect relationship between mutilation and strength, his idea of the sick artist, alienated from his society but the master of an art which it needs, is related to Freud's theory of the neurotic origin of art. He applies his argument to novelists including Dickens, Kipling, Edith Wharton, Hemingway, and Joyce. In the first two essays, on Dickens and on Kipling, Wilson finds that traumatic childhood experiences and subsequent circumstances determine the writers' themes and viewpoints. Of all the essays in the book, that on Dickens is the most fully developed.

The dualism of the title of "Dickens: The Two Scrooges" applies not only to the manic-depressive personality of Ebenezer Scrooge, shared by his creator (perhaps by all artists?), but also, and more significantly, to the two imaginative roles of the criminal and the rebel projected by Dickens in his novels. Both roles are natural to "the man of spirit whose childhood has been crushed by the cruelty of organized society"; they are manifested by the prominence of the image of the prison and by a persistent hostility to social institutions of all kinds. Dickens' neurosis was rooted in the six months that he spent as a twelve-year-old boy pasting labels in a shoe-blacking factory when his father was sent to debtors' prison, an experience that left him with an unforgettable sense of despair and betrayal. (It becomes apparent that the debtors' prison of his fiction is a microcosm of the middle-class world outside.)

In this long essay Wilson marshals social, economic, and political evidence from Dickens' life and writing to support his psychological interpretation. It effectively combines psychological interpretation with a devastating analysis of a middle-class society and is remarkable not only for the fullness of this sort of information but, more importantly, for the extent to which it is applied in formal analysis of theme, character, and imagery. Although Wilson is primarily concerned with psychological interpretation, he makes surprisingly little use of Freudian or any other technical psychological terms. He mentions the *censor* in the Kipling essay, and in his discussion of the Philoctetes legend he refers to the *Oedipus complex.* Scrooge is described as a *manic-depressive,* and childhood experiences are *traumatic.* But, for the most part, Wilson employs lay language to communicate psychological insights—without any loss of effectiveness.

Lionel Trilling is described by Louis Fraiberg, in *Psychoanalysis & American Literary Criticism* (1960), as the contemporary critic who has most effectively made use of a comprehensive knowledge of Freud's ideas. This interest is represented by two selections in *The Liberal Imagination: Essays on Literature and Society* (1950). "Freud and Literature," which had first appeared in 1940, considers the relevance of Freudian to literary theory. Trilling objects to Freud's lack of esteem for art but approves of his recognition that the human mind, which deals in metaphors, is essentially a "poetry-making organ." He also remarks that literary criticism has gained from the Freudian system both "the license and the injunction to read the work of literature with a lively sense of its latent and ambiguous meanings." The aspect with which Trilling is most concerned, however, is the idea of the repetition-compulsion introduced in *Beyond the Pleasure Principle,* where Freud takes note of the tendency of the victim of battle neurosis to re-enact in dreams the situation that had precipitated his shock, interpreting it as the effort to restore control through the development of fear. Speculating upon the function of tragedy, Trilling goes beyond the Aristotelian idea of catharsis to define what he calls the "mithridatic" function, "by which tragedy is used as the homeopathic administration of pain to inure ourselves to the greater pain which life will force upon us."

In "Art and Neurosis," first published in 1945, Trilling considers the "myth of the sick artist" so widespread in modern culture and rejects the idea of any causal relationship between neurosis and creativity. The coexistence of a sense of pain and suffering and of artistic achievement is acknowledged, but it is not accepted as an explanation of the artist's genius. Our knowledge of the artist's suffering tells us something about his materials but it does not explain his power. What distinguishes him from the ordinary neurotic is his ability to control and shape the common experience of pain. Trilling quotes with approval Charles Lamb's differentiation of the true poet, who "dreams being awake," from the neurotic: "He is not possessed by his subject but has dominion over it."

The controlling psychological concept of *The Opposing Self* (1955) is most fully developed in the opening essay, "The Poet as Hero: Keats in His Letters," which first appeared as an introduction to *The Selected Letters of John Keats* (1951). Acknowledging his indebtedness to Freud for the insight that personality is shaped by a conflict between the "self" and the culture, Trilling finds in Keats a pronounced development of both the pleasure principle and the reality principle and a full recognition of the claims of both the creative self in quest of identity, mastery, and fulfillment and the implacable world of circumstance with its "certainty of pain and extinction." The containment and balance of these opposed forces is the foundation of that paradoxical personal quality, or intellectual power, that Keats called "Negative Capability," or the capacity for "being in uncertainties, mysteries, doubts, without any irritable reaching after fact and reason." This quality, which Keats considered necessary to a "man of Achievement, especially in literature," Trilling identifies with the poet's (any poet's) way of seeing life, a vision expressed in the line, "Beauty is truth, truth beauty," which conveys Keats's belief that the poet, in Trilling's words, "looks at human life, sees the terrible truth of its evil, but sees it so intensely that it becomes an element of the beauty which is created by his act of perception." Through the mediation of beauty, the truth of fact or circumstance becomes a truth of life that affirms the strivings of the creative self. The self is thus justified in art through an aesthetic transmutation of the fact of evil.

The same theme appears in *Freud and the Crisis in Our Culture* (1955), in which Trilling assumes a likeness between literature and psychoanalysis in their common concern for the opposition of the reality and the pleasure principles. Although Freud possessed a scientific rather than a literary mind, he was bound to the tradition of "literary humanism" in regarding the individual self, rather than the culture, as the "first prime object of attention and solicitude." Literature asserts the authority of the self "in its quarrel with its society and its culture" and is a valuable subversive force because the culture has lost an adequate awareness of the nature of the self. This lack of knowledge and of a "right relation" between the individual and his society has brought about what Trilling calls "a crisis in our culture."

Although Freud helped to disseminate the idea of culture through his emphasis on family environment, his attitude toward it remained ambivalent. He saw it as something to be resisted, something against which the self must react in order to find its identity. Writing at a time when McCarthyism was an urgent issue, Trilling stresses the need of resistance when the forces of conformity and repression are in the saddle. The importance assigned to biology by Freud is helpful because it imposes limits upon the power of culture: "It suggests that there is a residue of human quality beyond the reach of cultural control, and that this residue of human quality, elemental as it may be, serves to bring culture itself under criticism and keeps it from being absolute." He finds hope for the future in the "irreducible, stubborn core of biological urgency, and biological necessity, and biological reason," which resists culture and which will eventually judge and revise it. In this theme of resistance, which Trilling finds in *Civilization and Its Discontents,* Freud is "at one with literature."

Trilling's application of Freudian concepts to literary theory is skillful and effective, but a few questions remain to trouble his reader. Although he recognizes Freud's rationalism and commitment to science, Trilling identifies his interest in the unconscious or hidden life with the romantic tradition of the "night side" of human nature. He thus finds an affinity between psychoanalysis and the antirationalist romantic tradition, a relationship which Louis Fraiberg, for example, considers both unjustifiable in view of Freud's positivistic orientation and unsupported by evidence in Trilling's essay.

Trilling's own concern for the "self" in his essay on Keats seems very much in the romantic mode in its assertion of an individuality in opposition to the normalizing influences of society. The word *self* offers difficulties when it is removed from a context of romantic speculation. In Trilling's *Freud and the Crisis of Our Culture* it is not easy to determine to what extent the "self" is an irrational conservative force and to what extent it is a critical and rational agent of social progress or at least of ameliorative change. The emphasis upon an irreducible "biological" core which resists the pressures of culture supports the former view, but the reference to "biological *reason,*" which judges and revises culture, suggests the latter. The reader is left in the dark as to whether Trilling views biology primarily as a deterministic factor or as an instrument of will and reason.

6

The broader influence of Freudian psychology on criticism can be seen in articles published in such journals as the *Psychoanalytic Quarterly, The American Imago,* and *Literature and Psychology.* As the quarterly newsletter of a Modern Language Association discussion group, *Literature and Psychology,* edited by Leonard Manheim, is the most directly concerned with the relationship between psychoanalysis and literary study. In addition to articles and reviews, it carries a running bibliography of books and of articles appearing in other periodicals. *The American Imago* is an older journal. Perhaps because it is edited by a psychoanalyst and is not exclusively devoted to literature and the arts, it often supplies illustrations of the problems and pitfalls of psychoanalytical literary criticism.

The American Imago was founded in Boston, in November 1939, by Dr. Hanns Sachs, as "A Psychoanalytic Journal for the Arts and Sciences." Sachs thought of the magazine as an American continuation of the original *Imago* (1912-37) established by Freud and published in Leipzig and Vienna under the editorship of Sachs and Otto Rank; and the first issue of the American journal carried Freud's name as editor. A note by Sachs regretted that the magazine had, before its first number appeared, lost its guide, who had suggested its name and given it his blessing before his death. Sachs concluded, "Our aim can be no other than to keep the flame alive which he lighted and to try, as best we can, to continue in his spirit the science which he has founded and developed." Upon the death of Sachs in 1947, Dr. George B. Wilbur took over the editorship.

Relatively few articles on literature appeared during the early years of the journal. In "The Myth in Jane Austen" (1941), Geoffrey Gorer examines the four "central" novels and finds a recurrent pattern: in each a young woman is courted by a charming but worthless lover whom she finally rejects in favor of a man she esteems and admires. Since the heroine in each is opposed to her mother and marries a man who has paternal traits (who is a "father surrogate"), the "myth" is identified as a version of the Oedipus (or Electra) complex. Unlike the Jungians, the critic is interested not in isolating a rebirth archetype, but in explaining motive and plot in terms of Freudian theory. The Freudian critic is interested in myth, not for its own sake or as a substitute religious faith, but as it can be rationalized in Freudian terms or supported by parallel psychological interpretation.

During the postwar period, articles on literature appeared more frequently, sometimes outnumbering those on other topics. Among authors considered, Shakespeare received by far the most attention. Others whose names recurred include Charles Dickens, Henry James, Nathaniel Hawthorne, and Franz Kafka.

As might be expected, some of the least useful interpretation appears in essays in which the writer is psychoanalyzed through his work, a weakness particularly apparent in the criticism of Shakespeare, about whose life so little is known, most ludicrously when the Oxfordian theory is introduced, as it is in several *Imago* articles in which the plays are interpreted as the "confessions" of Edward de Vere, the "real" Shakespeare.

In *The Writer and Psychoanalysis* (1949; second edition, 1954), a number of chapters of which first appeared in the magazine, Edmund Bergler explains the process of composition as the defense mechanism of a "psychic masochist." Deprived, because he wishes to be deprived, of "milk, love, tenderness," the artist assumes the roles of both mother and child, and "gives to himself, out of himself," beautiful words and ideas, thus establishing an "autarchy." This special process of sublimation is at the same time rationalized by the writer as a social and altruistic act. Although this theory has been applied to literature in several *American Imago* articles, its usefulness would seem to lie in the clinical treatment of authors (an area in which Bergler has worked as a psychoanalyst) rather than in criticism, where it can supply only a narrow and dubious perspective for the analysis of themes.

Psychological theory is helpful as it provides an added dimension of interpretation. It is least valuable when it is simplistic and reductive—most so when it recognizes the complexity of literature and acknowledges that its function is contributory to a larger conception of form. But whether or not the psychological critic acknowledges the limited nature of his approach, the insight he provides may help his reader toward a fuller awareness of literary form. Thus a discussion of the "beast" imagery in Henry James's stories in relation to an Oedipal pattern or an interpretation of the behavior of Richard II as an example of narcissistic illusion can add to our understanding. An article like Helen B. Petrullo's "The Neurotic Hero of *Typee*" (1955) reveals one consistent principle of order in Melville's first novel—sometimes dismissed as a fictionalized travel narrative—by demonstrating the correspondence of the book's events with the pattern of the birth trauma theory of Otto Rank.

Some *Imago* criticism deals with individual works in a larger literary context. William Wasserstrom's "The Spirit of Myrrha" (1956) treats the figure of the heroine in James's fiction with respect for psychological, social, and literary values. In "Kafka and Dickens: The Country Sweetheart" (1959) Mark Spilka discusses the indebtedness of Kafka's *Amerika* to Dickens' *David Copperfield.* Although Kafka described his work as an imitation of Dickens', Spilka points out modifications of treatment resulting from Kafka's familiarity with Marx and Freud, but he also demonstrates the basic similarity of Dickens' naïve vision and Kafka's more sophisticated psychological perception. In their differing ways both were able to fuse "sexual and economic themes into a single psychic experience."

Unfortunately, a treatment like this, which integrates a psychological interpretation with a recognition of other literary values, is less common in the *Imago* than "documentary" analyses presenting a one-to-one relationship between the events of a literary work (sometimes related to the events of the author's life) and a Freudian theory. Still, this journal has made a contribution to literary study of the past twenty years by affording an outlet for psychological criticism.

7

Some eclectic critics have combined Freudian and Jungian ideas, or occasionally psychological concepts and those of other disciplines. Kenneth Burke, whose developing dramatistic theory has absorbed terms and concepts from various sources, has considered the possibility of synthesizing Freudian and Marxist theory.

In *Permanence and Change* (1935), Burke describes psychoanalysis as a "secular conversion" which "effects its cures by providing a new perspective that dissolves the system of pieties lying at the root of the patient's sorrows or bewilderments." He objects, however, to its reductiveness, calling it a "*conversion downwards* of the patient's distress by means of an unfit, incongruous terminology," in which his problems are explained as "autoeroticism, homosexuality, sadism, masochism, incest, and exhibitionism." Although Burke believes that any set of motives is translatable into another and that "Freudianism could 'explain' Marxists psychologically and that Marxism could 'explain' Freudians sociologically," he makes a qualitative distinction between the two systems when he calls one, the Freudian, "impious" and the other a "humanistic and poetic rationalization." And when, in his conclusion, he speaks of poetic metaphor as a guide to radical social changes, he is thinking of the communist rationalization as the inspiration of the society of the future.

The Philosophy of Literary Form (1941) treats psychoanalysis more sympathetically. In "Twelve Propositions on the Relation between Economics and Psychology" Burke notes that both Freudianism and Marxism are interested in shifts in identity or in allegiance to authority symbols and that they both work toward this end dramatistically: "Marx's concept of the 'classless' state following a maximum intensification of class conflict is precisely in line with the Aristotelian recipe for the process of dramatic 'catharsis.' The shock value of Freudian analysis exemplified the same process in tiny 'closet dramas' of private life (the facing and burning out of conflict)." The approach is " 'diagnostic' in that it invites us to note the psychological and material factors *furthering* communication (the coöperative act)."

The essay most concerned with the relation of psychology to literature is "Freud and the Analysis of Poetry," in which

Burke defines his subject as "the bearing of Freud's theories upon literary criticism." While acknowledging Freud's function as a pioneer and liberator in revealing a new dimension of human motives, hitherto denied recognition, Burke finds certain limitations in his theory and insists that a distinction must be observed between neurotic and poetic acts. As a correction of the Freudian tendency to interpret literature as wish fulfillment and to regard art as self-expression, Burke considers the motive of communication to be the basic category of literary criticism.

Accordingly, in considering the usefulness of Freudian ideas to the three modes of analysis introduced in *The Philosophy of Literary Form* (dream, prayer, and chart), Burke finds them most illuminating when the work is considered as dream, in terms of its unconscious factors. Here Freud's concepts of "condensation" and "displacement" are invaluable to the critic. But in the analysis of "prayer" (the communicative function) and of "chart" ("the realistic sizing-up of situations that is sometimes explicit, sometimes implicit, in poetic strategies") Freud provides very little assistance.

What is needed is an extension of Freud's theory in dramatistic terms that would point up the communicative and social functions of literature. Such a development would permit the reconciliation of Freudianism and Marxism: "Both Freudians and Marxists are wrong in so far as they cannot put their theories together, by an over-all theory of drama itself (as they should be able to do, since Freud gives us the material of the closet drama, and Marx the material of the problem play, the one treated in terms of personal conflicts, the other in terms of public conflicts)." To make Freud more useful to the critic, a bridge is needed from the familial to the cultural implications of the theory, and for Burke the bridge would be art as symbolic action in a community.

Louis Fraiberg, in *Psychoanalysis & American Literary Criticism* (1960), believes Burke deluded in thinking that the two systems of Freud and Marx can be integrated. Fraiberg contends that the idea of the conversion of terms is the weakest feature of Burke's argument because it denies the status of psychoanalysis as a science grounded in experience. By regarding psychoanalysis as merely a set of words, interchangeable with any other, phenomena are "converted downward" into terms, and any contact between Burke's psychological criticism and experience is severed.

Fraiberg's objection raises a very important question about Burke's idea of the function of language and of literary criticism. If all sets of terms are simply interchangeable and without verifiable reference to reality, how can criticism relate literature to experience and affect social attitudes, as Burke wishes it to do?

Insufficient light is thrown upon this question by *A Grammar of Motives* (1945), in which Burke develops further his theory of symbolic action by introducing the five "key terms" of dramatism through which literature and human behavior can be analyzed: *Act, Scene, Agent, Agency, Purpose.* These represent necessary categories of thought found to be "equally present in systematically elaborated metaphysical structures, in legal judgments, in poetry and fiction, in political and scientific works, in news and in bits of gossip offered at random."

Although any set of terms is translatable into another, the terms for motives will inevitably be ambiguous because of the enigmatic nature of the universe. This is a pleasing thought to Burke, who considers it his task to "study and clarify the *resources* of ambiguity" and to deal in many kinds of transformation since all terms are formally interrelated as "attributes of a common ground or substance": "At every point where the field covered by any one of these terms overlaps upon the field covered by any other, there is an alchemic opportunity, whereby we can put one philosophy or doctrine of motivation into the alembic, make the appropriate passes, and take out another." Burke thinks of his method as necessarily dialectical and metaphysical (defining dialectics as "the employment of the possibilities of linguistic transformation"): "Our speculations as we interpret them should show that the subject of motivation is a philosophic one, not ultimately to be solved in terms of empirical science."

Burke considers these transformations not as "illusions" but as "citable realities." Although positivists might classify all metaphysics, literature, political thought, and personal statements as nonsense, "these words of nonsense would," Burke argues, "be real works, involving real tactics, having real demonstrable relationships, and demonstrably affecting relationships." Burke apparently is assuming that the terms of his analysis have reference to a *reality* identified with whatever system or strategy he may be considering. Later, however, following a discussion of Kant under "Agent in General," Burke remarks that the test of a philosopher is what he can say about nothing and hastens to add that his own five terms are "all about nothing, since they designate not this scene, or that agent, etc. but scene, agent, etc. in general."

Burke may not himself know and it is not possible for the reader to determine to what extent he believes that language can have reference to reality and to what extent he believes that he must assume a verbal universe in which knowledge is purely metaphysical. He concludes that the attitude embodied in his method is one of "linguistic skepticism," in keeping with "linguistic appreciation" since "an attitude of methodical quizzicality towards language may best equip us to perceive the full scope of its resourcefulness."

But some of Burke's ideas are inconsistent with an attitude of skepticism: Self, which is "under the sign of Agent . . . , has the same universalized quality [as transcendental idealism], making it a super-self or non-self, that we noticed in the mystic paradox whereby absolute purpose becomes transformed into necessity." He illustrates the idea by the anonymous wanderer in the poems of Shelley: "The kind of super person thus envisaged *beyond* language but *through* language may be *generically* human rather than *individually* human insofar as language is a *collective* product and the capacity of complex symbolic action is distinctive of the human race. Hence the Self we encounter at the outer limits of language would be a *transcendent* Self, an individual 'collectively redeemed' by being apprehended through a medium itself essentially collective."

The idea of a generalized or "universalized" character is reasonable, in view of the collective nature of language and the necessarily abstract nature of both language and art. But when Burke speaks of a capitalized "*transcendent* Self" to be encountered at the "outer limits of language," it sounds as though he is very close to the myth critic's view of art as an object to be transcended rather than as a bond to the world of experience in which the reader lives and has his being.

A Grammar of Motives is the volume to which Burke's analysis of Keats's "Ode on a Grecian Urn" as a rebirth archetype is appended. Burke had commented in *The Philosophy of Literary Form* on the profusion of rebirth rituals in the literature of transitional eras, and his concern for them has a social emphasis, since he is interested in promoting a conversion from patriarchal-competitive to matriarchal-cooperative values. His discussion of Keats's poem and of Shelley's wanderer, however, resists containment by a social and experiential view of literature. Although he has depended heavily on Freud for his ideas and terminology, as his logology has developed he has left behind the empirical attitude of psychoanalysis, and his conception of the function of poetic language is closer to that of the Jungian archetype critic than to that of either the Marxist or Freudian critic.

Rewarding as much of Burke's criticism is, he is so involved in the terminological system he has created that it is difficult to ascertain what his commitment is or how his criticism is grounded in common experience. Not that the critic need establish any simple one-to-one relationship between the work and "reality." But literature, like all art, is concerned with the evocation and evaluation of experience. Critics tend to discuss the values of literature (they can be defined variously) from a selective point of view that represents their own experiential sense of reality. To this extent, at least, criticism has an empirical basis. Burke, however, is less concerned with the individuality of a work and its evaluation of experience than with its resources for the maintenance and development of his theoretical system, which despite his distrust of technology can perhaps best be thought of as a kind of autonomous machine, especially remarkable for the interchangeability of its parts.

Another eclectic critic is Leslie A. Fiedler, whose *Love and Death in the American Novel* (1960) is an unorthodox archetype study. Fiedler mentions, among various influences on his work, Marxist criticism, the theories of Freud and Jung, and D. H. Lawrence's *Studies in Classic American Literature;* and he announces that he has syncretically combined and freely transformed his borrowings. Despite its debt to psychology, his book seems closest to Lawrence's essays in its concern for the covert sexual themes of American literature and its record of conflict between conscious and instinctual forces.

While the idea of the archetype is Jung's, the love and death of Fiedler's title are Freud's Eros and Thanatos, the twin impulses toward life and death. The archetypal pattern isolated by Fiedler is not one of rebirth but rather of frustration and perversion resulting from the denial of mature sexuality in American literature, a reflection of the psyche of American society. The Oedipal situation supplies the basis for cultural analysis. Since the passing of the patriarchal Puritan order, the American male has habitually rejected the father as an image of authority and has substituted the figure of woman "as Maiden and Mother," represented by the idealized blonde heroine of sentimental fiction. The rejection of the father's role, and of maturity, has led the male to search for an innocent substitute for sexual love. The classic resolution has been an idealized homoerotic relationship, represented in literature by such devoted couples as Natty Bumppo and Chingachgook, Ishmael and Queequeg, Huck and Jim. To Fiedler this "pure marriage of males" is an archetype "haunting almost all our major writers of fiction" from Cooper to Hemingway. This love, innocent though it is made to seem, is sterile and self-destructive—the symbolic expression of a love of death.

The disguised forces of perversion in our literature stem

from the sentimental and romantic rebellion against the Enlightenment view of human nature as reasonable and innocent. Fiedler calls this reaction a "Break-through" in which the "darker motive forces of the psyche" refuse to be repressed and denied any longer. Their literary expression is indirect and symbolic, beginning in American fiction with the Gothic mode introduced by Charles Brockden Brown. The source of Gothic horror is the fear that "in destroying the old ego-ideals of Church and State, the West has opened a way for the inruption of darkness: for insanity and the disintegration of the self."

The withdrawal of sexual passion from art was responsible also for the "disguised masochism of the 'protest' novel," which Fiedler treats less sympathetically. He identifies social consciousness with sentimentality and comments that "the unemployed libido loves to walk on picket lines." But it would seem that modern protest novels dedicated to such issues as "anti-Semitism, racial discrimination, the atom bomb, McCarthyism, etc., etc."—which Fiedler cavalierly dismisses—are less the expression of the libido than of conscious ego-ideals important to the writer and his society.

Fiedler rounds off his study with detailed readings of three novels: *The Scarlet Letter,* "Woman as Faust"; *Moby-Dick,* "The Baptism of Fire and the Baptism of Sperm"; and *Huckleberry Finn,* "Faust in the Eden of Childhood." The Faust image is identified with the archetypal hero-villain of the Gothic romance and represents the isolated individual (and author) "challenging the mores of bourgeois society, making patent to all men the ill-kept secret that the codes by which they live are archaic survivals without point or power."

Love and Death is something of a tour de force in the

range and scope of fiction to which the author applies his thesis, and the book is admirable in many respects. Fiedler demonstrates the strength of the tradition he traces, seeing in the "tragic humanism" of Hawthorne and Melville the courage to confront the darker realities of life (a quality noted earlier by F. O. Matthiessen). He reveals the extent to which the Gothic tradition involves criticism of a decaying Western culture. His bold use of psychological concepts leads to fresh insights.

However, Fiedler's archetypal pattern is Procrustean, and the readings that support his interpretation are sometimes crude and insensitive. In discussing Twain's novel he characterizes Huck and Jim as sentimentalized "id-figures," while Tom Sawyer is Huck's "misguided ego-ideal." Huck is also a Faust figure whose pact with the devil occurs when he says, "All right, then I'll *go* to Hell," upon deciding to steal Jim out of slavery. The "American theme of loneliness" pervades the book, and in periods of "lonesomeness," when he says, "I most wished I was dead," Huck is "obsessed by, more than half in love with death." And in his isolation, after he has accepted his "terrible freedom," Huck seems to Fiedler "the first Existentialist hero, the improbable ancestor of Camus's 'Stranger,' or the protagonists of Jean-Paul Sartre, or the negative characters of the early Hemingway."

Although literary meanings are manifold, these particular interpretations are surely arbitrary and thesis-ridden. While Huck and Meursault have certain traits in common (they often take refuge in nature—in swimming, for instance—as an escape from an absurd and hypocritical society), there are important differences between them which Fiedler ignores. Huck is not morally and emotionally insulated from his fellows; his world is not meaningless; his isolation on the raft is redeemed by the presence of another and by the values of a shared life—by "ego-ideals" that have institutional support (the "Widow's Providence") even though they are largely denied in Twain's antebellum fictional world.

Another conspicuous defect of the book is its many extended passages of classroom explication that could profitably be replaced by more selective and discriminating criticism.

8

In *Fiction and the Unconscious* (1957) Simon O. Lesser attempts to apply Freudian psychoanalysis to literary theory by exploring the disguised appeals of literature and the unconscious responses of the reader. Although his aim is to be as scientific as possible, he describes his theory as "admittedly speculative" since the empirical knowledge amassed by psychoanalysis is not yet adequate to the needs of a completely naturalistic aesthetic.

One of the chief functions of fiction, Lesser believes, is to relieve anxieties and guilt feelings, although, unlike such other "auxiliary constructions" as drinking or asceticism, reading involves a confrontation of disagreeable facts and a reconciliation of the pleasure and reality principles. Assuming that fiction is concerned with basic emotional rather than intellectual or moral issues, he asserts that a novel like F. Scott Fitzgerald's *Tender Is the Night* is at no point "centrally concerned with moral problems"—a judgment that many of Fitzgerald's readers would question.

He acknowledges, however, that this novel, like any other, appeals to deep instinctive wishes by dealing with "what might be called sacred crimes, transgressions of the tabus on which human society is founded." It is able to do so in a disguised fashion, through the mediation of form, which delights and placates the ego. With the relaxation of the ego's vigilance, the reader is able to perceive, unconsciously, the depth meanings of literature in psychological truths unrecognized by the ego. In one of several illustrative analyses, Lesser discusses "My Kinsman, Major Molineux," one of the most compelling of Hawthorne's tales, which is to the conscious mind simply a "story of an ambitious youth's thwarted search for an influential relative he wants to find." To the unconscious mind, however, "it is a story of the youth's hostile and rebellious feelings for the relative—and for the father." By finally identifying himself with the mob that has tarred and feathered his kinsman, the Major, the hero is "destroying an image of paternal authority so that, freed from its restraining influence, he can begin life as an adult."

Although Lesser's analysis has been criticized as reductive, a reader familiar with Freudian psychology could not easily resist it as one of several possible interpretations, supported as it is by the dreamlike imagery and atmosphere of the story. Whether this meaning is actually perceived *unconsciously* is more difficult to determine. With the general dissemination of Freud's thought, writers, critics, and the reading public have come to share a sophisticated consciousness of patterns of unconscious behavior. This development, which has brought aspects of the unconscious into the ego's domain, has undoubtedly contributed to the current shift toward ego psychology.

Lesser does not minimize the importance of the ego. The principle of form, opposed to our destructive impulses, is identified with the conscious mind: "The solicitude form displays for everything it touches is only one of the means it employs to inform us that it respects the values of the ego and superego. One attribute of form, mastery or control, could be looked upon as an 'objective correlative' of certain functions of the ego, those concerned with regulating the instincts and bringing them into harmony with the demands of conscience."

In an appended "Note on the Use of Scientific Psychological Knowledge in Literary Study," Lesser recognizes that the critic who makes use of empirical knowledge is liable to the charge of reductiveness; he counters this charge by defending Freudian psychology as an essential aid to the understanding of motives in literature. It seems to him unfortunate and limiting that a prejudice should exist among students of literature against borrowing, not only from psychology but from the social sciences in general. The common and largely successful effort to "excommunicate certain kinds of knowledge from the field of literary study" he considers harmful and unhumanistic.

In considering the problem of terminology, Lesser recognizes the dangers of jargon and the overuse of technical words. Certain Freudian terms that are well-established and generally understood, like *ego,* are indispensable, since alternative descriptive language would be either inadequate or cumbersome. But the critic has the obligation of subordinating his terminology to the conditions of literary study and of treating literature as literature and not as psychology—a discrimination that Lesser displays in his own work.

Modern psychology has exerted a very great influence upon literary critics, both directly and indirectly. Even among those who have resisted psychological theory, there has been an increased awareness of the complexities of literature and sensitivity to its deeper meanings. Among more receptive critics, the ideas of Jung have suggested expanded possibilities of interpretation, as the work of Maud Bodkin attests, while Freudian psychology has provided concepts for theories of the nature and function of literature, as well as for the analysis of character and motive within works. Jung's theory of archetypes, which has already contributed a great deal to criticism, points to possibilities of further developments through the study of historically conditioned type-images, which relate the individual work to other literature and to its immediate social environment. The influence of both Jung and Freud has been most salutary when it has kept open the relationship of literature to our larger experience. It has been least so when it has attempted to isolate the experience of literature as an aesthetically pure or transcendentalized religious event—or when it has reduced literature to irrelevant biographical terms or to a solipsistic verbal universe reflecting a private theory. (This latter is not to deny language as a vital aspect of experience. But the values of literature derive from the relation of language to other kinds of experience, individual and social.)

While the trend of recent psychological theory has been toward a renewed stress on social and environmental factors in personality, there has been something of a lag in the carryover of current psychological theory to criticism. A preoccupation with pioneers like Freud and Jung is at present more common among literary critics than among psychologists. The coming years will probably bring about a growing interest in post-Freudian psychological theory affirming the rationality and moral responsibility of human nature and the social values of art.

◆§ 8 §◆

HISTORIES, THEORIES, AND CRITIQUES OF CRITICISM

1—Norman Foerster's American Criticism; *2—Bernard Smith's* Forces in American Criticism; *3—Wellek and Warren's* Theory of Literature; *4—Wimsatt and Brooks's* Literary Criticism: A Short History; *5—Louis Fraiberg's* Psychoanalysis & American Literary Criticism; *6—Northrop Frye's* Anatomy of Criticism; *7—S. E. Hyman's* The Armed Vision; *8—W. V. O'Connor, Murray Krieger, and Richard Foster; 9—Textbook anthologies of criticism*

There have been a number of general works, including histories, critical and theoretical discussions, and influential textbooks, which have surveyed broadly the field of modern criticism. Most of these can be identified with the viewpoint of one or another of the major groups, and many contribute to a fuller understanding of the problems and the resources of American literary criticism.

1

One of the first of these is Norman Foerster's *American Criticism: A Study in Literary Theory from Poe to the Present* (1928). The author, a specialist in American literature and a follower of Babbitt and More, has been mentioned as the editor of the symposium, *Humanism and America.* In

American Criticism, written when Humanism was at the height of its influence, Foerster reviews the theoretical assumptions of four nineteenth century figures—Poe, Emerson, Lowell, and Whitman—and considers their relevance to contemporary criticism.

Among the early romantics, Foerster favors Emerson over Poe, as might be expected. Although recognizing Poe's rationalism, he deplores his assertion that poetry is concerned solely with beauty and not with truth or goodness and concludes that Poe's fatal flaw, one that vitiates his aesthetic, is his intellectual and moral deficiency. For Emerson, however, beauty embraced intellectual truth and goodness, and the imagination was ethical. Even so, Foerster cannot accept Emerson as a prophet. Although he minimizes Emerson's debt to the romantics and links him with earlier traditions of Greek humanism and neo-Platonism, he perceives and distrusts his essential mysticism. In Foerster's view the resigned Unitarian preacher remained primarily an advocate of an otherworldly faith, and the weakest feature of his poetic theory is a false union of art and religion in which the values of literature are subordinated to the spiritual revelation attainable *through* literature.

Somewhat ironically, Foerster's highest praise is bestowed upon James Russell Lowell, whose reputation has sunk steadily during the twentieth century. Although Lowell, "our most distinguished literary critic," was more concerned with practical criticism than theory, Foerster believes that his sound principles earn him a high place, if only as one of "those 'brokers' of thought who perform a great if secondary office in literature." Somewhat ambivalently, Foerster acknowledges Lowell's impressionism and lack of intellectual force and at the same time asserts his importance as a critic because of his great learning, his use of a historical perspective in criticism, and his effort to conserve and combine the "best ideas offered by the two great critical traditions, the classic and the romantic."

Although Walt Whitman described himself as a "hell of a critic," his theory is important for modern American criticism. Foerster describes his point of view, which combined Emerson's idealism with an un-Emersonian confidence in the scientific mind, as a "transcendentalized deism," a doubly derogatory term. Whitman not only shared Emerson's "naturism," but possessed other offensive qualities. Ignoring the claims of an intellectual and cultural elite, he was a firm believer in democracy and the "divine average." Foerster views democracy in a mood of "weary acceptance mixed with distrust." While "committed to it for lack of any other promising working plan . . . , we can discern few indications that democracy might show itself a substantial basis for any such grandiose structure as that which Whitman prophesied." Whitman's acceptance of science links him with the realists, who identify man with nature as an object of scientific study, and, in concentrating on man's life in the here-and-now, ignore the cultural heritage of the past.

Because he is a prophetic critic, "dominated with the idea that the future will be different from and better than the present and the past," Whitman is ranked below both Emerson and Lowell, whom Foerster describes as "traditional critics, men impressed with the fact that humanity is made up of more dead than living, and with the rights of the dead to a hearing and a suffrage in matters of perennial interest to humanity." Emerson and Lowell are both "appraisers of tradition, enemies alike of convention and revolution." Although it is strange to hear Emerson, who professed to reject the dead past, described as a conservator and friend of tradition, Foerster points out that he was indebted in his reading to neo-Platonism supplemented by Eastern mysticism and seventeenth century metaphysical literature, as well as to nineteenth century romanticism. What Foerster does not note is that Whitman also was indebted to the past through Emerson and his other reading.

Skipping over such representatives of realism as Howells, James, and Garland, Foerster moves to his concluding chapter on the twentieth century, in which he discusses briefly the ideas of John Macy, author of *The Spirit of American Literature* (1913), as the expression of a new Whitmanesque spirit of revolt for which he holds little hope. Other modern critics mentioned but relegated to a footnote as followers of Macy include Van Wyck Brooks, Randolph Bourne, H. L. Mencken, Stuart Sherman, Carl Van Doren, Henry S. Canby, Lewis Mumford, and Harold E. Stearns.

Foerster's conclusion makes it clear that he is really less interested in discussing criticism than in characterizing the modern spirit and offering an ideology and a moral discipline for a disordered postwar society. He lumps romanticism, realism, and naturalism as "naturism," a term apparently invented by the Humanist for the disparagement of a scientific world view. In contrast to Humanism, naturism recognizes a past of only about three hundred years, the period of the rise of modern science, which brought about a better understanding of external nature but undermined traditional human values and religious beliefs. As a panacea, Foerster advances the reconstructive discipline of the New Humanism, with its emphasis on the dualism of man and nature, its belief in the freedom of the will and in the necessity of control, its faith in reason but dependence upon a suprarational ethical "intuition" or "imagination."

In his conclusion, Foerster also presents a critical method and aesthetic. The first step in Humanist criticism is historical understanding. The critic must attempt to read the work as the author himself would, in order to "re-create the aesthetic experience of which the book is the external expression, to revive in its totality the intention of which it is the issue." With this preparation, he is in a position to judge the book's value, both quantitatively, as to the degree in which the intention has been successfully carried out, and qualitatively. The criterion for his judgment is "truth or nature—the nature of things, things as they really are." Aware that this standard is suspiciously like that of the realists, Foerster explains that for the Humanist reality, or truth, is not found in men as they actually are (the concern of the realist) but in men as they ought to be "with reference to the perfection of the human type."

Unfortunately, Foerster provides no practical illustration of Humanist criticism. Although his statement acknowledges the Humanist's interest in the historical context of literature and reveals his habit of judging its moral values by his own, it does not relate the historical and moral to the aesthetic and formal characteristics of a work—a matter upon which Foerster might have been enlightened by Henry James if he had not chosen to ignore him as a "realist." The four essays on nineteenth century figures are carefully developed, from a Humanist point of view. But they do not constitute anything like a representative coverage of American critical theory. The omission of any discussion of the leading nineteenth century realists and any reference to the

Imagist theory of the first-world-war period or to the liberal, psychological, and formalist criticism of the 1920's is a serious weakness in a work issued in 1928 as a "Study in Literary Theory from Poe to the Present."

2

The cultural disintegration lamented by the Humanist was intensified by the crash of 1929 and the world-wide depression of the Thirties. As the prestige of the New Humanists declined, that of the liberal and Marxist critics rose.

Bernard Smith's sympathy with Marxism is apparent throughout *Forces in American Criticism* (1939), which is a selective but systematic survey of American criticism from its beginnings to the 1930's. Smith, who had been associated with the *New Masses* as both an editor and contributor, begins his work by professing his belief in the use of scientific methods in literary study, his antagonism to mysticism, and his bias "in favor of the broadest possible democracy."

It was not until the emergence of the romantic spirit, which accompanied the beginning of the machine age and the rise of popular democracy, that the predominantly "classical" standards of early American criticism were displaced. Smith sees romanticism as a liberating and creative force in its rebellion against social and literary conventions and its promotion of the democratic idea. But he disapproves of its extreme individualism, emotionalism, and mysticism, qualities reflected in transcendentalist criticism, which is largely subjective and impressionistic. Smith finds the critical essays in *The Dial* (1840-44), the chief organ of the movement, to be more often rhapsodic than analytical.

It was not until the advent of realism, with its concern for "materialistic truth," that a solid basis for criticism developed. Although a forerunner of realism, Whitman was limited by his mystical preoccupation with the spirit. Howells, who adapted Whitman's ideas, was the first American champion of a "realism devoid of metaphysical connotations." Inheriting the Western tradition of equalitarianism and troubled by the plight of the working class, Howells read with sympathy Edward Bellamy, Henry George, and the American Marxist, Laurence Gronlund. But because of his gentility, which led him to idealize the Brahmins and identify himself with the cultured and wealthy minority, he was not really a socialist. He was courageous, however, in speaking out on social issues, as at the time of the Haymarket Riot. More important for criticism was his insistence that the values of art must be democratic; that literature is for the public, not for an elite; and that the novel should "speak the dialect, the language that most Americans know—the language of unaffected people everywhere."

Smith sympathizes with the socially conscious criticism that originated with Whitman and Howells and sees other developments as regrettable divergences. In a chapter entitled "The Quest of Beauty," he treats Poe and Henry James as advocates of a sterile formalism. Identifying both with an "art for art's sake" position, he places each in his cultural setting and explains his social and aesthetic values. Smith recognizes James's critical sensitivity and his contributions to the theory of the novel as a representation of life. But because James was committed to nothing *besides* art, he did not deal "with the ultimate things for which men go to literature." Despite his aesthetic sense, he remained the appreciative observer, the man of taste rather than passion, without an integrating philosophy to support his otherwise admirable criticism. Like Poe, he remains, in his different way, a "forlorn aristocrat," who will be prized most highly by critics "interested in the sensibilities of superior individuals and convinced that the purpose of literature is to add to consciousness for its own sake."

Aside from the work of Howells and James, the critical landscape of the late nineteenth century is, for Smith, a genteel waste land. The one critic of importance was James Russell Lowell, an unoriginal appreciator and a reactionary in his literary as well as his social attitudes. Noting that Lowell explained his detestation of realism on the grounds that there is a higher reality than the phenomenal, Smith remarks, "The metaphysics of idealism was, of course, a favorite weapon of all genteel critics, becoming at last one of the surest stigmata of a reactionary esthetic."

As his discussion approaches the early years of the twentieth century, Smith singles out three critical tendencies for comment: the impressionism of James Huneker, the expressionism of Joel Spingarn, and the early socialist criticism of Floyd Dell. Of these, the first two are aristocratic in their aestheticism and can appeal only to a minority. Socialist criticism, however, distinguished by its Marxist strain, offers a scale of values upon which literary as well as social judgments can be made in terms of an author's relation to his society. Critics like Floyd Dell have not realized the potential of Marxism for criticism, however, because they are not fully committed.

Smith views the criticism of the postwar period as largely a war of traditions and "a struggle between irreconcileable ideologies" embracing such diverse positions as those of the Menckenists, the liberals, the radicals, the New Humanists, and the "classicists." Liberalism—represented by Van

Wyck Brooks and Lewis Mumford, associated with magazines like the *Nation* and the *New Republic*—is useless, a dead end of idealistic individualism. A radicalism like that of Parrington, in his *Main Currents in American Thought,* offers more promise because he makes use of "a materialist approach, in the form of economic determinism" as a way out of what he called "the 'arid desert' of romantic philosophy on the one hand and the sterility of pure esthetics on the other." Ignoring Parrington's own affinities with romanticism, Smith sees him as a pioneer in the Marxist analysis of culture although he was not "an outright socialist or a true Marxist." T. S. Eliot, who had studied under Babbitt and to whom the "classicists" looked as a leader, acknowledged that "literary criticism should be completed by criticism from a definite ethical and theological standpoint"—a statement Smith interprets as a confession of the bankruptcy of formalism since it admits that "non-esthetic criteria are the ultimate tests of value."

Marxism offers a firmer support for literary criticism. The limitations of existing Marxist criticism result from a too exclusive political concern. Marxist critics are too eager to reject the literature of the past, ignoring its continuity with the present, and to push the thesis that art is a weapon in the class struggle. They have slighted the problems of aesthetic appreciation and of "the interaction of idea and form, of emotion and expression." However, they have already made a contribution to criticism by introducing "non-literary standards that change the rules of the game, that make it more of a science, that bring it closer to the rest of life." They "have a philosophy of history to explain the present and guide them to a desirable future. They have a faith. They have a unifying idea. And therefore as critics of literature they have principles by which any work may be rationally interpreted and which may inspire and direct the creative impulse. No critic can ask for more; no critic should be satisfied with less. He who cannot accept their principles is obliged to offer alternatives for which as much can be claimed and which are as susceptible to being tested by reason and experience."

Smith's history provides a fairly complete coverage of American criticism from a consistent though biased point of view. It is superior to Foerster's *American Criticism* in its scope, though less intensive in its analysis. Foerster's book reveals a close familiarity with the work of the few figures treated; Smith often relies on secondary sources in the earlier periods, although he gives evidence of supporting research.

While he recognized the need of adjusting aesthetic and ideological considerations, Smith has not succeeded in doing so in his own work. (One obstacle is his blanket rejection of formalism, even when the relevance of ideas and moral values to formal criticism is demonstrated, as in the theory of Henry James.) This weakness, which Smith shares with most Marxist critics, does not alter the fact that he has presented a thoughtful and thought-provoking discussion of American criticism. It is noteworthy that this Marxist history of criticism is superior to almost all of the great mass of Marxist practical criticism of the 1930's.

3

In closing his study, Bernard Smith considered the opposed viewpoints of the Marxists and the conservative "classicists" and asked, "To whom does the future belong?" To him the question was rhetorical: Marxism was in ascendancy and Eliot, the leader of the classicists, had just announced (in January 1939) the demise of the *Criterion,* the review he had edited since 1922. But Marxism had also suffered losses in the years between the Spanish Civil War and the beginning of World War II; and at the close of the Thirties Marxist criticism was being displaced by the New Criticism.

By the end of the following decade, during which the New Criticism became firmly established, there appeared an influential work, not a history of criticism but a discussion of the methods of literary study. This was *Theory of Literature* (1949) by René Wellek and Austin Warren. In the preface the authors speak of desiring "to unite 'poetics' (or literary theory) and 'criticism' (evaluation of literature) with 'scholarship' ('research') and 'literary history' (the 'dynamics' of literature, in contrast to the 'statics' of theory and criticism)" in an effort to provide an "organon" of method for literary study.

After a concise introductory section, "Definitions and Distinctions," discussing the nature of literary study and of literature, and an even briefer section on "Preliminary Operations," the major portion of the book consists of two parts entitled "The Extrinsic Approach to the Study of Literature" and "The Intrinsic Study of Literature"—a division which automatically has the effect of establishing a dichotomy between "historical" and "aesthetic" or formalist literary study. This effect is reinforced by the chapter headings in the "extrinsic" section, which include "Literature and Biography," "Literature and Psychology," "Literature and Society," "Literature and Ideas," and "Literature and the Other Arts." Among the chapters of the "intrinsic" section are "The Analysis of the Literary Work of Art," "Euphony,

Rhythm, and Meter," "Image, Metaphor, Symbol, and Myth," together with others on such topics as "Literary Genres" and "Literary History."

Because of a bias in favor of the "intrinsic" mode of study, the authors' theoretical position supports the formalist tendency of the New Criticism. Despite the wide range of topics, the coverage is surprisingly efficient, except in a number of the "extrinsic study" chapters, which are slanted in such a way as to ignore and foreclose the potential uses for criticism of the subjects treated. The discussion is supplemented by a generous system of notes and bibliographical references international in scope. Both provide useful leads for further reading in a broader context of scholarship than is usual for works of literary theory.

One of the admirable features of *Theory of Literature* is the authors' attempt to clarify and guide the usage of literary terminology by considering problems of definition. Even in those instances in which they do not succeed in settling the questions raised, attention is focused on the problem of terminology and on theoretical questions.

In the first chapter Wellek and Warren distinguish between literature and literary study, which must translate the "experience of literature into intellectual terms, assimilate it to a coherent scheme which must be rational if it is to be knowledge," even though literature itself contains "unrational elements." They are skeptical of the procedures of the natural and social sciences and believe that specialized methods and terms must be developed for literary study. (This attitude helps to explain the relegation of psychology, sociology, and the history of ideas to the "extrinsic" category.)

The authors decide to limit the application of *literature* to imaginative writing, both verse and prose. They make a distinction between its language and that of science on the grounds that literary language is not merely referential but highly connotative. Just what is the referential nature of literary language is a question not conclusively treated. Here the statement is made that the "reference is to a world of fiction, of imagination." In the next chapter, dealing with the function of literature, it is suggested that it may communicate knowledge or "truth" either in a systematic conceptual form—as it may exist outside—or in a "presentational" form, to use the term introduced by Susanne K. Langer in *Philosophy in a New Key* (1942). At any event, the communication of knowledge and truth is regarded as not the most important, but as only one among many possible functions of literature; its "prime and chief function" is defined but not explained as "fidelity to its own nature."

The least satisfactory part of the book is the section on the "extrinsic approach" to literary study, which is concerned primarily with literature in terms of "its setting, its environment, its external causes." In a sequence of five brief chapters, averaging thirteen pages in length, the relevance to literary study of biography, psychology, sociology, the history of ideas, and the context of the other arts is considered and dismissed as insignificant. The method employed is uniform: first to survey the actual and possible ways in which these sources of knowledge may be used and then to decide that they are largely concerned with external events and contribute little or nothing to the understanding of the literary work.

Thus in Chapter 8, "Literature and Psychology," the authors consider three possible uses in "the psychological study of the writer, as type and as individual, or the study of the creative process, or the study of psychological types and laws present within works of literature." Of these, only the third belongs to literary study "in the strictest sense." Strangely, most of the chapter is given over to a consideration of the first two while the third, the question of psychology in the work, is dismissed in about two pages. The conclusion is that "in itself, psychology is only preparatory to the art of creation; and in the work itself, psychological truth is an artistic value only if it enhances coherence and complexity —if, in short, it is art."

The very important question of the aesthetic value of psychology as an aid to understanding the interrelationship of the elements of the literary work Wellek and Warren leave virtually untouched as they raise questions of the "realism" of such devices as the stream of consciousness technique in Faulkner and Joyce. What they accomplish by this treatment is not so much an exploration of the possible uses of psychology in criticism as an avoidance of the subject for reasons that may stem from their bias against extraliterary disciplines.

The same bias and argument appear in other chapters of this section. That on "Literature and Society" begins with the promising statement that "literature is a social institution, using as its medium language, a social creation. Such traditional literary devices as symbolism and meter are social in their very nature . . . , conventions and norms which could have arisen only in society." But unfortunately the relation of literature and society is usually conceived more "narrowly and externally" by those with a sociological interest in literature. The chief weaknesses of the sociological approach, then, are its reductiveness and its extrinsic concerns. Taine's triad of *race, milieu,* and *moment* has led, in practice, to "an exclusive study of the milieu." Although Marx realized that the relationship between literature and society was oblique, "the vulgar Marxist tells us that this or that writer was a bourgeois who voiced reactionary or progressive opinions about Church and State." Wellek and Warren acknowledge that the best Marxist criticism "exposes the implied, or latent, social implications of a writer's work," but they cite no examples. They do not even comment upon the better non-Marxist criticism with a sociological emphasis, like much of Edmund Wilson's work.

On the whole, the authors find sociological thought to have very little actual or potential use for criticism. Only if the social determination of forms were to be proved, could "the question be raised whether social attitudes cannot become 'constitutive' and enter the work of art as effective parts of its artistic value."

One can sympathize with the judgment of the weakness of most sociological criticism, as in the tendency of Marxist critics to practice an "evaluative" criticism based on nonliterary political and ethical criteria. But instead of canvassing fairly the possible uses of "extrinsic" disciplines, Wellek and Warren forestall further consideration by pronouncements which have the effect of excommunicating from the body of true literary scholars critics who make use of them: "There is great literature which has little or no social relevance. . . ." "No biographical evidence can change or influence critical evaluation." Neither of these assertions can withstand close scrutiny. All literature has a "social relevance" which can be discussed in terms of the sources of knowledge virtually proscribed by Wellek and Warren, a relevance not restricted to any "content" which can be nonaesthetically conceived. Despite the authors' exclusions, attitudes and ideas from sociology and other sources can function as "constitutive" formal elements of the literary work. Moreover, they can do so in terms of the definition of the literary work of art provided by Wellek and Warren in their own discussion of the "intrinsic study of literature."

This portion of the book begins with a chapter entitled "The Analysis of the Literary Work of Art," in which a poem is described as "not an individual experience or a sum of experiences, but only a potential cause of experiences." From a viewpoint they call "Perspectivism," the authors describe the "real poem" as a "structure of norms, realized only partially in the actual experience of its many readers. Every single experience (reading, reciting, and so forth) is only an attempt—more or less successful and complete—to grasp this set of norms or standards."

The norms exist not as a single system but as a complex of "several strata, each employing its own subordinate group," and including, in a rising order, sound, meaning, and objects represented (the "world" of the novelist or poet). Above these are two not wholly separable strata—that of the "point of view" employed by the writer and that of the work's "metaphysical qualities." The latter permits the introduction of "questions of the 'philosophical meaning' of works of art without the usual intellectualist errors."

The authors recognize the necessary relativism of the poem as it is experienced by different readers. In one sense the literary work of art is like a system of language, which is never realized completely by any one speaker. But this relativism does not require the acceptance of an anarchic impressionism. The authors insist on a substantial "identity of 'structure' " for different readers of the same or different generations. The *Iliad,* for example, possesses this substantial identity, even though its structure must be recognized as dynamic, changing "throughout the process of history while passing through the minds of its readers, critics, and fellow artists." All these different ideas of the poem are not equally right. The authors insist that a "hierarchy of viewpoints" exists and that "all relativism is ultimately defeated by the recognition that 'the Absolute is in the relative, though not finally and fully in it.' "

The perspectivist idea of the structure of a work as a complex of interrelated systems of norms, partially and variously seen by different readers, is a valuable one for any theory of criticism that recognizes the validity of a multiplicity of approaches. But it has several awkward features as it is formulated by Wellek and Warren. One is the emphasis upon contextual meaning (although the possibility of philosophical meaning is admitted). This stress is achieved by slighting all possible uses of extraliterary disciplines in critical analysis. If the terms of grammar can function as norms for the definition of sentence patterns within the work and if the terms of philosophy can be introduced in discussing the metaphysical stratum, there is no justification for excluding the terms of history, psychology, or sociology as norms that might be used in the same way, especially since all norms must derive from some area or other of the reader's experience "outside" the work.

While it is obvious that all readings of a work are not of equal value, the authors' idea of a hierarchy of viewpoints is not supported by any standard or control other than the rather murky pronouncement that "the Absolute is in the relative, though not finally and fully in it." Could not this control more profitably be identified with the poem's objective order of words? Instead of contrasting "the poem itself" with various individual conceptions of its structural identity, it would be more useful to think of these separate views as representing simply aspects of *form* manifested by the objective order of words, which has a formal potential that can never be fully realized.

The chapters immediately following—"Euphony, Rhythm, and Meter"; "Style and Stylistics"; "Image, Metaphor, Symbol, Myth"—include discussions of problems of technique and theory in an order corresponding to the rising order of the strata of the literary work. In "Image, Metaphor, Symbol, Myth," the authors recognize that these terms are overlapping, pointing to the same area of interest and representing "the convergence of two lines, both important for the theory of poetry." One of these is sensuous particularity; the other, figuration or tropology—"the 'oblique' discourse which speaks in metonyms and metaphors." While the image, as a relic of sensation, is closer to the particular, and the symbol, as a representation, is closer to the figurative, all four of these essentially metaphoric devices necessarily possess both sensuous and figurative attributes. The authors point out that poets have not succeeded in writing purely imagistic or "physical" poetry and that Pound himself, the leader of the Imagists, defined the image "not as a pictorial representation but as 'that which presents an intellectual and emotional complex in an instant of time.' "

Is there any way, then, in which a term like *symbol* (in a literary rather than a logical or mathematical sense) can be distinguished from *image* or *metaphor*? Wellek and Warren suggest that the difference is in the "recurrence and persistence" of the symbol: "An 'image' may be invoked once as a metaphor, but if it persistently recurs, both as presentation and representation, it becomes a symbol, may even become part of a symbolic (or mythic) system." Although this distinction has not been commonly accepted, Wellek and Warren perform a service by focusing attention on problems of terminology and by suggesting solutions.

Theory of Literature has had a significant influence on analytical criticism on the graduate and professional level in much the same way that Brooks and Warren's *Understanding Poetry* has had on the undergraduate level. It has been criticized, more often by students than by teachers, for raising questions of theory and usage that it fails to answer. But the questions raised are important ones, even if no final solutions have as yet been found.

4

Another and later work sympathetic to the New Criticism is *Literary Criticism: A Short History* (1957) by William K. Wimsatt, Jr., and Cleanth Brooks. In introducing their selective treatment of literary criticism from the time of Plato and Aristotle to the present, the authors disclaim any idea that it should be viewed as a disinterested or relativistic historical account. It is, rather, "polemic" and "argumentative" and might more properly be called an "*Argumentative History of Literary Argument in the West.*" The authors are concerned with theoretical principles; they are less interested in presenting a history of aesthetics than "a history of ideas about verbal art and about its elucidation and criticism." The problem that serves as their unifying device is the difficult question of "the kind of knowledge which a criticism of a poem, or a poem itself, can lay claim to." ("What does a poem say that is worth listening to? What does criticism say?")

For Wimsatt and Brooks, the most satisfactory solution to this problem can be drawn from the poetics of tension and irony of I. A. Richards, the "impersonal" theory of Eliot and Pound, and the religious speculation of much of the later New Criticism. While the authors have avowedly "not been concerned to implicate literary theory with any kind of religious doctrine," it appears to them that the "kind of literary theory which seems . . . to emerge from the long history of the debates is far more difficult to orient within any of the Platonic or Gnostic world views, or within the Manichaean full dualism and strife of principles, than precisely within the vision of suffering, the optimism, the mystery which are embraced in the religious doctrine of the Incarnation."

The book consists of five parts comprising thirty-two chapters. Some chapters center upon certain heroic figures (Plato, Aristotle, Horace, Longinus) while others follow thematic lines ("Art for Art's Sake"; "Symbolism"; "Myth and Archetype"). As might be expected in a work attempting to cover so great an expanse in 750-odd pages, there are numerous omissions of figures and subjects and also a considerable unevenness from chapter to chapter. Some reveal a familiarity with original sources while others are markedly dependent on secondary materials. Some are effectively developed, even within the authors' limits of space, while others give the impression of incompleteness.

The subject of modern criticism is largely though not exclusively confined to the seven chapters contributed by Cleanth Brooks (25-31) and to the epilogue by Wimsatt (Chapter 32). In his discussion, Brooks treats sympathetically Richards' theory of poetic tension and Eliot and Pound's idea of an "impersonal art"; he is less favorably disposed toward the tradition of symbolism and the modern development of myth and archetype criticism, which depends in part upon it. As for nineteenth century symbolism, Brooks distrusts its purist tendency toward an "angelism" which would identify the aesthetic symbol with an ideal reality and deny the claims of human and animal existence.

Among philosophers contributing to the growth of myth and archetype criticism, Ernst Cassirer and Susanne K. Langer are singled out for discussion. Both are careful to distinguish myth from poetry, unlike many myth critics who have been more influenced by Jungian psychology and anthropology. Although Brooks disapproves of the monistic tendencies of Jung's theory, he sees in the idea of a psychic tension expressing itself as "the play of opposites" a confirmation of his own idea of irony and tension as principles of poetic structure.

Unlike most of the New Criticism of the 1940's, which did not customarily appeal to the authority of psychology, the *Short History* cites Freud as well as Jung. Brooks refers to "Wit and Its Relation to the Unconscious" in his discussions of comedy and of Richards' poetics of tension and acknowledges a critical debt to Freud for a "whole new psychological vocabulary" and for an enlargement of our awareness of "the richness and complexity to which a literary symbol may attain."

In considering Richards' "context" theory of meaning, which holds that words interanimate one another within a qualifying context and that poetic meaning is found only through a process of exploration, Brooks devotes most attention to the question of metaphor, which Richards had defined as a transaction between and a merging of two different contexts. Brooks is concerned with the fact that the joining of the two contexts produces a third thing, quite different from either, "a new meaning in which imagination pushes itself forward and occupies new ground."

An interest in metaphor as a key to poetic meaning appears also in Wimsatt's "Epilogue," the summary last chapter of the book, which examines metaphor as a device through which the critic may be able to break down or modify the idea of the strict contextual confinement of poetic meaning.

Wimsatt sees the whole movement of critical opinion as pointed toward "a certain kind of goal," which he discusses in terms of values and questions of truth and reality. Apparently to resist the tendency toward a complete subjectivity, Wimsatt argues that some values, even though they are not "objective," have the character of universals because they are *"intersubjective."* Though the poet is concerned primarily with the "inner moral and spiritual experience of man," as the realm of "our most clearly absolute, our most securely universal concepts of value," he does not leave behind those assigned to external phenomena and experiences. The experience of color, for example, has a value not only as a source of sensory pleasure but also of a symbolic and phenomenological language through which the poet "speaks about the inner and deeper realities of value." Even though the lessons of literary theory seem to tell us that stress must be placed on subjective and emotive experience, rather than upon the object "so far as that is outside *any* experiencing subject," this lesson does not relegate the values of poetry to "the whimsical and debatable": "A refraction of light through a crystal tells us something about the light, something about the crystal; the refraction itself is a kind of reality, interesting to observe. Let us say that poetry is a kind of reality refracted through subjective responses. This refraction itself is an area of reality. Does the refraction tell us something unique and profound about the reality beyond itself? We need not actually say much about this for the purposes of a workable poetics. (Much will depend on what we conceive the ultimate character of that reality to be.)"

Wimsatt believes that contextualist theory based on Richards' idea of irony can help to reconcile the claims of objective and subjective reality and that it is concerned with human and moral problems to an extent that has not been appreciated: "The 20th-century neo-classic irony of poetic inclusiveness, looking back to conversational ironic symbolism, and finding a theoretical hint in quotations from Coleridge by Eliot and Richards, has had a strongly emotive and at times moral accent. There is a direct concern with human affairs and human values here (human 'interests'), good and evil, pleasure and pain, rather than with the mysteries of knowledge and creation, the activity of that 'synthetic and magical power' the imagination. And so it seems to us that the recent ironists have put a hard problem very compellingly."

It is at this point that Wimsatt introduces his opinion that the poetics he favors is more compatible with "the religious dogma of the Incarnation" than with any other world view. The idea seems to be that just as the figure of the Christ embraces the physical and the spiritual, unites the universal with the individual spirit, and reconciles goodness and evil, the poem too, through the operation of irony and tension, embraces and reconciles the widest possible range of human values and experience, subjective and objective. "'Irony' may be usefully taken . . . as a cognitive principle which shades off through paradox into the general principle of metaphor and metaphoric structure—the tension which is always present when words are used in vitally new ways."

Poetic metaphor alone provides the "most radically and relevantly fused union of the detail and the universal idea," and through metaphor poetry can convey a truth, which Wimsatt describes as truth of "coherence" rather than "correspondence." He would encourage "a double or paradoxical theory" which through its stress on metaphor can avoid the alternative reductions of aesthetic values to either sensory qualities or "conceptualized ethical and religious values." The special character of poetry or imaginative literature is "a tensional union of making with seeing and saying," a union that comprehends the Aristotelian emphasis and the Platonic and romantic. The aesthetic to which Wimsatt appeals in conclusion is that of the neo-Thomist Jacques Maritain, who thinks of poetry as a principle of subjective communion with objective reality and as the essence of the arts.

Wimsatt and Brooks's short history is typical of much New Critical theory in its endeavor to defend the contextual integrity of poetry, to establish a cognitive function for it, and to prove that it has something to say about a society's common values. It goes beyond earlier contextualist theory, and in this respect it is typical of its time, in its willingness to admit general truths and values to the poem. By conceiving of metaphor as a "fused union" of the particular and the universal, Wimsatt pushes Ransom's idea of the "concrete universal" further than Ransom himself was willing to go. But by insisting that poetic truth is a truth of coherence rather than correspondence, by refusing to admit referential propositions to the poem in the form of either direct statement or metaphor, Wimsatt remains in the familiar contextualist dilemma. This plight cannot be relieved by positing a "double or paradoxical theory" if it denies referential meaning to literature.

As the authors admit, the book is highly selective, argumentative, and even polemic. For this reason it seems unfortunate and even misleading for them to call it a "history," a term that suggests comprehensiveness. In comparison with a history like Bernard Smith's *Forces in American Criticism,* the work is deficient. Writing from an equally biased point of view, Smith nevertheless includes other critical perspectives, something Wimsatt and Brooks fail to do. Their work gives no idea of the range and variety of modern critical approaches and theories. Sociological criticism is discussed by Wimsatt in a chapter entitled "The Real and the Social: Art as Propaganda," in which fewer than four pages are assigned to modern American criticism; these are largely devoted to disparaging references to Parrington, Edmund Wilson, and Marxist criticism. Wilson's contribution is ticked off in one misrepresentative sentence: "Edmund Wilson in *Axel's Castle,* 1931, made gestures acknowledging the social responsibility of the artist but only as if in atonement for his having dwelt at such length among the mysteries of symbolism." F. O. Matthiessen, who attempted to combine aesthetic and social considerations in his work, is not mentioned in the short history (except for an early reference to his work on translation as an Elizabethan art). This omission is typical of the neglect of many important individual modern critics.

5

The influence of classical Freudian psychology is the subject of Louis Fraiberg's *Psychoanalysis & American Literary*

Criticism (1960). As a background for the discussion of the practice of six critics, Fraiberg surveys the writings of Freud and three of his colleagues as they bear on art and particularly literature. The treatment of the four psychoanalysts is economical and efficient, although less rewarding in the chapters dealing with Freud and Ernest Jones than in those devoted to the relatively unfamiliar work of Hanns Sachs and Ernst Kris.

Disturbed by the extent to which psychoanalysis has been associated in the mind of the public and of most critics with the concept of the unconscious, Fraiberg is eager to emphasize the importance of recent work in ego psychology, which takes account of the conscious control and craft that goes into the production of art and also of its social and communicative functions. This interest is apparent from the first chapter, on Freud, in which art is described as a "mysterious combination" of intuitive choice and deliberate and conscious craftsmanship. The same emphasis is present in Fraiberg's summary of Freud's ideas about art: "Psychoanalysis as Freud conceived it stresses the value of the social function of art, its communication of mind with mind and psyche with psyche. This involves the transmission of the artist's ideas and psychic states by the use of symbols capable of carrying both conscious and unconscious stimuli which together evoke in the appreciator a combined intellectual and emotional response. Their power is enhanced by their patterns (artistic form), especially when these approximate the patterns of the basic human experiences which both artist and audience have as their common heritage."

The principal work of Hanns Sachs is *The Creative Unconscious* (1942). Although Sachs (editor of the Vienna *Imago* and the later *American Imago*) was investigating the unconscious, and preconscious, roots of creative activity, his findings also emphasized its conscious and social characteristics. The ascending order of such mental activities as individual fantasy, mutual daydreaming, and artistic creation reveals a movement away from the isolation of wishful individual fantasy and toward a shared social experience. The work of art gratifies the unconscious wishes of its audience and pleases by its formal elements (symmetry, rhythm, euphony, and so forth), which are lacking in the personal fantasy. Although the literary work inevitably reflects a conflict between the id and the ego, between impulse and inhibition, it cannot threaten the security of the super-ego if it is to be aesthetically successful, for to Sachs the absence of anxiety is an "indispensable condition" for beauty. The gratification of the super-ego allows it to suspend its usual function of censure and control over the ego and permits, in aesthetic appreciation, a pleasurable integration of the id, ego, and super-ego, which are ordinarily at war with each other.

The work of Ernst Kris gives the greatest scope for Fraiberg's interest in the relation of ego psychology and art. In his *Psychoanalytic Explorations in Art* (1952) Kris combines his training and experience in art and psychoanalysis. He makes it clear that simply to identify a recurrent theme or motif in literature, like the Oedipus complex or the rebirth archetype, is of slight critical value. What is more important is the way in which the recurrent pattern has been shaped and modified by a conscious artist working within a particular social context. While much of the force of literature comes from unconscious impulses, the work, as art, is subject to ego controls and is evaluated by criteria that have little or no connection with id-impulses. Fraiberg renders Kris's view thus: "Art is a function not of our animal nature—although it may be said to grow out of this—but of that which makes us human; it does not come from our isolated selves but from that part of us that reaches out to the rest of humanity. It expresses not only our relationship to the world as it is but also to the world as we wish it to be, and it thus opens the way to limitless human aspirations."

Of the critics discussed by Fraiberg, three whose work belongs to the Twenties and early Thirties have been considered previously as early psychological critics: Van Wyck Brooks, Joseph Wood Krutch, and Ludwig Lewisohn. Fraiberg thinks that none of these men succeeded in integrating psychology and criticism. While Van Wyck Brooks achieved a kind of social criticism in his biography of Twain, his knowledge of Freud was rudimentary and often misapplied. Krutch had a slightly better knowledge of Freud at the time he wrote his biography of Poe, but, since he was more interested in psychoanalyzing the author than in treating his writing critically, Fraiberg classifies his work as "psychography." In *Expression in America,* Ludwig Lewisohn subordinated both psychology and criticism to ethics in developing his argument that Puritanism had inhibited American literature.

The remaining three figures—Edmund Wilson, Kenneth Burke, and Lionel Trilling—are more highly regarded as critics, but not always as students of psychoanalytic theory. Edmund Wilson is a critic of taste and competence who looks upon psychoanalysis as a tool of the historical criticism in which he is primarily interested. Fraiberg considers Wilson a fair student of the earlier Freud, with a special talent for applying the interpretation of dream symbols to literature. The most questionable feature of Wilson's use of psychology is his "wound and bow" theory developed in the essay on

Sophocles' *Philoctetes.* Fraiberg believes that Wilson, like others who have made use of Freud's discussion of the neuroticism of the artist, has failed to consider the full context of Freud's remarks. He points out that Freud's famous statement about the artist as a man who turns from reality to fantasy is followed by an important qualification: "But he finds a way of return from this world of fantasy back to reality; with his special gifts he moulds his fantasies into a new kind of reality, and men concede them a justification as valuable reflections of actual life."

But one wonders if Wilson's use of the story really implies that the artist is cut off from society? Philoctetes was needed by the Greeks and contributed to their victory. Perhaps the difficulty with Wilson's use of the legend is that he did not spell out all its implications and its relation to his own criticism but used it metaphorically, contenting himself with a comment on the association of the traumatic "wound" with creativity.

In "Kenneth Burke's Terminological Medium of Exchange" Fraiberg objects to Burke's use of interchangeable terms from various disciplines without regard for their reference to observable phenomena, thus ignoring the scientific basic of psychoanalysis. In Fraiberg's opinion, Burke regards verbal symbols simply as a "kind of universal medium of exchange, with added magical properties." It is not possible to combine religious and scientific vocabularies or even the terms and concepts of various fields of knowledge without violence. Fraiberg is particularly disturbed by Burke's attempt to integrate the ideas of Marx and Freud, a union which cannot be achieved, he believes, without "destroying what is essential for one, or both."

Fraiberg reserves his highest praise for Lionel Trilling as

the critic who has made most effective use of Freud's ideas, especially in his recognition of Freud's conception of the mind as a poetry-making organ and in his idea of the mithridatic function of tragedy. Trilling's discussion of the relation between the writer and his society in *The Opposing Self* and *Freud and the Crisis in Our Culture* reveals an awareness of ego psychology as it concentrates on "the interaction between a writer's artistic impulse and its environment."

In his summary last chapter, Fraiberg decides that the chief weakness of most of the critics discussed is an incomplete knowledge of psychoanalysis which shows up in their tendency to regard published findings as a closed theory and to ignore the interaction of theory and clinical experience. If the critic chooses to use psychoanalysis, one of several extraliterary disciplines, he has the obligation of acquiring a competent working knowledge of its history, theory, and practice, a knowledge that should ideally be acquired through a combination of study and experience. Such a critic would learn the necessary lesson that psychoanalysis is a science and that it is not "confined merely to pathology or even to individual psychology, but that it has the means for studying all aspects of human behavior."

Within his established limits Fraiberg has produced a careful and responsible study. By stressing the importance of ego psychology, he encourages the further development of a psychological criticism of literature in its social setting. By emphasizing the empirical foundation of psychoanalysis, he demonstrates the relevance of science to criticism and thus calls attention to a neglected resource in an area too long regarded with aversion and hostility by many scholars in the humanities. Fraiberg's claims for psychoanalytic science are not excessive. He admits the limits of its competence and the question of "how much it can ultimately reveal about the shaping, controlling and creating functions of the mind and about their influence upon finished works of art." But yet this science *can* contribute to our understanding of the literary work, and a creative criticism "will take from psychoanalysis what it has to offer and use it within the larger critical context." His final point, an extremely pertinent one, is that "the values of the critic can hardly be compromised if they take into account the little that science can tell us about the truth."

6

Another scholar interested in the relation between criticism and science is Northrop Frye. His *Anatomy of Criticism: Four Essays* (1957) is presented as a tentative "synoptic view of the scope, theory, principles, and techniques of literary criticism." In its method and aim it is the most ambitious work of its kind to appear since Wellek and Warren's *Theory of Literature* attempted to set forth an *organon* of critical methods.

Frye's "Polemical Introduction" considers the relationship of literary to scientific study. In Frye's opinion, criticism is ideally "an examination of literature in terms of a conceptual framework derivable from an inductive survey of the literary field." It is thus a kind of science, though not a fully developed or pure one. While criticism must deal with literature in terms of a conceptual framework which is not that of literature itself, Frye believes that the framework should be determined by the nature of the work, rather than by the biases and preconceptions of the critic. He flatly opposes, as unscientific, all determinisms in criticism, "whether Marxist, Thomist, liberal-humanist, neo-Classical, Freudian, Jungian, or existentialist," because they substitute a critical attitude for criticism and "attach criticism to one of a miscellany of frameworks outside it."

As a rudimentary science, criticism stands in need of a theoretical development that will assimilate "its work into a unified structure of knowledge" comparable to those of the older sciences. Such a development requires the formulation of general terms lacking in literary study and of methods of classification of data. For Frye, as for the Chicago critics, Aristotle offers the best guidance. Because Aristotle approached poetry "as a biologist would approach a system of organisms, picking out its genera and species," Frye regards him the progenitor of the science of criticism and acknowledges a debt to him for his choice of method and for much of his terminology.

Frye recognizes the importance of Eliot's conception of tradition as an existing "ideal order" of literary works, but he has misgivings about the "magic word" *tradition* as an organizing principle because the term implies simply a temporal sequence according to which a "miscellaneous pile" of discrete works is "strung out along a chronological line." In contrast to this chronological perspective, Frye speaks of a "total literary history" which "gives us a glimpse of the possibility of seeing literature as a complication of a relatively restricted and simple group of formulas that can be studied in primitive culture." These formulas or patterns seem to draw toward a focus or point of convergence. Frye wonders whether literature may not be seen "not only as complicating itself in time, but as spread out in conceptual space from some kind of center that criticism could locate." He favors some atemporal principle of organization, the specific nature of which is not developed in the introduction; it later becomes apparent, however, that the "formulas" are archetypal patterns and that the "center" is the literary symbol as "monad."

Frye disapproves of literary value judgments as projections of social attitudes. He recognizes that Arnold's touchstone system, with its premium on high seriousness and the decorum of the aristocratic forms of epic and tragedy, was developed as a kind of "scriptural canon" that culture was to take over from religion. He observes that "every deliberately constructed hierarchy of values"—whether conservative and romantic, as in Arnold, or radical and ironic, as in Shaw—"is based on a concealed social, moral, or intellectual analogy." Because distinctions such as those between high, middle, and low styles are determined by the class structure of society, it behooves the critic to look at art "from the standpoint of an ideally classless society." The implication is that criticism, in its historical phase, must tend toward an "indiscriminate acceptance" of all literary phenomena rather than assume a selective attitude toward "tradition," in the manner of Arnold, Eliot, and the subsequent (unnamed) New Critics. Because of its lack of discrimination, historical criticism should be complemented by an "ethical criticism," which Frye describes in his introduction as "a communication of the past to the present . . . , based on the conception of the total and simultaneous possession of past culture." Ethical criticism is to be thought of neither as prescriptive (it imposes no moral or aesthetic mandates on the artist) nor as evaluative.

The introduction, which repeatedly stresses the disinterested and inductive nature of criticism, closes with a note of qualification: Frye acknowledges that he himself has proceeded deductively and has been rigorously selective in his examples and illustrations. Recognizing the highly schematic plan of his own work, he regards it as a kind of preliminary scaffolding, much of which may be knocked away when the structure of critical theory is more satisfactorily developed.

The reason for Frye's precautionary note becomes clear as one turns to the four essays that make up the body of the work. Organized into what one reviewer has called a "fearful symmetry," they discuss historical, ethical, archetypal, and rhetorical criticism as complementary and interlocking perspectives.

The first essay, "Historical Criticism: Theory of Modes," establishes a classification of five literary modes: myth, romance, high mimetic (epic and tragedy), low mimetic, and ironic. These are correlated with historical periods, during which the emphasis in Western literature is seen to have moved from myth in the pre-medieval period, through the subsequent development of the high and low mimetic to the ironic, which has been dominant for the past hundred years or so. As the ironic mode tends toward the re-emergence of mythical patterns in writers like Kafka, Joyce, and Yeats, the historical movement of the modes is seen to be circular; and the return of irony to myth is accompanied not only by cyclical theories of history but also by the renewed interest, so obvious in our own time, in sacramental philosophy and dogmatic theology. The classification of five narrative modes which correspond with historical periods is supported by evidence, but when Frye argues, simply on the basis of the re-emergence of mythic elements in modern ironic literature, that the movement of the modes is "circular," the reader's confidence is strained. A preoccupation with cyclical movement is more typical of the mystical than the scientific mind.

"Ethical Criticism: Theory of Symbols" deals with five phases of symbolism adapted from the medieval scheme of literal, allegorical, moral, and anagogic meanings. In Frye's plan, five phases of symbolic meaning (the literal, descriptive, formal, mythical, and anagogic) parallel the five modes of the first essay. The coexistence of these phases attests the principle of the manifold or "polysemous" meaning of the literary symbol, which is defined, very broadly, as "any unit of any literary structure that can be isolated for critical attention."

In its mythical phase, the symbol is the *archetype,* or typical or recurring unit of expression. Frye defines the archetype in a way that stresses its communicative value: "I mean by an archetype a symbol which connects one poem with another and thereby helps to unify and integrate our literary experience. And as the archetype is the communicable symbol, archetypal criticism is primarily concerned with literature as a social fact and as a mode of communication. By the study of conventions and genres, it attempts to fit poems into the body of poetry as a whole." The notion of the archetype as an integrating symbol follows Eliot's idea of the existing order of literature and implies a basically historical perspective. It also opposes the conception of the poem as a self-contained entity. As Frye points out, "A symbol like the sea or the heath cannot remain within Conrad or Hardy: it is bound to expand over many works into an archetypal symbol of literature as a whole. Moby-Dick cannot remain in Melville's novel: he is absorbed into our imaginative experience of leviathans and dragons of the deep from the Old Testament onward."

But Frye is less concerned with exploring the full resources of archetype criticism (the subject of his following essay) than with the archetype as a mythic bridge to the fifth or "anagogic" phase of symbolism, in which nature is "contained" by the literary universe which represents the "total dream of man." Shifting from the critic Eliot's idea of a historical order to the poet Eliot's mystical image of the turning wheel, Frye thinks of this universe, with its revolving cycle of modes, as having a "still center" like the still point of the wheel. This center is at the focus of the converging formulas, or archetypes, in the microcosmic individual poem, or work, in which the "whole" is revealed through an "epiphany." From this essentially mystical rather than historical or humanistic point of view, literature is seen as "existing in its own universe, no longer a commentary on life or reality but containing life and reality in a system of verbal relationships."

Frye tries to restrict this apocalyptic view to a humanistic perspective (the divine word is "the unlimited or projected human"), citing Coleridge as an example of the theorist who has subordinated criticism to religion. But he acknowledges that "anagogic criticism is usually found in direct connection with religion, and is to be discovered chiefly in the more uninhibited utterances of poets themselves." "It comes out," he feels, "in those passages of Eliot's quartets where the words of the poet are placed within the context of the incarnate Word." In reading this discussion of a series of symbolic phases, ascending from the descriptive to the anagogic, one finds it difficult to avoid the impression of "a deliberately constructed hierarchy of values," despite Frye's earlier rejection of value judgments in the critical process. When Frye speaks of the anagogic phase as one in which "the symbol is a monad, all symbols being united in a single infinite and eternal verbal symbol which is, as *dianoia,* the Logos, and, as *mythos,* total creative act," his terms, detached from any specific literary referents, merge into meaninglessness. At this point, for one reader at least, Ezra Pound's impatient dismissal of the original medieval scheme strikes home: "Anagogical? Hell's bells, '*nobody*' knows what THAT is."

In the third and fullest essay, "Archetypal Criticism: Theory of Myths," Frye announces that the aim of his work is "to give a rational account of some of the structural principles of Western literature in the context of its Classical and Christian heritage." These principles are to be derived from "archetypal and anagogic criticism," the only kinds that assume a larger context of literature as a whole. Using Biblical symbolism and classical mythology as a "grammar of literary archetypes," Frye ingeniously classifies Western literature from the medieval period to the twentieth century. Most of the essay is given over to a discussion of four narrative categories of plot structure, or *mythoi,* broader than, or prior to, the ordinary genres. Of these comedy is identified with the *mythos* of spring, romance with summer, tragedy with autumn, and irony and satire with winter. Illustrations of these types are drawn from a wide range of major works, among which Shakespeare's plays figure prominently in the discussion of comedy and tragedy.

Each of the four categories of *mythoi* involves six isolatable phases which so interlock as to organize the categories themselves into a cycle like that of the seasons. Furthermore, comedy, romance, tragedy, and irony are regarded as four aspects of one "central unifying myth." The citation of Joseph Campbell (*The Hero with a Thousand Faces*) and C. G. Jung (*Symbols of Transformation*)—together with references to Sir James Frazer, Jane Harrison, and Lord Raglan—provides support for Frye's effort to give the literary "monomyth" the status of the unifying law of science. What particularly distinguishes his theory is the identification of the monomyth with the Jewish-Christian myth of quest and salvation, under which all other versions of Western myth are to be subsumed. In a later consideration of "Specific Encyclopaedic Forms," the Bible is described as "a definitive myth, a single archetypal structure extending from creation to apocalypse," embracing the epic cycle of wrath, return, and rebirth found in the *Iliad, Odyssey,* and *Aeneid,* and also relating, through less fully developed forms of the same myth, to Western literature as a whole.

The archetypes also supply the analogies of form on which a study of genres is based. In his fourth essay, "Rhetorical Criticism: Theory of Genres," Frye notes the undeveloped theory of genre criticism. To complement the Greek *drama, epic,* and *lyric,* distinguished by contrasting modes of presentation, he introduces *fiction* to embrace the kinds of literature that reach their audience through the printed page. Within this most recent and now most important genre, the novel, the romance, the confession (or autobiography), and the anatomy are four intermingling formal strands. Joyce's *Ulysses,* for example, is described as a complete prose epic integrating the four equally important forms. The term *anatomy,* borrowed from Robert Burton, applies to a dissection, or analysis, in which the dramatic interest derives from the dynamics of ideas rather than of incident or character.

The fourth essay ends with a discussion of the rhetoric of nonliterary prose and leads into the proposal, developed in a "Tentative Conclusion," that "all structures in words are partly rhetorical, and hence literary, and that the notion of a scientific or philosophical verbal structure free of rhetorical elements is an illusion." Frye draws an analogy between literature and mathematics. After comparing the functions of the metaphor and the equation, he asks whether the "verbal structures of psychology, anthropology, theology, history, law and everything else built out of words have been informed or constructed by the same kind of myths and metaphors that we find, in their original hypothetical form, in literature" and concludes that all discursive verbal structures involve metaphorical identifications representing an "organizing structural pattern or conceptualized myth." Literature and mathematics are simply two different ways of "conceiving the same universe," and one of the most important activities of criticism should be the reforging of "the broken links between creation and knowledge, art and science, myth and concept."

This conclusion reveals a familiar concern for the "dissociation of sensibility," as Eliot called it, that is supposed to have contributed to the alienation of the artist (and the critic) since the rise of science in the seventeenth century. In attempting to bridge the realms of science and literature by attributing to the former an origin in "conceptualized myth" comparable to poetic myth, Frye is following a contemporary trend supported by such philosophers as Ernst Cassirer (cited in Frye's conclusion) and, even earlier, by I. A. Richards' argument in *Coleridge on Imagination* (1935) for the mythopoeic origin of all knowledge and the integrative function of poetic myth.

Frye is a perceptive reader, and his work is full of original insights and unsuspected relationships brought to light by his interest in archetypes. Its weakest feature is its claim to a scientific method and disinterestedness. Scientific law does not presume to integrate all natural phenomena, as Frye would have the total universe of Western literature revealed, apocalyptically, through the symbol as monad, in a vision which is more easily identifiable with the experience of the religious mystic than with the limited view of the scientist.

Why should Frye think of Western literature as constituting a "whole"? If we consider his own idea of the nature of the archetype as a formal element that helps us to "unify and integrate our literary experience," it is apparent that the conception will not allow us to detach Western from Oriental literature as a separate entity. Frye is concerned with a "literary universe" representing a specifically Western culture for reasons suggested by the scheme of his work. If *world* literature were being considered, the Biblical myth incorporating the Christian version of the rebirth archetype could not be singled out as the monomyth behind all the narrative patterns of the literary universe. Such use of the Biblical myth points to a cultural as well as a literary motive. The critic is not working disinterestedly in the manner of the scientist, but interestedly as a partisan of a specifically religious world-view. Would not Frye's critic be performing a function much like that of Arnold's with the difference that Arnold's ideal is of a secular critic of culture while Frye's is of a religious critic of literature with unspecified cultural implications?

Frye's conclusion returns to the discussion of criticism as an "ethical instrument, participating in the work of civilization." The idea of a free, classless society provides the "implicit moral standard to which ethical criticism always refers," but it "can never be formulated, much less established as a society." The precise relation of ethical literary criticism to society, except perhaps as the expression of a classless

Christian humanism working as a kind of leavening in the social lump remains unexplained although the question is among the most interesting raised by Frye.

One of Frye's main concerns is the language of criticism. He comments upon the lack of an adequate or precise critical vocabulary, and, building on Aristotle, he makes use of a number of terms which he is at pains to define and to use consistently throughout the *Anatomy,* to which a brief glossary is appended. Unfortunately, archetype criticism tends to make key terms diffuse and interchangeable, as in the quotation from the discussion of the symbol as monad, rather than precise. In both the text and the glossary, the definitions of such terms as *archetype, image, monad, myth,* and *symbol* illustrate this disposition toward overlapping and imprecision. Frye seems less aware of the problems of meaning presented by such words than Wellek and Warren in their chapter, "Image, Metaphor, Symbol, Myth," in *Theory of Literature.*

Despite the unscientific nature of Frye's archetype theory and the impression of a closed system conveyed by its schematic organization, *Anatomy of Criticism* presents a coherent discussion remarkable for its treatment of the literary work as a verbal complex of many meanings.

7

Stanley Edgar Hyman's *The Armed Vision: A Study in the Methods of Modern Literary Criticism* (1948) pursues a threefold objective: "First, to study the nature of modern critical method as exemplified by selected contemporary literary critics; second, to note the ancestry of their techniques and procedures, both as disciplines in themselves and as gradual developments in the history of criticism; third, to suggest some possibilities for an integrated and practical methodology that would combine and consolidate the best procedures of modern criticism." Hyman's method is to consider, in separate chapters, twelve American and English critics, and to identify each with a distinctive approach: "Edmund Wilson and Translation in Criticism"; "Yvor Winters and Evaluation in Criticism"; "T. S. Eliot and Tradition in Criticism"; "Van Wyck Brooks and Biographical Criticism"; "Constance Rourke and Folk Criticism"; "Maud Bodkin and Psychological Criticism"; "Christopher Caudwell and Marxist Criticism"; "Caroline Spurgeon and Scholarship in Criticism"; "R. P. Blackmur and the Expense of Criticism"; "William Empson and Categorical Criticism"; "I. A. Richards and the Criticism of Interpretation"; "Kenneth Burke and the Criticism of Symbolic Action." In each chapter, Hyman systematically defines the critic's method, singles out at least one of his more important works for analysis, considers his relation to his contemporaries and to earlier critical tradition, and evaluates the actual and potential usefulness of his method. While Hyman ranges widely over the field of modern criticism, displaying a broad knowledge of its backgrounds, he "makes no attempt to be impartial, but is frankly both biased and opinionated."

This warning, refreshing though it is in an area where personal prejudices are often veiled, proves superfluous when the reader turns to the first essay, in which not only a bias but a personal animus is evident. Hyman describes Edmund Wilson as a "translator" rather than a historical critic, a popularizer who won a wider audience for "difficult" moderns like Eliot and Joyce by interpreting their work through paraphrase and the analysis of symbolism. Hyman accuses Wilson also of using other critics' "researches and insights, sometimes without credit."

Hyman has harsh comments for a number of other critics, notably Van Wyck Brooks, but his consistently antagonistic treatment of Wilson has struck many readers as unjustifiable. In the hierarchic ordering of critics, Wilson ranks lowest. The last four (Blackmur, Empson, Richards, and Burke) are the most favorably regarded, and of these Burke—with his fertile imagination, his hospitable attitude toward other disciplines, and his desire to integrate them within his own syncretist system—comes closest to realizing Hyman's ideal.

The identification of twelve American and English critics with twelve distinct approaches illustrates the diversification of the modern critical enterprise. But Hyman's system has certain disadvantages. Under it, Miss Bodkin, who is much closer to Jung than to Freud, becomes *the* representative of psychological criticism. A survey of Freudian theory and criticism is provided, but no individual critic is given comparable treatment, and thus Freudian psychoanalytic theory receives less attention than Jungian archetype theory. Furthermore, the labels applied to individual critics sometimes suggest a narrower view of their functions than Hyman actually holds and obscure the interrelationships and common groupings that might be made among them. While Yvor Winters can be distinguished from many of his contemporaries by his effort to make value judgments about literature on moral and rational grounds, it is perhaps even more important that he is like R. P. Blackmur and William Empson in his use of close textual analysis.

When the question of analysis or exegesis is introduced, the inadequacy of the classification of Edmund Wilson as a "translator" rather than a historical critic becomes apparent. For the techniques of paraphrase and interpretive symbolic analysis that Hyman attributes to Wilson do not really distinguish him from such other modern critical exegetes as Blackmur, Empson, and Burke. The psychological critic, as well as the more formalistic New Critic, depends upon these devices in elucidating a text. Essays like Cleanth Brooks's or Kenneth Burke's on Keats's "Ode on a Grecian Urn" rely heavily upon the use of paraphrase, despite Brooks's banning of the device as a "heresy." To identify Wilson as a translator is simply to acknowledge that he employs some of the techniques in general use among modern analytical critics of whatever persuasion.

Hyman wishes to broaden the base of criticism and favors the use of as many of the extraliterary modern disciplines as possible, particularly the social sciences. Although he does not think of criticism as a science, he sees it as moving in the direction of a science—"that is, toward a formal methodology and system of procedures that can be objectively transmitted." In a brief conclusion, which considers "some possibilities for an integrated and practical methodology," he speaks of "an ideal modern literary critic" whose method would be "a synthesis of every practical technique or procedure used by his flesh-and-blood colleagues," omitting only "their special obsessions, preoccupations, and weaknesses." The result would be an exhaustive, integrative, analytical criticism beyond the scope of any actual critic or conceivable group of critics.

Hyman recognizes that his conception of an ideal critic is nonsense, "although perhaps useful nonsense as a Platonic archetype." Turning to the problem of the "actual critic," he notes that only Burke among our "best critics" has tended toward a broadly integrative approach while the others (Richards, Empson, and Blackmur) have been inclined "to do only one thing at a time," depending on the nature of the work under discussion. Because of the trend toward specialization in all fields of modern knowledge, Hyman believes that the same tendency will operate in criticism and produce "the specialist critic, the man using one highly developed method." In this situation, integration can be developed only through a collective criticism operating on some sort of symposium basis, planned rather than haphazard, and sponsored by such agencies as literary quarterlies, universities, and academic organizations like the English Institute.

Symposia have become increasingly common since *The Armed Vision* appeared, and they have undoubtedly helped to broaden critical understanding. But it is doubtful whether any symposium treatment of a literary work or the production of a single author has succeeded in producing as fully integrative a criticism as Hyman envisions. This observation is not intended to belittle his critical ideal but rather to suggest that the entire body of criticism relating to any given subject or work may best be thought of as a kind of symposium or dialectic, always developing but never complete, from which, as Hyman hopes for the collective criticism he proposes, tested truths may arise.

8

It is not possible to mention all of the scholarship or even all of the individual works dealing historically and critically with modern American criticism. However, a few others deserve brief comment.

William Van O'Connor's *An Age of Criticism, 1900-*

1950 (1952) is a historical survey of American criticism beginning with Howells and the genteel tradition in the late nineteenth century. Within his limits of space (the volume is one of a compact series on twentieth century literature in America), O'Connor provides a helpful introduction from a point of view sympathetic to the New Criticism. He speaks of a "pure literary criticism" as the ideal of the analytical New Critics, who are concerned with "the structure of the literary work, the way meaning and emotion are discovered in their appropriately imagined and created forms." Although O'Connor recognizes that literature is concerned with "ideas" as well as with "forms," he believes that the ideas, or "life values . . . exert a pull away from the literary object toward philosophy, or politics, or ethics, or social questions." While considerations of environment cannot be excluded, they should be subordinated to the analysis of literary structure; their primary value resides "in showing how factors out of a milieu or principles from an ethical system quicken the literary work."

In his last chapter O'Connor discusses the contributions of Richards and Eliot to modern analytical criticism, noting that the so-called New Criticism is actually a continuation of nineteenth century English criticism, with a particular indebtedness to Coleridge and Arnold. O'Connor includes Burke with the New Critics and illustrates the diversity of the movement by contrasting the close explications of Blackmur with the theoretical preoccupations of Burke. Although he feels that Burke is "the more characteristic of the movement in its liking for critical terminology," he does not point out that while Burke's terminology derives from many sources, including the social sciences, that of most of the leading New

Critics is more closely confined to literary and rhetorical traditions.

Murray Krieger's *The New Apologists for Poetry* (1956) is a dispassionate analysis of modern contextualist critical theory focused upon the same cognitive problem with which Wimsatt and Brooks deal. Krieger puts the question simply: "How can poetry tell us something about our world when for the contextualist it is not in any obvious sense referential?" He traces the development of modern organic theory, with particular attention to the contribution of I. A. Richards and then considers the "transformation" of Richards' theory by the New Critics, who emphasized complexity as a standard of value and asserted the status of poetry as the source of a "complete knowledge" of one sort or another, distinct from the knowledge of science.

Krieger's conclusion reviews the questions raised by contextualist theory. Several possible alternatives or modifications are advanced, but none resolves its problems. Although Krieger does not attempt to supply final answers, his analysis of the contradictions of New Critical theory is a valuable interpretive work that has helped to clear the air and provide a sounder basis for current discussion.

Richard Foster's *The New Romantics: A Reappraisal of the New Criticism* (1962) is a "characterization" of a selected group of New Critics designed to reveal the many ways in which these men, who typically assume the stance of classicists and antiromantics, are indebted to the romantic tradition. Foster traces the quest motif in the careers of critics like I. A. Richards, Allen Tate, and R. P. Blackmur, whom he views as pilgrims in a modern waste land, in search of truth and spiritual certainty. The model for the conversion pattern in their work exists in the earlier experience of T. S. Eliot. As a result of their essentially religious motives and interests, these critics have produced a theory establishing poetry as the source of a "higher knowledge" and giving it the status of metaphysics or religion.

Their concern for poetry, combined with their mystical tendencies and their distrust of logic as an ordering principle, has led many of them to conceive of criticism as a species of poetic expression employing symbolism and other devices of indirection. Somewhat satirically Foster interprets the techniques of the critic as poet in a chapter including such subheadings as "The Poetries of Love and Dread," "The Poetries of Fleeting Insight," "The Critic as Tragic Hero," "Approach as Supplicative Ritual," and "The Iconography of the Poem as Creature and Poetry as Deity."

Despite his irreverent treatment of the pieties of modern criticism, Foster is not wholly unsympathetic. The literary revolution accomplished by the New Critics succeeded in converting the university scholar-professor into a man of letters and made it possible for students to get a literary education that had formerly not been available. It also encouraged a new interest in theoretical questions. The "personal," "speculative," and even "impressionistic" qualities of the New Criticism have preserved the values of the traditional literary essay, which reflects the full "sensibility" of the discriminating appreciator of literature.

9

A knowledge of modern American criticism has also been disseminated and influenced by a number of collections of essays that have been widely used as textbooks in college and university courses. These include Mark Schorer, Josephine Miles, and Gordon McKenzie's *Criticism: The Foundations of Modern Literary Judgment* (1948); R. W. Stallman's *Critiques and Essays in Criticism, 1900-1948* (1949), with a foreword by Cleanth Brooks; M. D. Zabel's *Literary Opinion in America* (1937; revised, 1951); and Ray B. West's *Modern Literary Criticism* (1952). Of these, Zabel's is the only work concerned exclusively with American practice although the others provide a broad and representative coverage of American criticism as most important in the modern period. Zabel's work is distinguished from the others by its detailed introductory historical essay. Zabel's and Stallman's collections contain comprehensive bio- and bibliographical notes. Other less well-known collections are C. J. Glicksberg's *American Literary Criticism, 1900-1950* (1951) and C. A. Brown's *The Achievement of American Criticism* (1954). Brown's work consists of representative selections from the whole history of American criticism. It is divided into four parts (each provided with a scholarly introduction) of which the last is devoted to modern trends.

The extensive use of these collections shows the wide interest in literary criticism and its status as an intellectual discipline. The most influential of them, however, appeared at least a decade ago and stress the point of view of the New Criticism of the 1940's. The present need is for broader and more representative collections which take into account recent developments in criticism and theory.

⁂ 9 ⁂

CRITICISM AS A SOCIAL ACT

1—Recent criticism and critical theory; 2—The need for an idea of open form; 3—Literature and values; 4—The problem of method; 5—The problem of critical language; 6—Criticism as a social act

To place groups of critics in a roughly chronological order—early psychological critics in the Twenties, social and Marxist critics in the Thirties, and so forth—may tie each too closely to a particular period and obscure the fact that all represent parallel as well as successive trends. Each has a continuity that reaches beyond the period of its especial prominence.

During the post-World War I years, psychological, social, moralistic, and formalist criticism all flourished and all established lines of development for later work. Of these, the social and the formalist-aesthetic have received more attention because they represent what have commonly been regarded as polar extremes in a continuing debate in critical theory. Shifts of opinion from time to time have often been abrupt. The excessiveness of the emphasis upon political and sociological criticism in the 1930's provoked the apolitical and asocial New Criticism, with its stress on formal analysis.

The method of close textual analysis was not, however, an innovation of the late 1930's and early Forties. Although it was not cultivated in the universities until then, it had already been practiced by leading critics for more than twenty years. During the decade of World War I, Pound and Eliot were encouraging the criticism of literary structure and technique. During the 1920's, *The Dial,* to which Pound and Eliot both contributed, and *The Hound and Horn,* with which R. P. Blackmur was associated, were publishing "technical" criticism; Edmund Wilson's *Axel's Castle* (1931) dealt with figures later established in the New Critical canon; and F. O. Matthiessen's analytical study, *The Achievement of T. S. Eliot,* appeared in 1935, several years before the New Criticism of John Crowe Ransom and his associates was recognized as a distinct movement.

I

The special accomplishment of the New Critics was a theory that justified their practice of structural analysis, a theory advancing the idea of the poem as a self-sufficient language system and implicitly denying its social, intellectual, and moral relevance. This extreme position, understandable in part as a reaction to sociological and historical criticism, did not go unchallenged. Opposing voices were raised during the 1940's, not only by entrenched old-line historical scholars but also by younger men knowledgeable in criticism but also concerned for the social implications of literature. In "Literature as an Institution" (1946), Harry Levin noted that the sociological tradition, represented by literary historians like Taine and Parrington, had slighted questions of form. He advocated the reconciliation of the opposing claims of social and formal criticism by recognizing literature as a semiautonomous "institution," intrinsic to the general life of society but distinguished from its milieu by its conventions, which represent "a necessary difference between art and life."

In "The Responsibilities of the Critic" (1949), F. O. Matthiessen more directly attacked the New Critics for their scholasticism and neglect of social problems. Against the background of the violations of personal and academic freedom of the McCarthy era, he protested the moratorium on the discussion of pressing social issues—moral, political, and economic—observed by academic critics. Acknowledging that the critic's first obligation is to judge the work of art as a work of art, Matthiessen argued that such judgment involves broader social values. Knowing form and content "to be inseparable," the critic "will recognize his duty to both. Judgment of art is unavoidably both an aesthetic and a social act, and the critic's sense of social responsibility gives him a deeper thirst for meaning." Another assault upon the anti-social and political nature of the movement was made in Robert Gorham Davis's "The New Criticism and the Democratic Tradition" (1949-50), published in *The American Scholar.* Davis was less concerned with the practice of the New Critics than with the alien sources of their traditionalism in the reactionary clericalism of Charles Maurras. He pointed out that, through the influence of the New Criticism upon literary journals, such terms as "*authority, hierarchy, catholicism, aristocracy, tradition, absolutes, dogma, truths* became related terms of honor, and *liberalism, naturalism, scientism, individualism, equalitarianism, progress, protestantism, pragmatism* and *personality* became related terms of rejection and contempt." And this at a time when the United States was struggling against a totalitarian power "for world leadership in the name of democratic liberalism."

These attacks, on theoretical and ideological grounds, had little effect at the time they were made, for the prestige of the New Criticism was at its peak. What did happen was a gradual softening of the resistance to the claims of social and historical criticism, without any corresponding shift in basic theory. In a "postscript" to the "Letter to the Teacher" in the revised edition of *Understanding Poetry* (1950), Cleanth Brooks and R. P. Warren commented on changes that had occurred in the twelve preceding years. The aim of the first edition had been to bring "something of the critical attitude into the classroom" and to meet the need of "a sharp focus on the poem itself." With that objective won, they recognized the desirability, in their new edition, of relating criticism to other literary studies. The problem was, they felt, *"to see how history, literary and general, may be related to poetic meaning,"* and they attempted to illustrate the relationship by including extended discussions of Eliot's *The Waste Land* and Marvell's *Horatian Ode.* They mentioned, as a new emphasis, "the relation of the single poem to the whole body of the poet's work." In 1953, in "A Note on the Limits of 'History' and the Limits of 'Criticism'" (*Sewanee Review*), Cleanth Brooks made the point that "the literary historian and the critic need to work together and that the ideal case is that in which both functions are united in one and the same man." He then qualified his statement: "But historical evidence does not solve critical problems."

Such adjustments accompanied a gradual shift in practical criticism as the formalist concentration upon the individual work gave way to more integrative studies. Men who had been schooled in analytical techniques turned to themes characteristic of a literature or a literary period and related them to their cultural setting. Examples of works of this kind include Henry Nash Smith's *Virgin Land: The American West as Symbol and Myth* (1950) and R. W. B. Lewis's *The American Adam: Innocence, Tragedy, and Tradi-*

tion in the Nineteenth Century (1955). The relation of political thought to fictional technique was explored by Irving Howe in *Politics and the Novel* (1957). A more recent study combining an interest in literary form and its cultural matrix is C. L. Barber's *Shakespeare's Festive Comedy: A Study of Dramatic Form and Its Relation to Social Custom* (1959). The decade of the 1950's saw the beginning of a ground swell toward the recognition of the social and historical and away from the private and subjective. In psychological criticism this trend can be seen in the shift from a preoccupation with the unconscious to a concern for the ego and its relation to both the unconscious and the social environment.

In theory, however, it has been only recently that systematic efforts have been directed toward the reassessment and revision of the New Critical position. These have made it clear that the main problem of new theory is the relationship of historical and formalist criticism.

The keynote was struck by Philip Rahv in "Fiction and the Criticism of Fiction" (1956), a *Kenyon Review* article objecting to the unfortunate results of the application of New Critical methods to prose. Rahv saw the contemporary obsession with symbol and myth as an expression of the "reactionary idealism that now afflicts our literary life and that passes itself off as a strict concern with aesthetic form." He also called attention to the imbalance of the New Criticism: "If the typical error of the 'thirties was the failure to distinguish between literature and life, in the present period that error has been inverted into the failure to perceive their close and necessary relationship." Rahv's objections strike at the heart of the weakness of New Critical formalism without indicating how the difficulty can be resolved.

In the opinion of some critics, the solution lies in a breaking down of the dichotomy between historical and critical studies in such a way that history may be subsumed under criticism, or vice versa. In "The Current Revolt Against the New Criticism" (*Criticism,* 1959), Hyatt H. Waggoner takes note of a "subtle shift going on right now in the use of the word *criticism.*" Whereas Wellek and Warren's sharp distinction between history and literary criticism represented the outlook of the late 1940's, the attitude a decade later is more accurately represented, Waggoner believes, by Northrop Frye's *Anatomy of Criticism* (1957), in which both traditional literary scholarship and analytical formalist criticism are brought together under the "all-inclusive term *criticism.*"

On the other hand, Roy Harvey Pearce, a scholar-critic interested in combining cultural history and aesthetic analysis, has favored *history* as the more useful synthetic term. His "Historicism Once More" (*Kenyon Review,* 1958) explores the possibility of developing "a kind of criticism which is, by definition, a form of historical understanding." Resting upon a conception of literature as "a way, perhaps the most profound, of comprehending that dialectical opposition which characterizes our knowledge of ourselves in our history," this newer criticism would not be historical in the usual sense of the "historical placement and elucidation of the literary work" but would "go somewhat farther and establish between ourselves and the literary work a direct, existential relationship."

The dimension in which this relationship can best be studied is "language in its historical-cultural aspect," an aspect pointedly ignored by the New Critics (although T. S. Eliot has given evidence of an interest in it in his criticism since the early 1940's, collected in *On Poetry and Poets*

[1957]). Pearce sees the language of literature as the vehicle of the values of a culture, which as a "residual power" gives to the language of a poem a "creative power analogous to the poet's." In the foreword to his more recent study, *The Continuity of American Poetry* (1961), Pearce speaks of poetic language as transmitting values which have (and have not) made possible a communal life within a society and of literary history as a discipline which mediates between "cultural history" and "criticism." His own work, which aims to interpret the achievement of American poetry and to define its basic styles, Pearce identifies as "a study in cultural history."

Regardless of whether his commitment is to *criticism* or to *history,* the theorist performs a useful and necessary service in demonstrating that the two are not only interdependent but inseparable except as emphases. The literary scholar must develop broader systematic concepts of both criticism and history. Pearce points out that history involves an organic relationship between the individual and his culture and that the language of literature is peculiarly suited to the expression of this relationship.

Other scholars have been concerned with the further development of the concept of criticism, the function with which most students of literature would identify themselves. In "The Necessary Stylist: A New Critical Revision" (*Modern Fiction Studies,* 1960-61), Mark Spilka recognizes the "narrowness" of the New Critical formalism, which has ignored the relation of the literary work to its author and its social environment. He sees the growing reaction against this position as following two theoretical lines. The "eclecticists" include those who "would buttress formalism with an eclectic or synoptic mixture of methods." (Theorists of this persuasion have sometimes described themselves as "syncretists.") Others, identified as "formal revisionists," "would strike at theory itself: they would broaden the base of formalism by showing that quality in verbal art depends partly on external elements, like history and language, and on shared awareness of those elements." Spilka approves of the "connection between *form* and broader contexts" and contributes to this emergent theoretical position a discussion of style as "a characteristic use of language, and . . . a characteristic way of arranging experience for aesthetic ends." Since an author's style is a common element in his various works and since it also reflects social influences and conditioning, the concept of style provides a necessary bridge between literature and its cultural environment. (Both Josephine Miles in *Eras and Modes in English Poetry* [1957] and Roy Harvey Pearce in *The Continuity of American Poetry* [1961] have also been interested in style as a historical as well as a personal expression.)

The broadening of the base of formalism in such a way that the structural elements of the work are identified with environmental and historical factors promises the best resolution of the social-aesthetic critical dichotomy.

2

To recognize that literature shares the characteristics of its culture in language, social experience, and conventions requires more than simply a revision of New Critical formalism. It means a breaking through to an idea of form and of criticism which takes into account, in the fullest possible manner, these environmental determinants. The acceptance of such a view, a necessary foundation for *open criticism,* demands a rejection of some of the basic assumptions of contextualist theory and the development of new principles.

What conception of form will produce criticism that is, in Matthiessen's words, "unavoidably both an aesthetic and a social act"? The form of a literary work must be thought of as a complex phenomenon, inevitably conditioned by its changing social environment, infinitely variable and inexhaustible to analysis, yet requiring recognized controls for its interpretation. It must be conceived of as open and relative, subject to the broadest possible range of interpretation and to definition in terms taken from an unrestricted selection of relevant sources.

The idea of the poem or literary work as an organic complex is not a new one. Typical of both romantic and modern formalist thought, it has been most effectively set forth in Wellek and Warren's "perspectivist" theory, which acknowledges the complexity and variability of the literary work. The weakness of their version lies in the assumption of a "hierarchy of viewpoints" and in the resistance to norms or terms of formal definition drawn from extraliterary sources.

It is necessary to get rid of any such restrictions in order to arrive at an idea of organic form that recognizes the "openness" of the literary work and the identification of its elements with the shared experiences of its readers. This end can be achieved by thinking of literary form as comprised of interrelated patterns of sound, syntax, event, and meaning, within which all aspects of critical examination can be comprehended. These interrelated patterns of organization together constitute a "form" only partially apprehended by any one reader. While a high degree of differentiation and integration of the formal patterns enhances the interest of a work, complexity cannot be regarded as an arbitrary requirement or criterion. A comparatively simple work, which may seem disproportionately developed in any one formal dimension (like an early Imagistic poem by H.D.), may be extremely effective. Regardless of its relative complexity or simplicity, form can be perceived and defined only in terms drawn from the reader's experience—including his experience of linguistic and literary conventions.

An analysis of sound patterns would consider such devices as rhyme and meter (often over-emphasized in the discussion of the formal elements of traditional verse), alliteration, assonance, cadence, euphony, dissonance, and onomatopoeia, depending upon the nature of the individual work. Although sound is given most attention in the criticism of poetry, it is also important in prose, for which adequate analytical techniques are lacking. In both verse and prose such qualities as rhythm, pace, and pitch contribute to meaning. Syntax, the grammatical arrangement of words, may also be implicated in the dimension of sound, as when parallel constructions provide initial rhyming effects in Whitman's free verse. It is *necessarily* involved in meaning. Although the symbolist poet or the modern free verse poet like Cummings or the "stream of consciousness" novelist like Joyce or Faulkner may attempt to break down conventional syntax as a way of subverting rational order, the resulting pattern of language, fragmented though it may appear, has an order and a logic consistent with the writer's point of view. The events of a work include the imagined experiences represented by its words. Besides sensory experiences (with which the term *image* is most commonly associated), these may be actions, thoughts, speeches, feelings, and dreams. In this sense, the images and statements of feeling in a lyric poem are *events* as much as are the actions of a character in a novel. Taken together, the events constitute a "world" having a consistency and an integrity which, although not absolute, are sufficient to compel imaginative acceptance (Coleridge's "willing suspension of disbelief"). Although any event or combination of events may be isolated by the critic, as in an image study like Caroline Spurgeon's on Shakespeare, images or other events cannot be valued for their own sake or regarded as separable from other aspects of form. Both the imagined experiences themselves and the words that represent them are "charged" with ideas and feelings. For this reason the events have meaning not only as they relate to each other but also as they strain toward the level of extended meaning, or metaphor.

Meaning thus exists on two distinguishable levels, the plain-sense and the metaphorical. The latter includes both the argument or theme of a work, however defined, and the images and events which, as individual figurative devices, support it. In a more general and basic sense, metaphor is the product of the interaction between language and experience; as the term suggests, it reaches beyond the world of the work and invests it with values to an extent permitted by the reader's experience and perceptiveness. (These include feelings and moods, which the critic must conceptualize in his interpretation.) It is largely this interanimation of language and experience, as image and event rise into metaphor, that gives literature its dynamic and vibrant "life."

This idea of open organic form recognizes not only the interconnectedness of the verbal elements of a poem, but also their dependence upon a larger order of experience. A theory that ignores this truth is false to the natural process to which it appeals. Nothing in nature is self-sufficient. Just as a tree depends upon its physical environment, a literary work is dependent upon its social environment for its inception, development, and configuration. It is not a self-sufficient and self-integrated phenomenon but rather has an organic relationship to its environment as the expression of an individual artist whose way of seeing and writing has been influenced by the society in which he lives.

In this relationship, there is an interaction between poetic and common language, between fictional and experienced events, between the conventions of an individual work and those of a larger body of literature. In these ways the poem depends upon experiences of the reader, which are shared, to a considerable extent, by the writer and other readers. Their combined experience, which might be thought of as the social environment of the work, supplies formal *controls* that operate through the medium of words. In shaping his work, the writer draws upon common language with its shared meanings and values and upon literary language with its specialized conventions. These meanings and conventions are, in turn, guides to the critic's interpretation of form.

A reader's response to three novels like Hemingway's *A Farewell to Arms* (1929), Céline's *Journey to the End of the Night* (1934), and Mailer's *The Naked and the Dead* (1948) is conditioned by his personal and historical knowledge of two world wars and the years between and by his knowledge of literary conventions. His understanding of the ways in which war is used as a metaphor of life in these novels will be deepened by familiarity with type-images of war in other literary works; and his perception of the differing uses of the quest motif will be helped by a knowledge of this common convention. Meanings and values associated with common experience and with accepted conventions will so control the responses of readers as to insure a substantial agreement about the form of the three novels. The form of any one can never be thought of as absolute, but it does have a stability and a permanence supported by the continuity of linguistic, literary, and other cultural traditions.

Not only metaphor but all aspects of form are controlled in this way. The sounds of modern English have varied from period to period and from region to region. Despite these variations, there would be a substantial similarity in the sound patterns of a sonnet by Shakespeare for both an Elizabethan Englishman and an American reader today. Grammatical formulations of syntactical relationships also change, although slowly, in such a way that constructions are subject to differing interpretations with the passing of years. The same principle applies to the meanings of words. In all cases the changes are not in the text but in the reader's environmental conditioning. The order of words endures as an objective control for the variable responses of the reader, whose conception of form is affected by changes in all areas of his experience. Developments in such fields of knowledge as depth psychology and modern physics have deeply influenced both the general experience of readers and their ideas of literary form.

3

In defining literary form, the critic, who can know the work only through its environment, may draw upon values and "truths" from any relevant field of knowledge. The state of knowledge being what it is, relative and incomplete, literature cannot be expected to tell us the "whole truth" about anything, any more than science can. But literature, like any linguistic formulation, *can* be the source of verifiable truths. It is deeply implicated in our ways of knowing and valuing. Critics who have tried to distinguish between the verifiable truths of science and the "pseudo-statements" of poetry have not enhanced the status of literature.

In the same way, literature can be the source of moral values. A great deal of thought and many thousands of words have been expended on the subject of literature and morality, and the present time (any present time) calls for a few more. T. S. Eliot, in "Religion and Literature" (1935), recommended the application of Christian ethical and theological standards in criticism on the assumption that literature inevitably has a moral influence and that for the Christian reader the greatest literature will necessarily represent Christian values. Instead of regarding Christian standards as absolutes, Eliot might have gone on to say that for the Hindu, Buddhist, or Mohammedan reader the greatest literature would reflect the values of his particular faith (indeed, he later did come to say much the same thing in his *Notes towards the Definition of Culture* [1949]). On this basis, a reader who sees the world as one world would recognize the most "universal" great literature as that which incorporates the values common to all great religions, including democracy, which, ideally, accommodates them impartially. No one ethical system can be regarded as the source of absolute standards for the judgment of literary merit. It may, however, contribute to the understanding of form as it supplies the means of defining one among many variable aspects. But we must also recognize that, because of its importance to a reader, a system of ethics, or any set of values, may modify or block a response to other aspects of form.

The magnitude of the question of the relation of literature and morality, and the confusion surrounding it, can be seen in the controversy that followed the award of the 1948 Bollingen Prize to Ezra Pound's *Pisan Cantos.* In these poems, written while Pound was under arrest as a traitor, affirmations of Confucian and Jeffersonian principles mingle with violent anti-Semitic outbursts and expressions of sympathy for Mussolini's Fascist ideals. The committee awarding the prize attempted to forestall objections by insisting that its action was based upon aesthetic values having nothing to do with the author's personal opinions: "To permit other considerations than that of poetic achievement to sway the decision would destroy the significance of the award and would in principle deny the validity of that objective perception of value on which civilized society must rest."

In the heated discussion provoked by the award, two opposed positions emerged from the welter of opinion. Most critics who supported the decision prized the poems on "technical" grounds as the expression of a distinguished modern poet and regarded their value as poetry as apart from any extractable moral judgments. Others found the anti-Semitic and Fascist sentiments of the *Cantos* a barrier to appreciation. Even though these readers might admire Pound's accomplishments as an innovator and sympathize with some of his ideas, his poems were for them seriously flawed by their offensive statements. Some in this second group were so deeply shocked by passages in which Pound callously refers to the Nazi program of genocide that they were incapable of any but a negative response to the poems. For them the collection honored by the award was the expression of a deadly enemy to the civilized values that the Bollingen committee professed to defend.

What conclusions can be drawn from the dispute? Unless one takes refuge in the outworn idea of a form-content dichotomy to justify objectionable attitudes on the basis of excellence of technique, it is apparent that moral values grounded in the social environment are important features of the reader's conception of form. From this point of view, the Bollingen prize committee was not justified in dismissing the writer's personal opinions, when expressed as literature, as irrelevant to the question of his poetic achievement. Much of the emotive power and meaning of literature, in which no element is nonaesthetic, derives from its appeal to the reader's deepest convictions and moral commitments. These values are relative to the conditioning of the reader and variable in their influence on his conception of form. They cannot be thought of as absolutes, however wide an acceptance they may command.

To say this is not to minimize their importance. The moral values expressed in literature have a direct relationship to the values of society. The acceptance or repudiation of an author's moral values also affects the reception and judgment of his work. In an open society, both literature and literary criticism participate in a never-ending debate in which values are examined, tested against experience, and revised. Criticism which regards literary form as open and relative and grounded in the social environment will contribute most to this process and at the same time advance the understanding of the aesthetic resources of literature.

4

All possible sources of illumination are needed. Although they have not worked in a spirit of collectivity, the various groups of critics have collectively provided much light. The New Humanists, despite their rather narrow concern for literature as a bulwark of traditional culture, have testified to the seriousness of its statements of moral value. Psychological criticism has helped to teach critics to penetrate the surface of image and event and to explore the latent and unconscious meanings for which psychology has supplied a rationale. After a long period in which attention was focused on the unconscious, recent developments in ego psychology give promise of a fuller understanding of the artist as a conscious agent and his work as a social product.

The economic, political, and sociological emphases of the liberal and radical critics are enduring concerns. Even though the simplifications of much of the criticism of the 1930's provoked a reaction, it would be well for contemporary critics to review and assess some of the theoretical discussions of that period. In "The Responsibilities of the Critic," F. O. Matthiessen comments upon the continuing importance of Marxist theory for an understanding of American life and literature. Marxism is in poor repute today, partly because of its identification with a totalitarian polity. It is, however, not a violation but rather a confirmation of the principles of a free society to examine this or any other system of thought in an undoctrinaire spirit to determine what contribution it might make to a broader social criticism of literature.

The New Criticism, originating as a reaction against both the philological and historical tradition in the universities and the sociological criticism of the Thirties, has performed an inestimable service in focusing the critic's gaze upon the literary work. Despite the limitations of its theory of structure and its rejection of extraliterary disciplines, it has fostered an interest in criticism both in and outside the university.

The neo-Aristotelians, reacting against the New Critics'

ideas of structure, have called attention to the need of a supporting theory for criticism and have contributed to its formulation. They have also renewed neglected critical traditions and demonstrated the usefulness of scholarly discipline in criticism.

However great the resources provided by these various groups, even more are needed. There are limitless possibilities for drawing upon other fields of knowledge which may help to reveal further aspects of literary form. Economics, sociology, psychology, and even some of the physical sciences can contribute to criticism. A poem or novel is extremely complex, but it is simple in comparison with the world of experience of which it presents a selective view—and in which, by its very nature, it participates. Likewise, any critical interpretation is simple in comparison with the complex work of which it provides a partial and limited view. Because of this progressive simplification—from the world of experience, to the work, to the critical interpretation—it is desirable that criticism supply as many perspectives as possible in order to provide a collective idea of form which may approximate, although it can never equal, the complexity of literature itself.

To work toward this end it is necessary that criticism be inclusive rather than restrictive in its methods. What is needed is less an all-embracing *system* or *organon* of methods than a theory of form and of criticism that will be hospitable to all existing types of criticism and encourage the development of new viewpoints and new methods. Although symposia contribute to the broader understanding of literary form, they are restricted by the exigencies and preoccupations of their time and place and can never present as full a view as the dialectic of criticism, itself a complex, over a number of years. Such a "long view" does not require that critics sit in Olympian detachment from the ideological conflicts of their time, for criticism is advanced through such conflicts. Any one critic is necessarily limited by his talents and experience, but it is desirable that he subscribe to ideas and values consistent with his point of view, which, although not fixed and unchanging, has a basic stability. A commitment to definite social and political ideals can be a positive advantage to the critic who also respects the integrity of the work with which he is dealing. It demonstrates the social consequence of literature and helps to interrelate literary and social values. Since the 1920's and 1930's this kind of commitment has been less common among American than European critics—in fact, it has been almost nonexistent—and our criticism is the poorer for its absence.

5

It is generally recognized that the confusion existing in critical language is an obstacle to communication. Language barriers separate groups of critics, each of which has tended to develop a specialized vocabulary. Even within a single group, like the New Critics, there has been a proliferation of terms and a trend toward private vocabularies.

A certain amount of specialization is unavoidable. But the peculiar weakness of critical vocabularies is the absence of a common foundation and a lack of agreement about the precise meaning of basic terms. *Image, symbol,* and *structure,* for example, each has a broad range of application encompassing inconsistent and sometimes contradictory usages. The problem of definition is complicated by the fact that certain words gain acceptance as a matter of fashion even though they may often be undefined if not undefinable. (There is high fashion in criticism as well as in millinery.) Critics themselves are often not certain of the meaning of terms upon which their arguments depend—a fact that has been too frequently demonstrated in the discussion period following the presentation of critical papers. It is possible for two critics to conduct a technical discussion in which neither has an understanding of the other's meaning, except in his own terms.

Behind the confusion of critical language is a lack of agreement about the object of criticism. Psychological critics have tended to consider the work a construct of *dream symbols,* to be interpreted in terms of Oedipal relationships or rebirth archetypes. The New Humanists' concern for *dualism,* the *inner check,* and the *ethical imagination* restricts literature to a narrow scheme of moral, philosophical, and religious values. Marxist critics, interested in the relationship of the literary work to its social environment, have viewed literature as a projection of the *class struggle.* The New Critics, to whom the work is a self-contained language system, have focused upon *irony, paradox,* and *tension* as structural principles. The neo-Aristotelians, attempting to revive the doctrine of art as *imitation,* have relied heavily upon the terminology and genre classifications of Aristotle's *Poetics.* Because of the limited range of concepts within which literary form is defined by any one of these groups, their separate vocabularies tend to reduce the work and to limit and isolate their conception of form.

One of the pressing needs of current criticism is for a broader, generally accepted vocabulary drawn from all relevant areas of experience and adapted to a view of literary form as open and relative. It is easier, of course, to recognize the problem than to solve it. It would be vain to assume a prescriptive authority, since usage governs language; but usage can be influenced and controlled, to some extent, by generous reciprocal criticism and by such responsible persons as the editors of literary reviews, scholarly journals, and university presses.

If the common faults of overlapping and imprecision are to be lessened, critics must be encouraged to employ definable, mutually exclusive or at least distinguishable terms and to explain the application of doubtful or ambiguous words. Improvement can be brought about only as critics come more fully to think of themselves as contributors to a larger professional effort, drawing upon language resources for which all are responsible. It is possible that a dictionary of critical usage, prepared under foundation or university auspices, might help toward a greater feeling of professional solidarity and the improvement of critical language.

It is not easy to say to what extent the language of criticism should be specialized. One recognizes the great usefulness of a critic's critic like Kenneth Burke, even though the complexity of his language has limited his audience. Others, like Edmund Wilson and F. O. Matthiessen, and Eliot and Pound before them, have succeeded in treating technical matters in lucid and relatively simple language. Surely the best and most enduring twentieth century criticism, like the best criticism of the past, will prove to be written in a language that transcends the narrow circumstances of its origins and presents no undue difficulty to a mature and sophisticated reader. It is just as certain that criticism which is obscurantist rather than honestly technical or which is unduly dependent on current fashions in language will pass into deserved oblivion.

6

American literary criticism has made tremendous advances in theory and technique over the past half century. The multiplicity of its interests is appropriate to a free and open society, the life of which depends on the competition of values. But the claims of limited and special interests have also contributed to confusion and waste. Much of this confusion can be relieved only by an improved body of theory.

The most obvious need of critical theory today is the integration of aesthetic or formalist and social or historical considerations. Literature and criticism are social functions. Like the writer, the critic is responsibly implicated in the formulation of the values, aesthetic and social, by which his society lives. In establishing a work in a historical perspective, in interpreting its form in terms derived in part from other disciplines, and even in working out its own internal controversies, literary criticism is part of a larger social process. Isolationism is impossible. It makes no more sense to sit behind an aesthetic barricade buttressed by theories of pure art and preach the values of the humanities than it does to sit behind a tariff barrier and preach democracy.

The critic and scholar will increasingly realize that he is socially engaged in all his activities. It is his obligation to keep criticism open to new ideas and values so that it may continue to provide fresh knowledge of an ever-expanding world of interrelated literary and social experience. Criticism is not a cut-and-dried game played according to set rules. Although it makes use of the guides of the past, it is a co-operative venture which looks to the future and the life of possibility. The critic might well identify his role with that of the poet of the 1855 preface to Whitman's *Leaves of Grass,* who shares with his readers the discovery of the meaning of the forms of art and the common life expressed through them: "Whom he takes he takes with firm sure grasp into live regions previously unattained . . . thenceforward is no rest. . . ."

INDEX